ISBN: 978-0-692-17892-8 (Paperback)

Edited by: Beryl Pittman
Cover Artwork: Scott Nelson and Spencer McKay

First printing edition 2018

www.atrip4steve.blogspot.com

Walk With You

For the Harrington Family, in honor of Steve

1986-2005

...and of course, Mom.

I can still recall sitting in the dimly lit room in November of 2005 when the wheels for this adventure were set in motion. It was the end of one of the hardest days of my life, the day we honored and said goodbye to a dear friend, and yet it would seem a dream was born that night. Life was given to a plan to thru-hike the Appalachian Trail carrying a remnant of a great friend. Outside of my immediate family, Steve was my favorite person on the planet. My best friend. His smile and zeal for life were contagious. In such a roller coaster week of emotions, Spencer and I pondered at what was to come, and we set out on a trip for Steve.

Fast forward 18 months of waiting, planning, and training; and there we sat hot and sweaty at the end of day one of our journey to walk from Georgia to Maine. We were at the Gooch Gap Shelter and it dawned on me sitting at the picnic table that we were really doing it. 15 miles down, 2160 to go. I remember lacking confidence and the question "What have we done?" was within me. But after an eventful night's sleep (I was startled awake in the middle of the night with a mouse standing on my chest outside my sleeping bag); we repacked our gear, pulled on trail-runners and off we went on day two of our epic hike. Confidence was gained as each step brought us closer to Mount Katahdin in Maine as we called to mind we were not just hiking for ourselves.

In addition to gaining hiking confidence and many memorable experiences, I gained a lifelong brother in Warpzilla. Our bond evolved from childhood Boy Scout friends to a friendship like few others I have encountered in life. Spending three months with someone for virtually every moment of the day, both waking and sleeping, is a rare occurrence. The harmony and fun we enjoyed is even rarer. True to his on-trail perseverance and follow through, I smiled at first hearing he was writing a book to recount our incredible thru-hike.

The story in these pages that unfolded as the miles rolled on has been told countless times and each time in telling it, Steve's legacy lives on. Since our hike I have walked through many milestones: getting married, having children, buying a first home, settling into a career and all along the way, I've wondered what my life would look like if Steve was still with us. I miss him a ton but also find great comfort in knowing he was with us every step of the way for the journey of a lifetime.

"Bandana Ben" Burchardi
June 2017

Connect the Dots

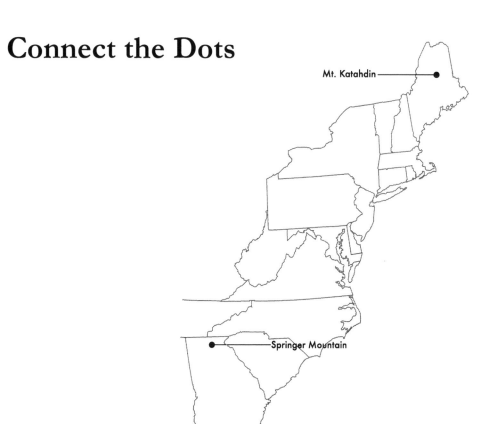

Sometimes, childhood dreams come true, but not exactly like you plan. I remember sitting in 10th-grade English class. Mr. Gillespie told us to write a list of things we wanted to accomplish or things we wanted to happen by the time we were 25. At the top of mine: thru-hike the Appalachian Trail. A lofty goal for a 14-year-old. I guess it falls under the whole "shoot for the moon, and even if you miss, you'll land among the stars" bullshit you hear when you're a kid. Like I said though, not everything went according to plan, at least not mine.

The Appalachian Trail (AT) is a footpath of over 2,000 miles stretching from Springer Mountain, Georgia to Mount Katahdin, Maine. The actual mileage may change from year to year according to the guidebooks because of changes in the path of the trail, trail relocations, and other reasons. One thing does not change though, is the fact that those who thru-hike the trail walk from Georgia (yes, the state of Georgia) to Maine (yes, the state of Maine).

My fascination with the trail started when I was young boy in Boy Scouts. I have fond memories, and some not so fond, of weekend and week-long trips on the Appalachian Trail with my Scout troop – Troop 215 in Raleigh, North Carolina. Our leaders wanted to make sure our troop was a "scout-run" troop. I am forever indebted to the leaders of my troop for the passion, respect, and love for nature they helped to teach. Tallying up 20 miles here, and 50 miles there on the Appalachian Trail trips over the years, it was hard to believe that, by the time I was an older scout, I had hiked nearly the entire trail from the start at Springer Mountain, Georgia, to Southern Virginia around the Grayson Highlands area.

Our first Scoutmaster, Mr. Charville, was the scoutmaster of all scoutmasters. He looks like Dale Earnhardt, and not Junior. I'm talking black-as-night mustache, serious as a heart attack and borrowing the late race car driver's nickname, he was the "intimidator." This man would rival Baden-Powell himself. He'd wake up hours early on a backpacking trip just to comb his hair and shave in a nearby creek. He could have written the Scout handbook as far as we were concerned. You knew when Mr. Charville was in the room, and if he had something to say, you listened. It was within his discipline though, that he shared with us one of his favorite things in the world: the Appalachian Trail.

On my first few AT trips, I discovered what chafing was. My fat little thighs were rubbed raw, and every step was a battle. My gait resembled that of a battered penguin. I tried everything to stop it: baby powder, Desitin, Desitin Creamy, Gold Bond, Gold Bond Medicated, but nothing could prevent the pain. I even had to leave one trip early. But somehow, I found the resilience to push on; something kept me coming back for more. I definitely saw it as a challenge. As adolescence passed, I finally grew out of my mom's 5'3 ¾ " genes. I also began running cross-country my freshman year of high school as a suggestion from my brother. I had never run more than a mile, I don't think. Sure, I had hiked 50 miles or so in a week, but that's a totally different ball game.

On the first day of cross-country practice, I ran four miles. The next day I woke up for practice and could hardly walk down the stairs because I was so sore. Again, that didn't stop me; I had never let my body hold me back from something that I wanted to do. I was determined to make it through a 5k race, and that's exactly what I did. From there, my goals grew. When my brother joined the cross-country team my sophomore year, I thought he was intruding on my turf. His expertise is basketball, and I tried to be the cool kid on the cross-country team. I became more interested in socializing during practice than in the actual sport. This lack of effort became evident in my performance on race days, but I couldn't understand the connection. I think this was a reaction to competing with my brother. For some reason, a healthy competition in racing my brother never formed while we were both on the team. He just seemed naturally faster and stronger than me, and that was not an easy realization.

Luke has always been there for me. We grew up in a broken family, and I was too young to ever remember my mom and dad together. It affected both Luke and me, consequences were both positive and negative. I think, overall, it made us stronger individuals because it was something we had to cope with at a young age.   We certainly went through all the confusion and pain of not having a normal family, but both our parents were completely involved in our lives. We had a "modern family."

Personally, I was never a skinny kid to say the least. I wasn't the fat ass either, despite my possession of a pair of "Husky" sized boy's pants growing up. Momma said I was big-boned, and that was all right with me. I've never missed a meal and don't plan on it anytime soon. I was active though. Playing basketball with my brother was one of my favorite things to do. We shot hoops from the time we got home from school at about 3 pm until late into the night every day. Luke often made the requirement that we could not go inside until we made 10 consecutive free throws. I played soccer as well and ran around with all the other kids in my neighborhood. I was a chubby momma's boy, and I remember the thought of spending a week in the woods backpacking as outrageous and scary. In fifth grade, which is when I "bridged over" into Boy Scouts from Cub Scouts, I went on what would become the most talked of trip in our Scout Troop to this day. It's infamously known as "the whitewater-backpacking trip." Not because we went whitewater rafting one day and backpacking the next -- oh, no. But because it rained from the moment we stepped out of the car until the moment we left. After going through what I have gone through now, that doesn't seem like a big deal. But when you're a know-it-all little fifth grader who gets his world washed inside out while carrying twice his body weight on your back because your mom packed everything but the kitchen sink, that's a different story; and that is exactly what happened. I don't even know why I came back to the next Scout meeting, but if it weren't for my brother and my step-father, along with other friends that went with me on that trip, I would have said "Sayonara" to that mess.

I wasn't the kid who would whine and complain about things in the Troop, but I had a hard time keeping up. I was at the back of the pack when all my friends and the cool kids were speeding away at the front. They saw everything first, and it seemed like they got to rest all the time because they were always waiting on the slow pokes, i.e. me, to catch up. I did, however, get to spend a lot of time with the leaders, whom I owe it all to. Luke, three years older, was also in my Scout Troop and an Eagle Scout as well. Even in Scouts, a healthy competition lived between us and we always tried to outdo the other. He always had the upper hand because he was older, but I was a crafty little guy. Luke took care of me on Scout trips when I was younger and helped me overcome many challenges. I often made fun of him for things like making sure I brushed my teeth and washing my hands on camping trips, but now I see that he was just trying to help.

Troop 215 always went on a week-long AT trip every summer for as long as I can remember. Mr. Charville leads a group of young men along the AT, teaching scouts not only outdoor skills but also camaraderie and respect for our environment. Whether we realized we were learning all of these things, I seriously doubt it. Looking back though, I see what a big impression it all made on me. It just so happened that, the 10th anniversary of our Troop doing a week-long AT trip (right after school got out in May/June), Mr. Charville decided he wanted to take us to the Southern Terminus of the trail, Springer Mountain, Georgia. Our Troop had never been to the trail in GA before, and we were all excited to see the very beginning and hike most of the 83 miles of the trail that goes through the state as it trickles into Western North Carolina. This trip was in 2005, the year I graduated from Sanderson High School. I was still active in the Troop and so were numerous other scouts my age as we had become close friends over the years, all starting with the "whitewater-backpacking" trip some 8 years before.

For every major backpacking trip, there was a shakedown at Mr. Charville's house where we made sure everyone had everything they needed, especially the younger scouts. We received our food rations for the trip and acquired Troop gear that we carry along the way (stoves, water purifiers, tents, tarps, etc.). I realized at these shakedowns just how much I have learned over the years of not only what I needed to bring, but also how to pack things in my pack and what kinds of conditions to expect. Heavier things go in the bottom; smaller accessories are placed on the outer pockets of the pack; items you might need in a hurry, such as a rain jacket or rain cover for your pack, in an area readily accessible. Precipitation was always in the forecast for our trips, or at least a possibility being in the Southeast. We were always instructed to have water bottles for "group water" to fulfill tasks such as cooking and cleaning as well as separate devices for personal use. Mr. Charville's attention to detail was impeccable. Topographic maps would be handed out with elevation graphs as well, showing how much up and down we would have. Also included was a detailed description of the actual trail by tenths of miles.

A running joke in the troop is that, many times in these descriptions, the phrase "Enter woods and ascend" reared its ugly head – a very specific sentence that could make everyone nod, cringe and laugh in the face of our fate. The older scouts on this 10th annual trip were Cordy and Don Stanley, Stephen Harrington, Ben Burchardi, Jonathan Booton, and me. To have this many older scouts on a trip of this length was unique. All of us had either just graduated from high school, were in college, or even out of college. If you grew up in our Troop, you would understand the bond between friends that kept us coming back for more. That is what I cherish most about the

Scouting program that I never quite realized as I was going through it. Sure, I have plenty of friends outside of Scouts, but those that I have made through Scouting are the best of friends. Together, we have been through so many different circumstances and an abundance of common ground.

Front Row: Cordy Stanley, Ben Burchardi
Back Row: Don Stanley, Spencer McKay, Stephen Harrington

Being at the start of the AT was a humbling experience. To know that we were taking the first steps that many people take as they embark on a journey to Maine, over 2,000 miles of mountains, was one of pure awe. The view that day from Springer Mountain, a mere foothill at the start of the Appalachian Range, was misty and blurred. But that didn't stop us from enjoying the moment. The picture of all of us sitting at the placard marking the beginning of the historical footpath is one I cherish greatly.

As the trip continued, so did the rain and mist that had greeted us on the first day at Springer Mountain. It rained every day of the 5-day trip, typical to say the least; but even with wet conditions, the sun would pop out sometime during the day, giving us just enough time to dry out and offering a glimmer of hope,… but then we'd get completely soaked again. Coming off 4 years of cross-country and track in high school, I was no longer faced with the physical liability that I faced as a young scout. I was at the head of the pack; I had made it. Now I was in the group getting to the top of the climbs first, setting my pack down, and descending the mountain to assist the younger scouts whose packs were twice their body weight. Other injuries including blisters and chafing affected the younger scouts as well; I could relate. All of us older scouts took pride in having the physical capability of helping out the younger guys because we knew how much it meant to them. They wouldn't even have to ask; we knew when a climb was hard, and we flew back down the mountain to give a lending hand to those struggling. I saw my younger self in the look on their faces, relieved as we came racing down the switchbacks with no packs on. They knew we were there to help, and just a simple, out-of-breath "thank you" was more than enough to let us know that we were doing them a great favor. A sigh of relief would come over the leaders as well, as you could see their patience had at times grown thin after repeating themselves "that's it, one foot in front of the other" or "keep going, we're almost to the top." I had been there before and providing relief for them was beneficial for everyone.

All trips come to an end, but this year was the first time Mr. Charville had offered an extended trip for the most willing and able Scouts and Leaders to keep hiking past the North Carolina-Georgia state line and, as a result, complete the portion of the trail in Georgia. It can be easily argued that this was merely for Mr. Charville's personal pleasure – to knock out an entire state from his miles left to hike on the trail. Although few would be brave enough to call out Mr. Charville on this fact, none of the willing scouts and leaders seemed to mind. There's actually a name for the style of hiking we had been doing. It's called section hiking, where instead of doing a thru-hike (hiking the entire trail in one go) you hike the trail in sections. There's no doubt in my mind that Mr. Charville, along with the other Scout-masters (Mr. Mazur, Mr. Haeseker, Mr. Booton, Mr. Johnson, and others) would love to be able to thru-hike the trail someday, but age and time (and fulltime jobs!) are so cruel that this is not always a possibility. Section hiking is more up their alley. By the end of this 10th anniversary trip, much of the trail between the southern terminus and southern Virginia would have been completed by numerous people in the troop.

After everyone returned from the 8-day excursion, Stephen Harrington and I began planning a trip to Maine. We were so curious from our experience at the Southern Terminus of the AT in Georgia, that we wanted to see the Northern Terminus in Maine at Mount Katahdin (kuh-tah-din.) A high school friend of mine, Garrett Dixon, (also an Eagle Scout but in a different troop) had a vacation home in Freeport, Maine. We had tossed around the idea before of heading to Maine to hike the Northern Terminus sometime, as Garrett's interest in the AT was as great as mine. Steve and I booked our flights, and we took off from Raleigh-Durham airport (RDU) on July 22, 2005.

I don't know if you've ever felt this way, but I can remember the smallest details from that trip: eating orange chicken at Panda Express, shopping, trying on way too expensive Bose headphones. It's as if my mind was preparing me to relive this vacation for some reason, a reason that I now know all too well. Garrett's mom picked us up from the airport in Portland, Maine, and took us to their lovely summer home overlooking the water in Freeport. On the first day we got there, we had to entertain ourselves because Garrett was working. So we took kayaks onto the water and paddled around for a few hours. Garrett finally got home from work, and we planned the finer details of our trip to the Baxter State Park, home to Mt. Katahdin, the Northern Terminus of the AT.

As we hopped in the car the next morning and drove along the most northern miles of I-95, we finally entered Baxter State Park, miles upon miles of wilderness and the home of Mt. Katahdin. I remember that first view of Katahdin. We pulled over and took pictures from the highway. It's a towering mountain that comes out of the remotely flat and pond-filled landscape that is northern Maine. It is truly a sight to see. We hiked around to stretch the legs and get a feel for the environment we were in, but our little stroll was cut aggravatingly short by the overly annoying number of black flies that annually pass through the area. These guys are ferocious, not your typical fly; they're actually big enough to bite – and they were everywhere. We were a bit, pun intended, worried that they might hinder our summit attempt the next morning, but our undying curiosity of the AT had brought us out here, and we weren't going to be deterred by bugs. Garrett, who had actually ascended Katahdin before, assured us that once we got above tree line on our climb the next day the black flies would subside. Fortunately, he was right. Sitting around the campfire that night swapping stories and camaraderie was shortened by the necessity of sleep to get an early jump on our climb in the morning.

We woke up around 5:30 am, drove about a mile up the dirt road to the base of the mountain and secured our belongings in the car. Standing at the Katahdin Stream Campground, with our bed-head hair and sleepy smiles, we gazed up at the Mountain we were attempting to summit. Our signatures were among the first in the trail log at the base of the mountain, and our steps now fell on the Appalachian Trail, some 2,170 miles north of where we walked just a month-and-a-half ago in Georgia. The trail started with seemingly normal conditions, we hiked three wide for the first few minutes, and then quickly formed a single file line as we began crossing streams and edged our way out of the tree line. I remember the first break we took when we were right at the threshold of where the hiking ended and the climbing began. Garrett had warned us of the rock scrambling and bouldering type maneuvers we were going to be presented with on our ascent. I think Steve and I took his story with a grain of salt; we were sure it would be tough but thought for sure Garrett was exaggerating. He wasn't.

Rebar had even been driven into the rock at some points so that hikers had something to hoist themselves up to the next level spot. It was some of the hardest hiking we had ever experienced. It was unlike anything on the entire Appalachian Trail. We remembered thinking how awesome it would be if our climb up Katahdin were us finishing a 2000-mile journey across the Appalachian Mountains. As fate would have it, we actually encountered a young man who was in that very situation. He was a college student from

James Madison University, and we had met his parents at the base of the mountain in Katahdin Stream Campground. He was hiking the final portion of his journey with his much younger brother, sharing the moment. It was inspiring to say the least.

As we continued up the rock scramble portion of the climb, we were unable to see the top from the trail because of the steep conditions we encountered. Finally, we arrived at the upper portion of the ascent where it leveled out greatly. The terrain reminded me of tundra conditions that for a majority of the year lie under foot upon foot of snow. We couldn't see Russia from up there, but it sure felt like we could. Rare types of algae and lichen grow on this plateau and aren't found anywhere else east of the Mississippi River. It's truly majestic to just turn a 360 and absorb the view of the vast wilderness. It is incredible to be standing on that rock thousands of feet above everything in sight. Humbled and excited, we pushed on as the white blazes marked the final yards of the AT. As the sign for the northern terminus of the AT came into sight, we couldn't believe how quickly we had made it up the 3500-foot climb. We talked ecstatically about our plans to thru-hike the trail someday. We were dead set that we had to now connect the dots plotted that summer. It was a big dream, but we were confident that it was something we would be able to do, perhaps after we all graduated from college but before we entered the "real world."

The weathered sign marking the end (or beginning) of the Appalachian Trail was powerful to behold. Etched in it were carvings made by thru-hikers that had finished their journey. It was the most beautiful day that we could have ever asked for, and I feel blessed to have shared that day with Stephen and Garrett. We took photographs around the sign and snapped panoramic pictures from the top. Lunch was in order, and we took pictures with our Payday candy bars in front of the sign. As if it were some sort of statement, this was our "payday" – experiences like this are what we lived for. The summit became crowded with people, but the first person to reach the summit after us was the thru-hiker that we had met on the way up. Although we didn't fully understand the accomplishment that we were witnessing, his emotions said it all, and it was moving to watch him take the

Spencer McKay

final steps of his hike. As he teared up and leaned on the sign, his joy was overwhelming and his triumph was great, one we all desired to share some day.

Hiking back down the mountain, we couldn't stop thinking about our future thru-hike. The 5-mile hike up Mt. Katahdin was the hardest and most fun I had ever had while hiking. With beautiful weather, wonderful friends, and aspirations to come back to this place, we eventually reached the base of the mountain where we had started. The next time we would return, it would be the end of our incredible journey through 14 states and over 2000 miles of ups and downs from Georgia to Maine. We prepared a meal fit for kings at the campground in complete car-camping fashion, whipping out a little charcoal grill and a big ol' hunk of steak and veggies. Our fajitas were washed down with Gatorade as our joints and muscles longed for rest. We slept like babies that night, absolutely exhausted from our experience.

My weeklong trip to Maine with Steve was coming to an end as we headed back to the airport and boarded our flight. I thought about what it would be like to, instead of flying from Maine to North Carolina, walk the terrain we were soaring over, an ambitious idea indeed. Like it always does, summer drew to an end, and exciting things like beginning college and living on my own filled my mind, but the AT seed had now been firmly planted in the back of my mind.

Thru-hikers are a breed of their own. What would make someone want to do nothing but walk for thousands of miles, traveling through the woods, miles from civilization? People decide to hike the trails for many reasons. The inspiration or reasons for thru-hiking range anywhere from a crazy weight loss program to "If I don't do this now, when will I?" to pursuing a bucket-list item, to honor someone, to raise money for a charity, to figure out life. Whatever the reason, it doesn't matter, the fact that you're doing it is commendable, and the hardest part is actually getting out to the start.

Perhaps it seems selfish for some people to hike the trail. At times, it does feel that way. However, as a huge advocate of the trail, I will say that thru-hiking has a ripple effect beyond the hiker. Those who know thru-hikers are inspired. Whether it be by following a hiker's blog or online journal, or seeing pictures and video from the trail, such an incredible feat is being attempted that people become addicted to following it. As support back home grows, it makes it easier to stay out there.

Some people hike just to get away from it all. One of the founders of the trail, Benton MacKaye, said that the trail was a "footpath for those who seek fellowship with the wilderness" and in turn themselves. There are two main groups of people that attempt to hike the entire AT. You have the just-graduated crowd (high school, undergrad, graduate, etc.) and the just-retired crowd. You would think such juxtaposing groups would have difficulty getting along. One is most likely in debt up to their eyeballs, hoping the forbearance on their student loans remains until they get back. The just-graduated class is looking at life ahead of them, wondering what they will do, and flying by the seat of their pants. The just retired folks has probably saved money, planned the trip from an office somewhere for years, and has all the details worked out. The retired group has most likely left a family, work, a mortgage and all the self-imposed responsibilities associated with the "real world" behind.

My inspiration for thru-hiking the trail entails many of the reasons listed above. I had always wanted to hike the AT since a young boy. I always figured I would fit into the "just graduated group." My freshman year of college at UNC-Charlotte was not your typical one, mainly because I was there for architecture school. It is a very demanding, time-intensive program. I don't even know why I had a dorm room because I lived in the Architecture building pretty much every day for the next 5 years of my life.

One night, I was working late in the Architectural studio fall semester during my freshman year when I somehow got a call on my cell phone. This was unusual because I got terrible service in the building. Yet somehow, the phone rang. It was my brother whom I hadn't talked to in a while; he was calling from college himself. This too was a fairly rare occurrence, so I raced outside to the patio to receive a better signal because I was sure the one I had would quickly fade. As I pushed open the door through the tall wall of glass windows into the nippy North Carolina November air, the voice of my brother was one I wish I had never heard. He said "Spencer,…" He never calls me by my full name, always a nickname like Spence, or bro, something along those lines. My brother, typically a serious guy, had "that" tone in his voice. The tone where you know something bad is following, the kind of bad that seems to shoot down through your ear from the phone and freezes you to the ground. That was the initial reaction when he told me that my friend Stephen Harrington had died. After the news began to sink in, I stormed out of studio, away from the architecture building, across campus. I had to go somewhere, frantically walking toward my girlfriend's dorm, calling her cell and trying to explain to her all I could between intermittent breaths of holding back streams of tears and disbelief.

Of course, she lived in the only all-girls dorm on campus, so I had to pound on the glass window for the security guard to let me in. It was always the same old guy sitting at a desk under fluorescent light, pretending to read a book as he drifted off into an effortless daze. He was startled and let me right in. As my girlfriend met me, we stepped back outside as I described to her what my brother had told me about my friend Stephen. Soon calls began coming in from other mutual friends as we all shuddered in disbelief at how such a thing could have happened.

Stephen was a good friend from Troop 215. Although never being best friends with Stephen, as Ben Burchardi was, we were close. Memories of our trip to Maine just a few months earlier began flooding my mind. The last time I talked with Steve, we discussed our plan to thru-hike the Appalachian Trail someday. It was not long until Ben called. Upset and distraught, we discussed our friend's death.

Travel plans for the funeral were immediately sorted out. I had a much shorter drive to Raleigh than Ben had. He was coming from college at the University of Florida. Ben moved to Florida before starting high school. He actively joined our Scout Troop on our AT trips during the summer though, and that is how we stayed close. Each time he came back to town, we just picked up right where we left off. As we began to get older, we all stayed active in our Troop. This is fairly rare because ordinarily, once kids get their Eagle Scout rank (before the age 18 deadline), they stop participating, or they quit scouts altogether due to fumes: gasoline fumes and girls' perfumes. Some skip out on the scouting program and see it as something that their parents made them do or as something that they finished and don't intend on returning to. For our Troop, though, some real friendships had been bonded not only across age groups of Scouts, but among Scouts and leaders, and between Scout Leaders themselves.

I wanted to call the Harringtons, Stephen's parents, but I couldn't. I would not have known what to say. Ben shared the same passion with me for wanting to hike the entire AT. I'm not sure either one of us really considered it possible though. What a ridiculous thing to want to do. Now, it suddenly did not seem so outrageous. The frailty of life had struck all too close. At just 18 years old, Steve's death affected me greatly. Classes were hard to attend; Though I went the next few days, it was hard to explain to people. Out of modesty, I told few people about it. I was not good friends with many people in school yet; it was still that awkward stage of seeing the same people every day, all going through the same things, but just not connecting with many yet. I didn't want people to feel sorry for me, professors and students alike.

That night, Ben and I began hatching a plan to hike the Appalachian Trail in Steve's honor. It would be a way for us not only to cope with what happened, but to give the Harringtons something positive to be involved with. When Ben and I arrived at their home the weekend after hearing the news that cold November night, Mrs. Harrington answered the door. We all broke into tears, embracing one another. All I could manage to get out was, "We are going to hike the Appalachian Trail in honor of Steve." The pain and agony on her face faded for a moment as a brief smile took over. "That would be wonderful," she said. Whether or not she thought we were serious, I'm not sure.

The funeral was powerful. For such a young man, Steve sure had made his mark on tons of people, including me. The sheer number of people who came was touching, including many Scouts and Scout Leaders donned in Class-A Uniform. A couple of them spoke in the service; Ben was one of them. How Ben got up there, I have no idea. I was torn up enough, but Ben, who was Steve's best friend growing up, did not even flinch. Ben's character is matched by few. A religious young man, the word of God is important to Ben. If anyone was capable of speaking that day, it was he. Garrett, who Steve and I hiked Mt. Katahdin with, was unable to attend the service because he was attending school at Cornell and was unable to travel on such short notice. Garrett was distraught over the news when I called him the night of Steve's death. I was surprised at first, but then recalled what we had all done together. When you share the same outdoor experience with someone, it is more meaningful than just a day around town. The wilderness bonds greater than man alone can, an appreciation not to go unnoticed. With hopes of one day hiking the trail himself, Garrett was included on the plans for an Appalachian Trail thru-hike in honor of Steve. Garrett wrote this on a blog we intended to use for our thru-hike.

Why the Appalachian Trail? Why honor your friend by hiking almost 2,200 miles through the wilderness? The answer for me is simple. Steve, Spencer, and I hiked the northern terminus at Mt. Katahdin in Maine in the summer of 2005 not long after Steve and Spencer hiked the southern terminus at Springer, MT in Georgia earlier that summer. We joked on our trip that one day it would be cool to hike the entire trail, for them, to connect the dots.

Garrett, a sort of engineering, intellectual, statistics guru, carries a sophisticated speak about him, Ivy League education and all. He can come off as jerk, but he's not. Slender and pushing six feet tall, his build is thin and handsome. Garrett has a knack for talking; sometimes it's hard to get a word in. But I regard myself as a good listener, so the dynamic seems to work out for the most part. He was the one counting ounces, planning calorie intake, nutrition, and researching the most recent hiking equipment. Garrett had also acquired years of weekend outings on the AT with his Scout Troop in Raleigh. He has also worked at Philmont Scout Ranch in

New Mexico. In fact, Stephen, Garrett, and I had all gone toPhilmont Scout Camp (Garrett and Steve, '01; and me, '02). Philmont is an extreme Scout camp, if you will. Each crew consists of a minimum eight scouts with two leaders. Your task is a ten-day excursion through the rugged yet pristine and diverse ecosystems.

Prior to our AT thru-hike, the Philmont hike was the longest trip I had ever been on. Ten days of painful blister-plagued hiking. This trip convinced me of my theory that traditional hiking boots are the devil. Not only are typical leather, waterproof boots like a rain forest for your foot, but if you don't have miles upon miles of experience with them, they will give you major problems and can hinder your entire hiking experience. Given I had hiked only around my neighborhood in them and a short weekend trip as well, they weren't broken in well. Considering all the warning and previous experience, I should have known it would happen. My blisters turned out to be only a minor speed bump on our trek. My friend Ryan was carrying an extra pair of trail shoes with him, and I ended up hiking the seven remaining days with trail shoes, carrying my boots tied to the back of my pack. Somewhere in my hiking experience, I remember hearing that boots are simply too heavy for your feet. If you compare the weight of a boot and the weight of a trail shoe, it makes sense. Although the difference can amount to just a few ounces, when walking over 2000 miles, carrying those extra ounces on your feet could have a severe overall impact on the amount of effort taken each step multiplied by whatever the amount of steps I was preparing to take. Makes sense, right?

It would have been far too ambitious to plan a thru-hike of the Appalachian Trail for the summer immediately following the blue November of 2005. Ben, Garrett, and I thought we could plan it better and would have a chance of being successful in our attempt if we shot for taking our first steps in the late spring of 2007. Ben was a construction management major at the University of Florida. As already mentioned, Ben is a devout Christian. He is heavily involved in spreading the word of God. Our thru-hike had a vibrant contrast of all types of personalities, and we were sure to meet many more. Ben wasn't always so "god squad" though. He was a typical high school kid. High School is an exciting time for a young man. Four spinning wheels, the freedom felt by that, and the exploration of the other gender. His high school days were filled with both. Somewhere along the road though, Ben decided that was not the way to go. I respect him greatly for that decision. Our thru-hike had a vibrant contrast of all types of personalities, and we were sure to meet many more. But somehow, our fates aligned in time to bring us all together for a summer between college semesters in attempt to hike the entire Appalachian Trail.

According to the Appalachian Trail Conservancy (ATC) website (www.appalachiantrail.org) the average thru-hiker takes just under six months to finish their hike from Georgia to Maine. In an effort to reduce the number of people starting on March 1st-vMarch 15th, the first day of spring and April 1st, all of which are the most popular start dates, the ATC suggests starting on a weekday and offers a voluntary thru-hiker registration to reduce overcrowding, trampled vegetation and sanitation issues. It is safe to say that most people start the trail between the beginning of March and April. Hikers departing during this time frame may encounter winter conditions as far as 500 miles up the trail, as well as the end of their trip. The average, or optimal, time to finish a thru-hike is projected on the ATC website as well. If you are lucky and are one of the few to make it through, you should arrive in New England and eventually in Baxter State Park to summit Katahdin between September and early October.

Our logic in taking an extra year to plan for our hike seemed like a good idea. However, in all honesty, we did little to prepare for it. The majority of real, sit-down and figure-this-beast-out planning came just two weeks before we prepared to venture in to the woods. Garrett was at Cornell, Ben was 1,100 some-odd miles away from him, and I sat somewhere in between at the University of North Carolina-Charlotte. We had shot a few emails back and forth to each other about when our start date would be. Garrett had set up a blog for us to post on as we traveled along the notorious footpath, updating it as we went into towns along the way for resupply. In a year-and-a-half of "planning," all we had done was order 20 boxes of Clif bars and acquire bits and pieces of gear.

Ben was the first to finish with his spring semester exams (May 4, 2007); I shortly followed (May 10, 2007). Ben and I immediately headed for Raleigh to set up base camp and plan our grand undertaking. The Harrington home was rejuvenated with life during the two weeks we frantically tried to pull everything together. The Harringtons were as excited about our trip as we were. Ben and I spent all hours of the day, and night, planning our journey. We had so many things to cover. We developed an itinerary planning our day-to-day mileage. This was something most people did not do, but because we had a total of 90 days, absolute maximum, between our projected start date of May 21 and when my fall semester started on August 20, we had little room for error. I'll do the math for you. If the Appalachian Trail is approximately 2,175 miles and we had a maximum of 90 days, then that's an average of 24.1 miles a day. That's with zero days off and a zero tolerance for pretty much anything to go wrong. Attempting such a feat would seem ludicrous to most; actually pretty much everyone we even mentioned it to thought it was crazy.

But by golly we had a plan, and we were damn sure it would work. If all else failed, we would just call upon our X-factor, Steve, to help get us through. It was a trip that would test our true grit. What could we handle? What were we capable of? Would we all get along? I remember, as my Dad shaved my head before leaving for the trip, he asked what we'd do if one of us got hurt. It was a mutual understanding among all of us that, if someone gets hurt, that the group must push onward. There was so little room for error, perhaps it was foolish to plan such a hike. It needed to be done though; it was not just for us, it was for Steve, even more importantly, for the Harringtons.

I was the common factor between all those included in our trip. Steve and I were in the Scout Troop and friends. Stephen was Ben's best friend growing up. I was also friends with Ben through scouting. Garrett is my friend from high school, and we had all earned the rank of Eagle Scout. Garrett was our ticket to Maine when Steve and I went to visit and hike Katahdin. Garrett and Ben were actually in the same Cub Scout pack when they were growing up. I felt like the glue holding everything together. Whether or not that glue would hold, I had no idea, but we had to try.

As the weeks left of planning turned to days, and as the itinerary was completed in the wee hours of the morning just one day before departing, our excitement grew. Unlike Ben and me, Garrett had little time to mentally prepare and help plan for our trip. His finals at Cornell commenced just 2 days before we planned to travel down to Georgia for our first steps on our 3-month journey. I can only imagine the pressure placed on him as he knew Ben and I were frantically planning our hike while he had to focus at the most immediate task at hand. Garrett also had to move home from New York and was hindered earlier that winter with a shattered collarbone. The situation was controlled chaos. So there we sat at the Harrington's home; Ben, Garrett, and me, hurriedly packing resupply boxes the night before we planned to drive to the Southern Terminus of the Trail. We had about 14 boxes labeled according to our daily itinerary that Ben and I had made, telling us where we were going to resupply and giving us notice of how many days' worth of food we had to place in each mail drop box. Now this seems like a simple task for one, but when you are supplying 3-5 days' worth of food for 3 people in one mail drop, everything becomes 3 times more complicated and 3 times more bulky. Nevertheless, we finished our mail drop boxes to the best of our ability.

At a final ceremonial dinner in Raleigh, North Carolina, we dined at one of my favorite establishments, the Sawmill Taproom. Accompanied by my parents, Garrett's parents, Ben, the Harringtons, and other family members, we excitedly talked about our final preparations and setting forth on our journey. It was a happy yet serious dinner. Had we prepared for everything? Were we going to make it? Would we be safe? All these questions and more filled our minds. We presented everyone with a copy of our itinerary. This comforted our parents, knowing they could look at a piece of paper, Google the location, and get a general idea of where we would be laying our heads each night. The blog was up and running at this point, and our parents were given access to post on it as well, in case we were only able to make a phone call and didn't have internet access to update all those interested in our whereabouts.

It was hard to sleep that night to say the least.

After I finally fell asleep that night, when my eyes shut for the last time, it seemed like 5 seconds after that it was time to get up and head to the Harrington's home one last time before we drove to Georgia. I said my goodbyes to my Mom (Zoe McKay-Tucker) and my Step-Dad (Randy Tucker) and rode with my Father (Jim McKay) to the Harrington's. Ben had been staying with the Harringtons during our pre-trip planning. Garrett also met us at their home. There we all stood, in their driveway, three young men, three Eagle Scouts, ready to attempt to hike the entire Appalachian Trail in just three months. No picture, writing, or piece of art could capture the emotions of everyone on the back deck of the Harrington's home as Tim Harrington poured Stephen's ashes into our 4 oz. Nalgene bottle from his urn. A powerful moment.

We drove half a day to Dahlonega, Georgia, from Raleigh to get as close to the trail as possible before my Dad and the Harringtons dropped us off at the Southern Terminus, Springer Mountain. Corey Smith, then an up-and-coming country/folk music singer even had a song about the small Georgia town. That night we feasted on steaks and mashed potatoes. The next morning at the Holiday Inn Express' continental breakfast, we could have taught a class on carb-loading 101. Gut-wrenching nerves curbed my appetite, though.

Setting Forth

Springer Mountain

A long and winding washed-out dirt road leads you up to Springer Mountain. There's an eight-mile (optional) approach trail from Amicalola Falls State Park in Georgia you can do that takes you to Springer as well. This is not part of the Appalachian Trail; therefore, we did not do it. In the group was Dad, Mr. and Mrs. Harrington, Ben, Garrett and me.

Getting back to the Southern Terminus was not as easy as we thought. There's a parking lot about .6 of a mile from the Terminus at Springer Mountain. Ben and I were the only ones who had been there before; I led the way from the parking lot to the start of our journey. After about 20 minutes of walking, far longer than it should take to walk just about half a mile, we still hadn't reached the mountain overlook that I sat on just a couple years ago. We were following the white blazes of the AT, so at least we had that part figured out. Yes, in our 2,175-mile journey, we started out heading in the wrong direction. I take full blame for this mishap. Once we figured it out, we headed back the way we had just come and then crossed the parking lot we had parked in and headed towards what had to be the Southern Terminus. It was a little warm-up hike if you will, giving my Dad, and the Harringtons a little taste of what the trail was like.

That day on Springer, May 21, 2007, was a beautiful day. There was not a cloud in the sky. We could see what had been hidden by fog and rain two years before. I signed the trail journal and tucked it back in its inconspicuous compartment hidden in a rock close to where the first blaze of the Appalachian Trail is painted.

As we spread some of Stephen's ashes at the wooded overlook at the top of Springer Mountain, we all reflected on the purpose of our journey. Steve had been here before, he had been to Katahdin as well, and it was now time to connect the dots of everything in between. Emotions ran high as we took photographs marking the beginning of our three-month trek. We sat on the cool, still damp from morning dew rock, which marked the beginning of the AT. Ben, Garrett and I all sat beside each other, holding a bottle filled with the ashes of our lost friend. With shaved heads, new shoes and packs jammed full of everything we thought we needed until our next resupply at Neel's Gap, we walked back down to the parking lot with everyone and said our final goodbyes. The next planned time we would see anyone we knew was in Damascus, Virginia, some 450 miles north of our current location.

Tears were held back only by the excitement of what we were embarking on. We were finally here, we were finally doing it, a lifelong dream had started. Great challenges lay ahead; there were so many factors we could not control. Things like weather, wildlife, and trail conditions all made the list. Those things weren't worth focusing on though: all we had to do was walk, and that's all we wanted to do.

I knew the pace we had to walk was a feverish one. None of us were really in tip-top shape although we knew for a year-and-a-half what we had to prepare for. Truth be told, there's only so much you can do to prepare for something like this. You just have to jump in headfirst. Just like jumping in a pool with water so cool it gives you goose bumps. Why stick a toe in and slowly walk through the shallow end? It's aggravating and takes too long. Cannonball into the deep end, feel the rush of the cool water. That sensation is the one we were going for. Ben had done the most training out of all of us, but Garrett led the way on the first few days. The first day, we covered a swift 14.9 miles and arrived to Gooch Gap Shelter at about 5 or 6 in the afternoon. What we would be trying to develop over the next couple of weeks were our "trail legs." In preparing for a marathon, you often run farther than 26.2 miles in the final weeks of preparations for the race. Obviously, in training for a 2,175 walk, you cannot do that. You just have to get out there, fight through the first couple of weeks, get some miles under your belt, work out the kinks in your equipment and keep your nose – or feet in this case – to the grindstone.

The advantage to a thru-hike over a section hike is that you soon get in a high-performance groove and can stay in it. On a section hike, about the time you start feeling comfortable on the trail with your pace and equipment, your blisters have started to heal and you're muscles start to not hate you quite as much, it's time to go home. We planned on taking full advantage of this fact.

As we arrived at Gooch Gap Shelter that night, the adrenaline had worn off, and we were preparing our first meals on the trail. The thru-hiker diet is an interesting one to say the least. There is no way you can consume as many calories as your body needs every day. If you did, the weight of your pack would be unbearable. The staples in our diet were Clif Bars. We had accounted for three Clif bars a day each, along with trail mix, other snacks like Snickers, Butterfingers, Paydays, and Zero candy bars. We were also armed with electrolyte gel packs and other items. Ben and I had pre-made pasta dinners for each night as well, ranging from pesto, four cheese, and traditional marinara, all supplemented with packaged meat.

That night was a quiet one. As we all lay in the upper bunk section of the shelter laying three abreast, I can only imagine the compilation of thoughts that were going through our minds. In reflection of that first night, Ben told me "I was nervous and lacking confidence then." We certainly had a long way to go, and who knew what lay in store for us.

Outdoor enthusiast/adventurer Andrew Skurka (www.andrewskurka.com) was an inspiration to all three of us while planning our hike. He completed a thru-hike of the AT in 2005 in the same time frame as we planned. I think we had more prior experience than he had on the trail and to backpacking in general before he attempted his hike. Andrew Skurka is now a hiking phenomenon who has somehow managed to make a career out of taking outrageously long trips, including an Atlantic to Pacific Ocean trek across North America and the Great Western Loop , which consists of 6,800 some odd miles of the most rugged and beautiful terrain the United States has to offer. We all credit him with coining the phrase caloric-drip. A sort of trickle-down theory applied to eating. If you constantly eat through-out the day your body will always have something to burn. Every day, from the time we got up until the time we went to bed, we tried to eat as much as possible. Believe it or not, our appetite wasn't as strong as when we were in our normal day-to-day routine back home.

We knew that we would encounter some interesting people on the trail. The only thing is, you never know when or where you're going to see these people. The Appalachian Trail sees a lot of foot traffic due to its close proximity to many major cities along the East Coast: Atlanta, Charlotte, Washington DC, Baltimore, New York City, Boston and so on. In preparation of the trip and to this day when I tell folks about people on the trail. Everyone seems to think crazy people live up in the mountains. Although people that think this aren't totally wrong, there are crazy people everywhere. Not clearly displayed in statistical fashion anywhere on the ATC website are the number of violent crimes recorded on the trail. However, the tips on personal safety are spot-on. It's obviously increasingly safer if you hike with other people. As three young men together in the wilderness, we never felt threatened by another human being. It was typically quite the opposite. The only overwhelming characteristic of strangers was their kindness and generosity. Eventually we met one character early on in our trek who would challenge that.

One set of trail personalities we encountered made quite the team. Their names were Phil and George. Both attended Warren Wilson College in nearby Asheville, North Carolina. Phil, an adventuresome guy with a hint of "free spirit" swagger to him, and George, who we soon found out (from Phil) had Asperger Syndrome, similar to autism, but with less nonverbal impairment, quickly won us over. It was George's dream to be a country singer, which came to light through one of his many nonsensical stories. We knew this one had to be true because he constantly sang country music songs. Every lyric quoted perfectly. I'll never forget that first night at Gooch Gap shelter and the next few days ensuing. Every time he saw us, he'd be singing, mostly from the late, great Hank Williams: "Red necks, white sox, and blue ribbon beer." A nervous clapping of hands and over-excitement followed each stint of song. We could see why Phil was hiking with this fella'. He provided endless hours of entertainment. George was a good guy. I think he understood why we were hiking and its significance. Good ol' George took a liking to us so much that he even offered to hike the rest of the trail with us. Talking to Phil and the three of us "You know, I think I might just tag along with you guys to Maine, I mean I've got nothing to do the rest of the summer." Phil quickly responded, "I don't know if you should do that, George; your parents might not like that." The three of us stared at each other before George's answer. "Yea, you're right, they'd be pissed."

While we were meeting folks like George and Phil, we were also making some decent mileage on our trip. In the first two days we traveled 30 miles afoot. This of course is not an enormous or outrageous feat, but with just hopping on the trail and cranking out that kind of mileage, it is fairly impressive. Our first re-supply was on our second day. We planned this out so that we could ease into our hike by carrying a lighter load on the first couple of days. That first re-supply was at Neel's Gap, a simple little state highway crossing. The trail crosses highway 19 and goes right under a breezeway of the Mountain Crossings at Walasi-Yi general store/outfitter. This is often a breaking point for many people attempting the trail. Out of the 1,300 hikers (average number of hikers that attempted a thru-hike from

2004-2009) only 1,169 hikers (average number of hikers from 2004-2009) continue on. This means, in just the first 30 miles, around 1% of the entire trail, the dropout rate is 10%. That's 131 hikers that throw in the towel after just a few days on the trail.

I guess people quit for all sorts of reasons, maybe the trail experience isn't what they thought it would be, or it was just too hard. Maybe they already miss their loved ones and the thought of continuing on for another 5 months is just overwhelming. It does seem a bit overwhelming though. Two days of busting your butt, getting into the groove, and you're barely 1% complete. For us though, getting there wasn't the entire goal. It was about spending time with each other and honoring Steve in the best way we knew how.

The Mountain Crossing store is notorious among thru-hikers and trail enthusiasts. This store is the first sign of civilization in the first few days of one's thru-hike. The sound of vehicles on the highway is like music to a hiker's ears. An appetite for "real food" has most likely been worked up as well. Also, it is the first place where hikers can re-supply, just like we did, and send home things that hikers realize they do not need. Extra junk is often littered and ditched at the shelters that lay between the start at Springer Mountain and Neel's Gap. I remember one recollection of a hiker who said he saw someone carrying a samurai sword at the start of the trail and later found it in one of the shelters along the way. As we re-supplied at Neel's Gap, organizing our next 5 days' worth of food on the picnic tables, we wondered how we would even fit it all in our packs. Through strategic cramming and rearranging, we managed to squeeze it all in. This was also our first opportunity to phone home. We were not able to post on our blog site, but my Dad was able to post something for us.

Spencer reports that they made it up Blood Mountain and arrived @ Neel's Gap just fine yesterday afternoon. They were hoping to be able to post a blog; so far I haven't seen anything. The only other interesting comment was they had mice crawling around their heads in a shelter on Monday night.

The Blood Mountain that my Dad is referring to in the blog post is the highest point on the AT in the state of Georgia. It is 4,458 feet high, and is the first true physical test of the trail. I recall vividly the 2005 10th anniversary hike of the AT with my scout troop. Steve and I flew up this section of the trail and were the first ones to reach the top. Reliving that moment, this time on a thru-hike, and without Steve made it a very emotional climb for me. My physical ability to reach the top with as much ease was still there, but emotionally it was very difficult. When we reached the top, I finally broke down; my final steps were blurred by tears in my eyes. As if I were looking through the bottom of a pint glass, I tried to take in the view. Ben and Garrett were there to cheer me up, as they began to understand why I was so upset.

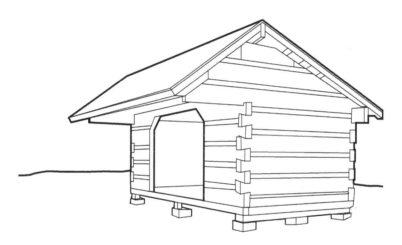

Typical Shelter on the A.T.

It is a steep descent from the top of Blood Mountain to the highway crossing at Neel's Gap. While we hung out at Neel's Gap, waiting for the sun to go down, we indulged with entire cans of Pringle's and soft drinks. It had been only 2 days since our last good meal, but you would have thought we had been on the trail for weeks. With no more room in the bunks that the Mountain Crossings store offers, we were planning to just pitch our tent in the yard surrounding the outfitter. An employee working the store told us we couldn't camp there though because it wasn't their property; it was actually part of a Georgia State Park, which apparently doesn't allow camping. It would have been nice to know this when we arrived at the store; when we were told it was basically sundown. All of our gear was once again repacked into our packs, and we continued up the trail on our personal, far less significant, trail of tears to find a spot to camp. We were informed that there was a nice little spot to camp about .3 miles up the trail.

When we arrived to the alleged "good place to camp" with headlamps and tempers on edge because we had to move from the picnic area, we saw the perfect place to pitch our three-man tent. Which it was, except for the fallen tree lying in the middle of it. In a last ditch effort hindered by fatigue and darkness, we tried our best to clear a spot for our tent. What would ensue was one of the worst night's sleep ever. Since we had never set up this particular tent that Garrett was carrying, it was the classic case of "how many Eagle Scouts does it take to...." Come morning, the three of us were scrunched up in a human puzzle at the bottom of the tent. Icing on the cake, there was an infestation of bugs that must have come from the top of the pine tree that was lying across our campsite.

It was after this horrible night that we decided from there on out we would try to sleep in as many shelters as possible. Shelters, also referred to as a lean-to, are a 3-sided structure with a roof and one open side. These shelters are typically a raised platform constructed of wood or stone. The volunteer hours and efforts to build these structures must be outstanding. There are more than 250 shelters along the AT. Their location is often determined by proximity to a water source and is usually equipped with a nearby privy, or outhouse. Shelters are occupied on a first-come, first-served basis. Fortunately for us, a shelter was typically available every night – one of the perks of starting 2 months later than most.

The next day's light could not have come soon enough. When we woke up and began packing, we looked at our haggard, makeshift camp and just had to joke about how terrible it was. Our awful night's sleep didn't help our performance that day, but nevertheless, we pushed on for our biggest day yet of 17.8 miles. Before arriving at Blue Mountain Shelter that night- we ran into a group who was out hiking for a few days on the trail. They had lost someone in their group. Unable to get a connection with their lost party member on a two-way walkie-talkie, they were becoming worried. We couldn't offer much help as we were extremely worn out. All we could do was inform them we hadn't seen anyone. That night at Blue Mountain Shelter was the most exhausted I had been yet. Muscles screamed out, "Why are you doing this to me?" I fetched water for us while Ben and Garrett hung sweat-drenched clothes to dry. Slowly bending over to fill my last water bottle, I could tell that a storm was moving in. Thunder became louder and inevitably closer. A stray water particle made its way through the densely wooded forest canopy. I achingly and hurriedly limped back to the shelter, racing an inevitable downpour. Thunder and lightning crackled as our dinner pots came to a boil. We soon heard a sound foreign to that of a summer thunderstorm. Was it the lost person's group? As distorted voices came rapidly closer, the hootin' and hollerin' was unmistakably from our fellow hikers Phil and George.

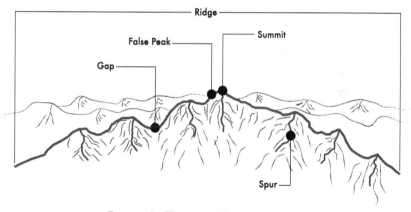

Georgraphic Features of Mountain Ranges

Literally sprinting into the shelter and beating the onslaught of rain by a matter of seconds, we couldn't believe our eyes. George's goofy laugh was cracking us up, and we temporarily forgot about our aching bodies. While we boiled water for our standard backpacking pasta meals, Phil asked George if he was ready for his dinner. Part friend, part caretaker of

George, Phil pulled out a commercial-sized pack of hot dogs from his pack as George's eyes lit up with excitement. We began to start expecting the unexpected with these two. Hysterically laughing and, truth be told, kind of jealous, we asked where one would even acquire such a bountiful supply of hot dogs. Phil explained that they didn't make it to Neel's Gap until that day because they camped the night before in the shelter on top of Blood Mountain. They had purchased the hot dogs from the Mountain Crossings store, where they hung out until about 2:00 that afternoon. This explained the hootin' and hollerin' of our friends arriving to Blue Mountain Shelter that night; they ran from Neel's Gap to the Shelter, 17.8 miles. Pretty impressive, all things considered.

Phil and George were not early risers to say the least, and as we packed up the next morning, ready for more, they still lay dead asleep. As we continued through Georgia, I found it comforting in our first few weeks that I had the confidence to complete this part of the trail because I already had done most of the AT from Springer to Southern Virginia. Having this experience also led me to wonder what existed further beyond in the miles north of Southern Virginia that I knew so little about. A perpetual excitement grew, but I had to focus on the task at hand, and that was just making miles, getting my trail legs, and enjoying the moment. The nostalgia of retracing my past footsteps wore off at times in the green tunnel of summer-rain soaked rhododendron.

One of the many complaints from hikers on the AT, especially those unfamiliar with the dense vegetation of the southeastern United States, is that even at the tops of most mountains, there is rarely a view. They are covered with trees and foliage, which can be somewhat demoralizing, because one great part of getting to the top of a climb is the rewarding view you expect when you get there. Instead, what happens is you get to the top of a climb and are instantly faced with a steep descent, only to get to another gap and then be faced with another climb with another disappointing non-view. After a few days of this, with just a handful of views for the numerous climbs you have done, you can see how frustrating this may be to someone expecting much more. With the possibility of bad weather, the few views you do have can be reduced to low visibility, crushing the soul of a thru-hiker. The three of us knew what to expect for the most part during the first few hundred miles of hiking, and were thus better prepared in our expectations.

A question we often get about our hike is people wondering how we knew where to go and where we were? The AT is an extremely well-marked trail. The blaze, or trail marking, that indicates where the trail goes (as if one cannot determine it by the some 3 million people that hike on the AT every year) is a 2-inch wide by 6-inch tall white rectangle often painted on trees, rocks, or posts placed in the ground. Variations of this are also used when the trail is not straight. Two stacked white blazes mean the trail takes a sharp turn or marks a trail intersection with another trail. Most other trails that intersect the AT are typically marked with a blue blaze of the same dimensions. The most common side trails marked by blue blazes lead to shelters that are not directly on the AT or that lead to water sources. The same marks apply for sharp turns and trail intersections on blue blaze trails.

Thus, the marking of the trail is straightforward. There are also an array of different guidebooks published by independent hikers and one by the Appalachian Trail Conservancy that are compact, fairly light and very resourceful. These guidebooks are intended to be carried with you as you hike. Typically arranged in similar ways, these "Thru-Hiker Companions" (as the Appalachian Trail Conservancy has so aptly named their guidebook) contain basic information about the trail. Those who are uber-concerned about the weight of their pack even rip out the individual sections of the part they are currently hiking so that they save weight by not having to carry a book that has information you'll need hundreds of miles away. I wasn't that gung-ho about saving weight although we were conscious about what we were carrying.

One important question we receive over and over again is how we knew how far we had been, how far we had to go, and how far we were from various terrain features. These guidebooks keep a running tally of how many miles you are from Mt. Katahdin and Mt. Springer as well as mile marks for significant trail features such as road crossings, water sources, shelters, low and high elevation points and other geographic noteworthy elements. These guidebooks are essential to the day-to-day planning that happens on the trail. We used the guides to determine how much water we needed to carry until our next water source, what shelter we were headed for that night as well as what services were available in towns on or near the trail. At most every major road crossing in my guidebook (I carried the "Appalachian Trail Conservancy's Thru-Hiker Companion") were a series of letter symbols representing specific services. For example "F" for food, "W" for water, "S" for shelter, and so on.

On just our fourth day as we passed over Kelly Knob, one of the first clear mountain tops of the Southern Appalachian Trail, we took in the view, took a break, and looked at our guidebook. Just down the top of the Knob was a highway crossing, one that led some 11 miles east to the town of Hiawassee, Georgia. In the spreadsheet format of the book, all the numerical and mileage data is provided. These sections are broken up into different parts, typically by state. Bold text on the spreadsheet pages encourages the hiker to keep reading for additional information like specific directions to shelters, or water sources, as well as towns. There are even a few fun facts thrown in there with short history tidbits and little nibbles about flora and fauna so you can promptly sound like the biggest dork on the trail.

We looked suspiciously at the acronym AYCE in the additional information section for the services in the town of Hiawassee, Georgia. "A-Y-C-E" we spelled out as we asked ourselves, what could this be? Then written in italics in the guidebook "All You Can Eat." The temptation was great, but we had to stay focused; we couldn't venture off the trail already – it had been only four days since we even started. Granted, we were making pretty good time, and so far had stuck exactly to our Itinerary that Ben and I conjured up at the Harrington's home the week before our trip.

As we meandered down the trail to the road crossing of US 76 at Dicks Creek Gap, we spotted a van parked on the side of the road. The presumed driver of the vehicle was walking around aimlessly where the trail met the road. I'll have to admit, it was a little off-putting as I pictured us in the makings of a suspicious story on the front page of a local Georgia newspaper: "Man captures three hikers on Appalachian Trail in Georgia." I reminded myself of how much previous time I had spent on the Appalachian Trail over the years and that there was nothing to worry about. No banjos were playing quite yet.

It was as if the trail was sending us a message that we should take a ride in to town to refuel on some food, do some laundry, take a shower, and a have a good night's rest. As if it were some sort of consolation of a few nights back at Neel's Gap. Turns out, the owner of the van was the man walking near the trailhead at the road. His name was Ron Haven, and he was a trail angel. Not only was Ron a trail angel but a trail enthusiast of the highest caliber. In our small talk (before he offered us a ride), we discovered he too had spent a number of years in Raleigh, NC. He claimed to be an amateur wrestler on the once-CBS affiliate in Raleigh, WRAL. Subtracting a few decades and a few pounds, it was believable enough. We were just glad the costume stayed at home.

Nevertheless, he convinced us that we ought to go to town and that he knew of a few hostels along the way. The main hostel he was thinking of and the one that we first read about in the guidebook was Cloud 9 hostel. However, due to our late start date, the Hostel had already shut down for the thru-hiker season. We ventured farther down the highway to the Blueberry Patch Hiker Hostel. Strike two. This Christian-run hostel was closed for the season as well. Ron finally decided that he would take us all the way into town to the Hiawassee Inn. He had heard that the owners were quite hiker-friendly and could probably shuttle us back to the trail the next morning. As we pulled up to the motel, Ron was still commenting on how he didn't know if we would be able to complete the trail in our short timeframe, a comment we were not short of hearing in our first couple hundred miles. We all took it as a "we'll see about that" kind of challenge. Our optimism was oozing from ear to ear.

While checking in to the motel we met the proprietors, Ron and Sam. Ron and Sam were very fond of us and enthusiasts of the trail as well. We had a hunch that Ron and Sam were also quite fond of, well, each other. They offered us a ride to and from the all-you-can-eat buffet at Daniel's Steakhouse. Immediately accepting their offer, we went to our room and showered up, and made ourselves presentable to a non-hiker, public restaurant. We feasted on plate upon plate of mac n' cheese, fried chicken, green beans, made multiple dessert trips, and washed it all down with glass upon glass of sweet tea. Before we knew it, our ride was there, the bills were paid, and the walk to the car was almost harder than the previous 60 miles of trail over the past 4 days.

Before we got out to go into our room and got laundry started, we were invited to a free breakfast in the motel office the next morning before our shuttle back to the trailhead. The rest of the night was filled with phone calls to family, journaling, and talking about the next resupply. As we began doing laundry, we quickly ran into a dilemma. In the effort to carry as little as possible, there was nothing left to wear whilst doing laundry. Each of us donned a motel towel about the third the size it needed to be, severely decreasing mobility. Rock, paper, scissors for who has to get the laundry from the outdoor corridor, anyone?

Going in to town always seems like a great idea, but it's the next morning, having to leave town, that becomes difficult. All the same, you get on with the grind; at this point in the trip, we were still eager to get on with it. Sitting down for breakfast in the motel office, which also happened to be the actual kitchen of Ron and Sam, we couldn't help but notice the décor. It was a rooster, or for lack of better term, cock motif. Ron and Sam's hospitality was nothing short of fantastic.

Georgia countryside on the route back was filled with fields of grass being cut for hay. The ongoing moan of the tractors made gentle by distance, bailing hay released a sweet, pollinated aroma into the air. The sun warmed our faces while cutting shadows from the car frame across our torsos as we quietly made it back to the trail. Our short, unexpected trip away from the trail was a much deserved and an efficiently utilized one. We slung our packs back on, tightened our shoes, checked our next water source/break point, and started walking.

While we were in Hiawassee, Garrett had talked to some family members and learned that his great aunt's health was failing her. After losing his grandmother at a young age, she filled the same role under a different title. Unfortunately enough, Garrett's immediate family had gone on vacation, and there was no logistical way, if anything were to go wrong, they would be able to make it. Ben and I weren't fully aware of how dire her health was, but we were there to support Garrett in whatever happened.

In the case that her health completely failed her, a plan was made on how we could make it to Belmont, North Carolina (just Southwest of Charlotte, North Carolina) to get to the service so Garrett could mourn with his extended family members. An aunt from Charleston would pick us up somewhere between our Hiawassee restart to somewhere across the North Carolina border. We soon reached our first significant milestone of the trip, the Georgia-North Carolina state line. Shortly after we stopped for a break on a relatively open ridge-line, resting for a moment, Garrett opened up the top of his pack and checked his cell signal. Sure enough, he had a couple bars and checked a voicemail that brought the disconcerting news that his great aunt had passed. Another series of phone calls organized us a ride as we gave Garrett the nod to confirm a pick up for us tomorrow afternoon at Winding Stair Gap at US 64.

In order to meet this deadline, we pushed on to our longest day so far of 24 miles. This was a considerable yet necessary leap in mileage in order to support our friend and his family. It was an effort, in a nutshell, that defined the reason of our trip. Hiking for the loss of our friend, we were hiking that day for the loss of another. To lighten the mood a bit, when we arrived at our destination for the night, at Carter Gap Shelter, we were greeted late by some recently met acquaintances. Hiking right up until dark, we had just enough time to claim our spots in the shelter among a silent Asian couple as we began preparing dinner and a much-deserved good night's sleep. Right as we finished our supper and were cleaning our bowls, the all too familiar hootin' and hollerin' of what was unmistakably Phil and George filled the air once again. The dynamic duo was not even planning on staying in the shelter. They had a night hike planned to the top of Albert Mountain, which sits at a stern 5,200 ft.

Being the only one in our threesome that had actually hiked this portion of the trail, I knew that the climb to Albert Mountain was no easy task. In fact, it's a huff, but I wasn't going to ruin the surprise. George and Phil were in for it that night as we fell soundly asleep worrying about getting to the pick-up point on time. Sure enough, the next morning, as we climbed up the final steps to the now unmanned fire tower that sits atop Albert Mountain, Phil and George were just waking to their nine o'clock sunrise at the base of the tower. It was a stupendous view from the top of the fire tower. As to the two guys below us, another country tune quickly followed our arrival. In honor of what was sure to be our last moment shared on the trail with Phil and George, George picked out a fine country tune to grace our departure:

I walked in and the band just started
the singer couldn't carry a tune in a bucket
was on a mission to drown her memory
but I thought no way with all this ruckus...
One round with Jose Cuervo...

George recited every line word for word, nine rounds; he also managed to hit a note or two. Once again blown away by the memorization skills of George, he shared his lifetime dream of becoming a country singer with us in more detail.

One morning in grade school while riding on the bus, he was talking to the bus driver. I picture the same George in a miniature frame, yapping the lady's ear off. She asked him what he wanted to be, surely in attempt to hear something valid come out of his mouth. "I'm going to be a country music singer." His fate was sealed as years later he roamed the Appalachians carrying an arsenal of country songs, serenading any hiker he came in contact with. Even if George never makes it on the billboards and doesn't topple George Strait's record of number one hits, he'll always be our country singer. And, just in case he does go big, I'll be able to release a viral You-Tube video of his days as a hiking singer. I look forward to that day.

We made Winding Stair Gap with time to spare. We were beginning a trend of crushing deadlines, a task we needed to get in the habit of doing. Arriving at US 64 with a little free time, we couldn't help but think about the food that sat just a few miles down the highway in Franklin, North Carolina. We referenced our trusty guidebook, more specifically, the map of the town of Franklin, and even more specifically, the fact that they had a Wendy's. The temptation was irresistible. It was time to test out our hitchhiking thumbs anyway. As cars whizzed by, we remained optimistic. Eventually we were picked up by an older woman who must of assumed that we were harmless, a correct assumption, minus the smell.

Despite doing laundry just 2 days before our first hitchhiking attempt, we still smelled. Trail funk was hanging all over us. What we hadn't accounted for, regardless of relatively clean clothes, was our packs and gear smelling. When asked our desired destination, we rang out unanimously "Wendy's." I was unfamiliar withFranklin being a town frequented on the trail by thru-hikers, but I'm sure it sees a fair amount of hiker traffic. Orders were filled, trays stacked high with value menu item on top of value menu item, and we chose the nearest table for immediate chow time. Like starved animals coming out of captivity, we once again started our binge eating. However, a few bites into our meal, we couldn't help but notice an unusual number of flies hovering around us. At first thought, we were in a Wendy's. On second thought, we didn't notice an overpopulation of flies when we first came in and were ordering, nor did they seem to be bothering any of the other customers. It didn't take long to realize they were there because we brought them in.

For a thru-hiker, trail funk is inevitable. It starts with your clothes, which can be temporarily fixed by doing laundry every time you go into town. Even that doesn't last long though. Once you start hiking in your clothes again, the smell comes right back. Deodorant isn't an option either unless you want to attract animals of all kinds: mice in the shelter, black bear and even wild boar in some areas. Those aren't things you really want to mess with. Besides, deodorant might smell nice, but you also have to carry it, and we weren't down with that.

While we finished our meals, fly friends and all, we did everyone else in the restaurant a favor and showed ourselves the door. The timing was great as our ride had just arrived. We loaded our gear into the truck and headed east back to Hickory, North Carolina, to stay with Garrett's grandfather, a.k.a. "Pops." Pops was no stranger to scouting, the outdoors, or the Appalachian Trail. He spent a fair amount of time hiking in the Great Smoky Mountains and the Grayson Highlands in Southern Virginia. Before we arrived in Hickory, we took a detour to a family reunion of Garrett's extended family that was happening nearby.

Meeting some of Garrett's family was nice, and they were all thoroughly impressed with the miles we already had in the bag. It felt good to hear such impressed opinions although the road ahead was still long. Most of the family members, along with both Ben's and mine, were avidly following our blog, checking on our progress. As we feasted on a crab boil for supper along with other traditional southern fare, it felt somewhat odd. Topping it all off with a pontoon boat ride around the lake where the reunion was being held, I felt a bit out of place. Though we totally supported Garrett and helping him get through his loss, I longed for the trail. After all, this wasn't in the itinerary.

Our Pleasure
Is our Pain

Nantahala Outdoor Center

We ended our long day arriving in Hickory by showering up and once again taking full advantage of a washer and dryer. Then we had to figure out what we were going to wear to the funeral the next day. As we ransacked Pops' closet, we threw some outfits together, stuffed our feet into dress shoes, and planned on getting some rest in a bed. At this point, we hardly felt like we were roughing it on our thru-hike: two out of six nights were spent in a bed after a shower and a home-cooked meal. We knew this trend wouldn't last for long though.

The day of the funeral service was going to be a zero-day. To put this into perspective of our trip itinerary, we planned for two zero days on the entire 90-day trip: one in Damascus, Virginia, the undisputed "friendliest" town on the trail; and one in Harper's Ferry, West Virginia, the unofficial halfway point of the trail (the actual halfway point is just north of the general store at Pine Grove Furnace State Park in Pennsylvania).

Pops and his wife Dot woke us up early, as we had to make the journey to Belmont, North Carolina, for the service. Packed in the backseat of his Cadillac like a can of sardines and awkwardly shoved into dress clothes, we arrived at the family farm where Garrett's Sisterhood of Great Aunts lived. Garrett and I had actually traveled here before a few months back while he was visiting me at UNC-Charlotte, and he was on holiday break. At least I felt some sort of connection with the family, having previously met Garrett's aunt. Ben, on the other hand, must have been in his own world of contemplation.

It was hard to believe I was just under an hour from my apartment and friends, knowing life was carrying on without my presence. I missed it all a little bit but tried not to think about it too much. The importance of what I was doing over the summer went beyond fulfilling a dream of mine; it was a dream of ours. If anything, the funeral service reminded me of being at Stephen's funeral. Not in the circumstances of death, nor the people that were attending. More in the sense of how you cope with death. The lives of Stephen and Garrett's great aunt were, in reality, juxtaposed: one's was lived to full potential, the gift of long life; the other was cut short, empty pages of unwritten chapters.

One thing was for sure during our time away from the trail: we weren't going hungry. After the service, we traveled back to the farm. Ben and I sat in the living room, the very one that I had met Garrett's great aunt in, as Garrett took some self-reflection time with his family. We ate until our stomachs could have popped, and the time finally came to travel back to Hickory for the night while we settled in for a third night of sleeping in a bed. Pops had promised us a "big scout breakfast" in the morning, which sounded promising though we had no idea what that meant.

Waking to the smell of bacon and eggs wasn't what we expected the 7th day of our thru-hike, but hey, I'll take it. Fresh fruit and orange juice accompanied the bacon and eggs and sure beat the hell out of a Clif Bar. We began another ride back to the trail, this time long before sunrise. Although we were coming off a zero day, it was still a fully emotional one. Pop's driving was beginning to worry us a little bit, so Garrett took over driving about 30 minutes in.

I was aware of the day's hike we had ahead of us and knew that it wasn't too bad. The only difference in the section we were about to hike compared to when I hiked it just a year prior with Troop 215 was we were going to it in one day instead of two-and-a-half days. Despite my previous traverse of this section, I was not deterred in believing we were fully capable of making it to the Nantahala Outdoor Center (NOC) that night. During the final descent down the ridge to the NOC, disaster struck on our long, exhausting day. Garrett fell while taking a step down off a rock outcropping in the trail and twisted his ankle. With ongoing shin splint pains in the previous days of hiking adding to his injury, the rest of the final descent was painful for Garrett. We figured the shin splints were just part of getting his trail legs under him, despite neither Ben nor I having the same problem. As a runner in high school, I know all too well about shin splints. Every step becomes painful, and the only thing that doesn't hurt is to sit down. That wasn't exactly a treatment our schedule allowed us to fulfill.

In spite of Garrett's injury, we remarkably made it to the NOC with daylight to spare. The three of us even had time to grab a bite to eat at the River's End restaurant in the small tourist haven just outside of Bryson City, North Carolina. The Nantahala River runs right through the middle of shops, restaurants, lodging and guide companies. There are cabins for rent as well as community bunk rooms. It's a neat little place to relax after a long day of hiking as you can enjoy a meal while watching rafters and kayakers make their final runs of the day.

We checked into one of the bunks that are available at a reasonable price and claimed our spots among other hikers. The next destination was the River's End restaurant, which literally hangs over part of the river. This added another decent meal to the trip, which the trip was not lacking so far. The appetizer and/or entrée dilemma was not nearly as crucial as that of

Garrett's worrisome situation. After being battered up a bit on our descent into town, we were worried. Sure, there would be the obvious adjustment time while starting out. But it was a tight timeline, and the margin for error was so incredibly minute – and we hadn't really thought about potential problems before we started.

As much as you'd like to tell yourself you're somehow unique – no snowflake's the same, they say – well, guess what? The trail doesn't care. You are just a tiny little cog in a great big machine. Weather, terrain, the availability of water, and mental stress are all the things that can hinder a thru-hike attempt. So now we had a decision to make. Do we go on with one of us hurt? Do we lower our mileage in hopes of making it up later in the trip? Does Garrett go home, get healthy again, and then return to hike with us in a couple weeks, skipping about 150 miles of the trail? Do all of us stop and wait for Garrett to return to full health?

We saw Phil and George again that night at dinner, bringing some relief from our tough decision-making. Attracted to one of the girls who was sitting at a table of river guides finishing up dinner, George went over to talk to them at the table right beside where we were sitting. Intrigued by George's capability of smooth talk, we watched him awkwardly strike up a conversation with the group. I thought to myself, Oh Lord, what is he going to do now. A few small talk questions gave way to song. After finding out his female prey was from Louisiana, he began belting out "Callin' Baton Rouge" by Garth Brooks from his arsenal of lyrics

Operator won't you put me on through gotta send my love down to Baton Rouge. Hurry up, put her on the line, I gotta talk to my girl just one more time....

As if to never disappoint, George once again delivered. He danced away in rhythm and song all the way out of the restaurant. Poor girl, I thought, she has no idea that this happens all the time. Part of me wished he were joining us on the rest of our journey, ensuring no dull moments.

Spencer McKay

Teetering right before our eyes was the decision whose weight would completely change the entire trip. We decided to buy some time by sleeping on it that night. But none of us did. By the next morning, our only decision was to bum a ride into Bryson City and get Garrett to a hospital or clinic. After loitering around the parking lot of the outfitter and restaurant for about half an hour, we were finally able to get a ride from an adult leader on a Youth Group rafting trip on the Nantahala. The group was from Southern Florida, and Ben was able to keep a friendly conversation rolling on our way to town. "Sitting on pins and needles" was the overall mood as we stalled around town and in the waiting room. I'm not sure a doctor's opinion was really what we wanted. As we expected, he had a severe strain and signs of overuse syndrome.

"Overuse Syndrome." No shit, we're traveling on foot from Georgia to Maine. We failed to find the humor in it at the time. Considering the doctor's only suggested treatment was "time-off," it seemed our decision had been made for us. Garrett explains his situation on our blog.

I am safely home as of 11:00am May 31 2007. The injury that I have acquired is called overuse syndrome, which is in my case is an inflammation of the muscles and connective tissue in my ankle. My body has not taken the adjustment to the terrain and mileage for one major reason. The shoes that I started the trail with lacked cushion and did not provide my feet and legs enough protection from the rock filled terrain that we have encountered so far, this factor combined with the 27 mile segment that we accomplished Monday led to severe pain in my right leg from the shin to the foot. I decided that with the doctor recommending at least 2-4 days off of my feet followed by tapering my mileage back to our planned pace that I would come off of the trail. I decided that it is more important for me to not accomplish a thru hike at this moment, but rather to not be injured or jeopardize the entire trip. I will be rejoining Spencer and Ben as soon as possible, and in the meantime will be resting my feet for another couple of days. Then I will taper in a training regimen in the time between now and getting back on trail. I would like to thank all of the people that sacrificed their time and effort to get me from such a remote part of North Carolina back home. I will be in touch with Spencer and Ben and will attempt to keep you updated during this time. We will blog more about some of the proverbial good Samaritans that we have met along the way in the near future.

Parting ways with Garrett, we got our ride back to the trail and began hiking. The afternoon resulted in a gain of 7 miles on a brutal ascent to Sassafras Gap Shelter. Our previous 27-mile day was catching up to us as we took our final steps to rest that night. A nice couple joined us at the shelter that night along with a four-legged trail companion as well. I felt pity on the stray dog, perhaps similar to it with one of our team members gone. The shelter was absolutely filthy. The floor of the shelter where we slept was covered with a layer of dirt, undoubtedly tracked in by a mud-covered crew. Clumps of mud were dried up and left for others to deal with.

There is a certain amount of trail etiquette people should oblige to. Some of the most common ones have to do with groups of hikers vs. solo or small groups of hikers. There's also a bit of a battle between thru-hikers and all other hikers. Some thru-hikers believe that they are subject to every right-of-way and perk on the trail. For example, when arriving to a shelter at night, some expect a spot in the shelter to be reserved for them. As if it's a Holiday Inn or something.

Another situation happens during actual hiking, not in a shelter or at camp. When a hiker is traveling downhill and comes in contact with someone traveling the opposite direction, they ought to yield to the hiker who is climbing. This is typically the case, but some people just don't think about it. There's also an argument on trail etiquette about single/ small group hikers vs. large groups such as Boy Scout and church groups. Solo hikers think the large group should step aside on the trail, if the terrain enables them, and make room for the single hiker to pass. The other side of the argument is that instead of an entire group stopping and moving aside, why not just one person or a small number of people step aside, if possible, and allow the group to pass. This becomes an increasingly difficult situation when the two parties are traveling in the same direction. The thru-hiker typically travels much faster and frequently catches up to groups. In this case, good luck. Most people in a large group of hikers are typically inexperienced and take a bit more time. You have to just try and get around them as politely as possible.

Fortunately enough, there was a broom head in the corner of the shelter and we swept out as much of the dirt and dust as possible. Talking with the older couple, we unraveled our thru-hike plans to them. Impressed by how little we were carrying and our speed of travel, they wished us the best. Another hiker was passing through the shelter that night that we had seen on the trail. Ben and I had gave him the nickname "Riddick." Every time we said it with a deep, raspy voice. The main reason we called him this was because he had these red tinted glasses and a shaved head, which was enough similarity to relate him to the Vin Diesel's character in"Chronicles of Riddick". Riddick took the dog with him, and when we passed him the next morning saw that he had even fashioned a leash. We weren't sure if Riddick was planning on a thru-hike or what, but we didn't stop to chat and find out. Our sights were set on entering the southern boundary of the Great Smokey Mountains National Park.

Arriving at the shelter, just a few hundred yards away from Fontana Dam, we saw the sign posted on the side that reads "Fontana Hilton." Just short of a Hilton indeed, minus the bar/ restaurant in the lobby and premium room service. A few others arrived late to the shelter that night. Appreciative of their effort to go right to sleep in lieu of staying up and swapping trail stories. Quiet voices carrying on a conversation would have been preferred over the logs being sawed. A snorer was among us in the shelter. This is one of the downsides to a shelter; you are subject to experiencing everyone else's sleeping behavior. Disclaimer: if you snore, and you snore really, really loud, get a tent.

After a scorching day before and a terrible night's sleep in the "Fontana Hilton," we traveled across the Fontana Dam at the crack of dawn. Passing the Visitor Center the day before, we caught up on a bit of history about the Tennessee Valley Authority (TVA) project built to power World War II efforts. While crossing the dam, we were surprised when a worker popped out of a manhole and stared across Fontana Lake focusing on the shoreline across the way. When we approached him after another minute of walking he called us over. Hey, hey, y'all look over there.

What is it? we responded, intrigued by the tone of his voice. Two black bears right over there up on that ridge. Our reaction was nonchalant -- Wow really -- while on the inside, we were a bit terrified. Unable to locate the bears ourselves, we asked the worker where the trail goes. Pointer finger raised up, following his line of sight. We waited as he approximated the path of the trail, as if having hiked it hundreds of times. He then came to an abrupt pause, Well, I guess the bears were right on the trail!

Nervously continuing, we weren't sure what to expect once we got off the dam and started walking on trail again. The Smoky Mountains are one of the greatest sections of the Appalachian Trail. The park has almost 10 million visitors each year. Before thru-hikers enter the park, they must fill out a Thru-Hiker's Backcountry Permit. All hikers that start at least 50 miles away from either end of the Smokies are exempt from needing a permit, but they are asked to state your projected campsite each night. If we were not thru-hikers we would have needed to register for a hiking permit months ahead of time due to the park's popularity.

The shelters in the Smoky Mountains are notorious for bear problems, more so than any other section on the trail, most likely due to the high volumes of people that visit the park. Bears are not stupid. People equals food to bears. Not people as food, not to black bears, but food that they can take from people. During 2007, the shelters in the Park had metal fencing covering the entire entrance to the shelter. It was like sleeping in jail for the night. However, to my knowledge, they have been removed because of a few instances when a bear would wait outside the fence with people inside the shelter, creating a sort of AT standoff between hiker and bear. How frightening that must have been for those hikers. Although most bears, especially black bears, are afraid of you, that's a tough conclusion to come to when you're in the presence of one.

We were not too awfully surprised when we rounded the corner of the trail to the approximate location of these bears and found nothing. What we did find in the trail were 2 hikers sitting in the middle of the trail playing chess on a mini travel board. Not looking for a conversation, we politely nodded and continued walking. Whoa Dudes! they called out, you don't want to go up there; there's a bear up there. The 2 young men turned out to be from New Jersey. Had the show "Jersey Shore" come out 3 years earlier, we could have assigned all kinds of stereotypes but tried to keep it to a minimum. Unwavered by their exclamation, we noticed a piney, nearly skunky aroma of some not-so-legal smoke still lingering.

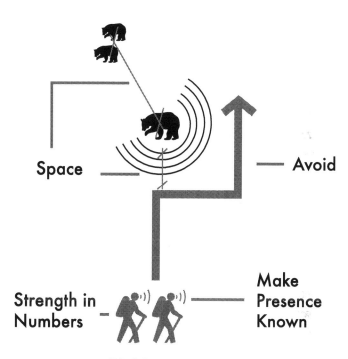

Black Bear Avoidance Tips

They elaborated a bit more, proclaiming a bear about half a mile up the trail wasn't letting people past. Apparently, a group of about 4 adult hikers had a problem with it as well and told the boys about a standoff with the bear. There are a few theories on what to do in the presence of a bear. Rule #1: do not get between a Mama Bear and her cubs. Simple enough, right? Rule #2: try not to startle the bear or sneak up on it. Problem solved by keeping a conversation going while hiking and making plenty of noise. This, for us, was not hard seeing as how we talked frequently enough, were hiking with trekking poles, and hiked fast enough that we made plenty of noise.

If travelling alone and you fail to let the bear know that you are there for some reason, which is probable, the next course of action is to begin making plenty of noise, talk to it, stay still, and let the bear make its next move. Odds are, the bear will run off and you might have time for a picture, or at least a mental picture and a good story. That night as we rolled in to Derrick Knob shelter, as predicted on our Backcountry Permit, we shared the shelter with a group of older adults hiking. Turns out, they were a group of friends from college that get together every year and hike a section of the AT. They started this tradition somewhere around 2002 and had done everything from Springer to our current location.

It was nice to see good friends sharing the outdoor experience together and the camaraderie of the trail. After all, that is what brought Ben, Garrett, Stephen and me together. They were impressed and touched with our story about why we were hiking and in further awe of our hiking pace. It was the classic "Do it while you're young" response. The old college buddies were chowing down on their freeze-dried backcountry meals, drinking their GNC recovery drink, and popping ibuprofen like Pez. They reminded me of the scout leaders Ben and I had become close to over the years.

After completing multiple 20-plus mile days in a row, we felt as if we were on a roll and finally started feeling confident in our ability to make large amounts of miles in a day. We started falling into a routine, now familiar with what we had to do each morning and each night to make getting started easier. For example, we made sure we had water purifying overnight so we could drink some first thing in the morning and have some to get us on our way to the next water source. In 2007, much of the Eastern Seaboard was hit hard by drought. Starting without water each day would have been to our detriment.

Great Smoky National Park was no different. At times, where we expected a healthy flow of water, it was down to a mere trickle and a less-than-appetizing static pool nearby. We just had to make do with what we had. Perhaps we weren't drinking enough, especially considering the amount of work we were asking our bodies to do. Dehydration is one of the most common mistakes among hikers and outdoor enthusiasts everywhere. The humid and wet conditions on the Appalachian Trail don't help much either.

We were extremely excited for our day after departing Derrick Knob Shelter because en route to our next night on the trail, we would be passing over the highest point on the entire trail, Clingman's Dome. At 6,643 feet, a large concrete observation tower sits atop with an elegant ramp that wraps around it 50-60' above the ground. It was also a mileage milestone for us as it sits just under 200 miles north of Springer Mountain.

The observation tower was filled with tourists, seeing as how a road leads right up to the thing. The infamous haze of the Great Smoky Mountains denied an opportunity for a spectacular view. We didn't let this deter us from making a few phone calls from the tower and taking in what we assumed to be an otherwise great view. Sitting atop the tower for about half an hour or so, people were curious as to where we had hiked from. Telling folks about our journey seemed to create a sense of astonishment. I guess people always hear about hikers walking from Georgia to Maine, but meeting someone in the act makes them feel like they were part of it.

Among the kudos and infatuation, one young boy, who could not have been more than 8 or 9, sticks out in my mind. After we were finished talking to the boy and his father, and they had descended from the ramp, I heard the young boy yell out, Dad, I wanna hike the Appalachian Trail. It gave me that warm and fuzzy feeling inside, hoping he'd hang on to that thought for a long time. With the passing of Clingman's Dome, we made the sarcastic assumption that it must be downhill from here. With a bit of a laugh, we continued on.

The descent from the highest point on the AT leads you to Newfound Gap/ US 441, the only major road crossing in the national park. Flooded with tourists traveling by car and RV on their Memorial Day holiday, we approached the road. Just before we emerged into a whirlwind of families on vacation, we found a little cooler on the AT labeled thru-hikers only. Under the lid of the white Styrofoam cooler lay 2 - count em - two, ICE COLD Pepsi's. This was some much-needed trail magic. As we carried them up to the parking lot, we snapped a couple of pictures at the North Carolina-Tennessee border sign and continued on after disposing of the Pepsi cans. Just before we began following the trail again, a Park Ranger approached us aggressively; notifying us that there was a Red Ozone alert that day. He suggested we hitch a ride into nearby Gatlinburg, Tennessee. We took it as a joke and headed onward. Feeling fine and a bit irritated by crowds of people on the trail due to a mountain overlook that was promised just a few tenths of a mile north on the trail, we were ready for isolation again.

In the frustration of fighting over room on a crowded trail, I took a big step down off a rock and a shooting pain developed instantly just above my right knee. Continuing to walk, I figured it was a mere tweak. It didn't hurt enough to make me stop so I just kept on going. I guess Ben started to notice a bit of a limp in my step. He asked me about it only because he was feeling something in his leg, too. We weren't sure what the problem was, but we were still able to walk and make pretty good time. Our trail legs were under us, and we didn't have any trouble making good mileage the past 3 days.

Discussing our dilemma, I asked Ben where he was hurting. My leg, he said. Where, I asked. Just above me right knee, Ben responded. Bizarre as it was, we both had developed a cramp in the exact same spot at the exact same time. Steps were becoming more and more painful as we began getting tired of overcompensating on every step. Our pace slowed to a mere hobble as we prayed for the shelter to magically appear around every bend. With unclear signage and fatigue building into hindrance, we finally stumbled into Peck's Corner Shelter to finish our 28-mile day. Although a high mileage day that included crossing over the highest point of the trail, it came at a price. The trail was fighting back. Almost as if to say, I'm here, and you're not getting away that easy. Who do you think you are, hiking 28 miles on a red ozone day in the Smoky Mountains? Fortunately enough, while on Clingman's Dome, we confirmed with 2 of my college roommates, Jason and Todd Chappell, that they along with their parents, would rendezvous with us 20 miles down the mountain at Davenport Gap. We ate and drank all we could, hoping we'd wake up and the cramp would sort itself out overnight.

Perhaps the pressure to perform day in and day out was getting to us. Nevertheless, we woke up the next morning feeling pretty good. At least that's what we told ourselves, and we hiked on, motivated by meeting up with some friends just 20 miles down the trail. In poor planning, we did not actually agree on a specific spot to meet up; we just knew that we were going to meet in Causby, Tennessee. There was no map of the town in the guidebook, which should have been a red flag to begin with. So, when we got to the road at Davenport Gap, we just figured a hitchhike in that direction would get us started. Hopeful for a cell signal in town, we assumed we could just make a phone call.

Causby is the proverbial "blink and you'll miss it" town. Not even a 1-stoplight town, unless you count a flashing yellow light as a stoplight. Causby is an unorthodox place to stop along the AT. However, for the sake of our schedule and the Chappell's, this was our best opportunity to meet up. We weren't complaining, but when we got into town, we failed to receive a good signal on our cell phones. Tired and thirsty for something other than water, we were dropped off at the town gas pump/convenience store/movie rental/arcade to gather our thoughts. After purchasing some refreshments and throwing our packs back on, I saw the twin brothers Jason and Todd whiz by. Frantically calling out and waving got their attention. That might have been it, or maybe it was that we were the only people walking around with backpacks on, better yet, the only people around period.

They got our gear in the car and we drove, oh, I don't know, 50 feet, to a cabin just down the street that we could literally see from the convenience store. What a nice surprise. The Chappells figured it was just easier to get a cabin for a night than to figure something else out. Besides, Causby didn't have much to offer. Jason and Todd brought another one of our friends along, Chris Barth, who is also an Eagle Scout. We all attended architecture school at UNC-C. It was great getting to see everyone, especially Mr. and Mrs. Chappell who are fantastic in the kitchen. Dinner consisted of BBQ chicken, steak, buttery baked potatoes, fresh summer corn, salad, bread, pasta salad, and, to top it all off, Italian Wedding Cake. Having dealt with our cramp the past few days, we saw their visit as a blessing. Ben and I were able to take our minds off it, enjoy some laughs with friends, and truly relax along with some hot tub time.

Heading out the next day, we were accompanied by Chris, Jason, and Todd. They trotted along at our pace. It was nice having some extra company for the short time that they hiked with us. At lunch time, we devoured the leftovers from last night, thanks to Mrs. Chappell, and said our farewells. And then, there were two. Just like that, resupply complete and back on the trail.

Climbing the ridge of a mountain and hiking towards us was an odd site. We just thought it was a bum of sorts, a hiking bum, or a vagabond perhaps. He stopped to chat us up. We were intrigued by his appearance: everything he owned was either fashioned of or covered with TyVek, an impermeable water barrier used in the construction industry. His thought to use the extremely lightweight waterproof membrane was not ill advised. In fact, our ground cloth for our tent was fashioned out of the same material. We had just never seen it used in such an abundant manner. He aptly introduced himself as TyVek...Holy Shit. The Holy Shit came later, he explained. TyVek Holy Shit wasn't his given name, of course. That was his trail name. A trail name is a nickname you earn while on your journey. It is bestowed upon you by someone else thru-hiking; it is the essence of you. Some choose not to use a trail name, but those who do tend to stick with it. It can be given or self-assigned; no one can know for sure. Each trail name has a story behind it, unlike most nicknames, which usually have something to do with your given name, just shortened or phonetically changed. Case in point: TyVek Holy Shit.

As we continued talking to TyVek, we began to notice another interesting detail about him: he was barefoot. That's right, barefoot. Ben asked him how long he had been hiking barefoot. His answer wasn't quite what we were expecting. 1973, he said. Ben and I swapped surprised faces as awkward silence ensued. He then asked us what our trail names were. Having only been on the trail couple weeks, we didn't have enough humorous experiences to earn our own trail names. TyVek Holy Shit quickly followed with, Well, I would give you one, but would probably something condescending like Cum Shot… but I don't know you well enough. Thank goodness he didn't know us well enough. We awkwardly got out of that conversation and continued to hike in silence for about 15 minutes, knowing we had to decide on trail names, and fast, for obvious reasons.

For whatever reason, mostly optimism, we thought we had seen the last of the terribly painful leg cramp that both Ben and I experienced in the Smoky Mountains. One afternoon/evening of rest, good friends, great food, and a soak in the hot tub, and we were cured. But the trail had a different, more frustrating, idea. After crossing under Interstate 40 and making our way up towards Max Patch Summit, I began feeling the comeback of the woeful cramp.

I wasn't about to start saying anything to Ben about my leg, mainly because I didn't want to be hurting still and him not. What kind of a wuss would that make me? Besides, I was looking forward to Max Patch. I had heard it was one of the most beautiful places on the trail, and in the Southeast in particular. Disappointingly though, the overcast, storm-threatening skies further plastered the grimace on my face. With no view, a storm approaching, and a cramp in full force, it was a hurdle we could not cross. Atop Max Patch, Ben revealed he was having the same pain again. We quickly decided that we would not push it much further that day and would hike to the nearest shelter, Roaring Fork Shelter, just a couple miles away. This was the first time our physical ailment had hindered our mileage. Luckily, there were a couple of hikers ahead of us, and we could keep a pace by judging their distance from us. Those last couple of miles were far more laborious than they should have been. What should have been pleasant views and relatively easy hiking was in reality painstaking and frustrating.

As we descended slowly into the woods, we finally stumbled upon the side trail to the shelter. Aching and emotionally worn out, we set our packs down, claimed our spots in the shelter and chatted small talk with the hikers we had seen in front of us. While Ben kept chatting, I went to hang the bear bag. I had the line, spotted the perfect limb to toss it over and then tie a rock to the end of the rope. I gave it a toss and missed the limb. Again, I took aim, gave the line a toss, missed again. With Ben in the shelter with the two other hikers, now watching carefully, wanting me to get the line over, like sinking a game-winning free throw, I just couldn't do it. Toss after toss angered me exponentially more. The cramp was affecting me both mentally and physically now. I was frustrated at how such a silly little cramp, something that I had never experienced before in my life, could have such an impact on me.

Finally, I said to hell with it, no bear bag tonight, and went with Ben to fetch water. He too was frustrated as we hobbled back up the trail whence we just came to the water source. We were obviously both hurt. And the worst part about it was we had no idea what it could be. We were drinking up to 8 liters of water a day, just while hiking. Our diet was relatively healthy, consisting mainly of Clif bars, pasta with chicken or tuna for dinners, and a few Snickers or Little Debbies here and there. So with water and diet were ruled out, could it really have been due to the trail itself. We had been on the trail before and never experienced anything like this. We were both athletes in high school and never had problems such as this. Both Ben and I were vexed as to how we could resolve this problem.

On that short walk to fetch water, I had a million ideas racing through my head. What were we doing wrong? Why was this happening? Why was this happening now? Why is it happening to both of us? What if it weren't happening to both of us? What if we can't make it to Maine? What if we can't make it out of North Carolina? What if we can hardly make it to the next town? Would we have to quit? What would people think of us if we quit? We can't quit, we're doing this for Steve. Oh my God, we might have to quit? No, we cannot quit. We've got to push through but how. The pain is unbearable, what if this cramp never ceases?

Questions like these and more are the frequent dialogue many thru-hikers have internally. It is a dangerous rabbit hole to go down. Negative thoughts like these are often the downfall of many hikes. Spinning out of control, these thoughts were racing through my mind as I knelt down to fill up my first water bottle. At that moment, the quickly moving water was silent, the light was grey and dreary, and my negative thoughts of just the idea of quitting the trail had snowballed into real emotions. I just sat there, holding my full water bottle in the stream. After years of dreaming and months of planning for this journey, this handicap seemed insurmountable. I reset, took a deep breath, grabbed my other water bottle, and just as the water began rushing into my container, so did those same negative thoughts. I turned to Ben after topping off my second bottle as our emotions began to get the best of us. I asked Ben, What are we going to do?

We both knew what we had gotten ourselves into, but we were not expecting something like this. This journey was not for us, this entire endeavor was for Steve. I shouted, We cannot quit, I'll crawl to Maine if I have to. Ben flashed a witty smirk as soon as I said it, knowing it to be half true. Turns out, we were no more untouchable than Garrett. We were miles from anywhere, vulnerable and exhausted. Exhausted from pain, exhausted from dealing with it. We were in it. This was it, our proverbial "come to Jesus moment" on the trail. In all truth, yes, we were hiking for our own passions and pleasure. At that moment, and from there on out, we decided that those personal accoutrements took a backseat to the real reason that brought us out there in the first place. No, Hell NO! We're not quitting on you, Steve! We can't, and we won't!

Warpzilla and Bandanna Ben

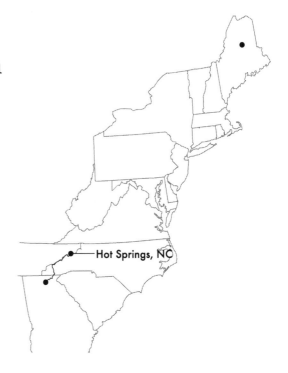

Hot Springs, NC

Hobbling back down to the shelter, we rummaged through our makeshift first aid kits, knowing full and well what we had at our disposal. Vitamin I (Ibuprofen) and Glucosamine for our joints. Ben and I wished that, by some chance of magic, there were a cure in our packs. One of the hikers curiously looked over, unavoidably eavesdropping on our dilemma. He revealed he was a physical therapist from Florida. What a great asset to have in our shelter at this time. Although he provided no real explanation of our situation, he offered up what he had. What he had was muscle relaxers and sleep aids. Kids, don't take pills from strangers. Against our better judgment, we were at the point where we had few options left. Without dinner, changing out of our hiking clothes, and to be honest, without much second thought, we accepted his offer. Moments later, trying to journal, wearily scribbling the pen with little to no sense, I blinked my eyes and looked at the watch: 7:15 PM. Another blink and check of the watch: 7:20PM. Lights out.

Ben and I awoke the next morning at 7:00 AM, almost a full 12 hours of sleep. I felt as if the weight of the world, of the trail, had been lifted off my shoulders. Perhaps sleep could have been what we needed. There was no doubt that we were pushing our bodies to the max. The cramp had been proclaiming that for days. Now, we were ready to attempt hiking again. With a long day in the saddle ahead, due to stopping short the night before, we had 27 miles to get to the town of Hot Springs, NC.

A relatively easy trail took us towards town. We were making excellent time, too. It was the draw of the town. Whenever a trail town is near, the pace picks up with thoughts of burgers, pizza, ice cream, showers, and other rare treats. The first sight of a road, sound of an automobile, or view of rooftop down below the ridge is enough to get any thru-hiker moving. The last bit of the trail before you make the descent into town was like a roller coaster. Just when you thought you were making the final descent into town, the trail would roll right back uphill. The trail is a master of mind games.

Towards the end of the descent into town, our cramps were returning. This was the norm, the morning miles were not bothersome. It was not until the afternoon, when we really pushed the miles that we had a problem. In this instance, we were both much more vocal about how we were feeling. There was nothing left to hide. If we were going to operate as a well-oiled machine, there had to be no secrets between us. That included when we were hurting, when we were hungry, happy, sleepy, sad, mad, and, well... you get the point. With communication lines more open about how we were feeling, we were able to comfort each other that we were almost to town, and we could rest there.

Descending into Hot Springs, North Carlolina, the trail comes right out to a sidewalk on its way towards Main Street. AT plaques are even set into the concrete as you walk along. We had made plans to stay at Elmer's, a hostel in town, and made a beeline for it. It's a convenient location in the small town. Elmer put the host in hostel. His hospitality was very generous. He does live a contemporary lifestyle. His lifestyle change that so aptly suits that of trail life was Methodist preacher turned practicing Buddhist. A unique switch indeed. A fully organic, vegetarian dinner is also available if you wish to partake. Hopefully, there were no hard feelings when we softly broke the news to him that we would be heading to the local restaurant for a hunk of red meat. We didn't use that description exactly, but I'm sure it wasn't the first, nor the last, time he was turned down for a carnivorous treat. Since it was just past lunch time, we ate at the burger joint on Main street for a late lunch. Then we hung out at the Outfitter in town for a little while and posted a blog from the use of their hiker computer.

We have just now made it to Hot Springs, North Carolina at about 1:30 this afternoon. We were recently in Cosby, Tennessee, being resupplied by the Chappell family and Chris (my roommates). They rented out a cabin for the night, and we got an excellent meal, a shower, and some time in the hot tub. It was hard to get back on the trail. Sunday morning we headed back to the trail at Davenport Gap, and we stayed the night at Roaring Forks Shelter. Ben and I have had some trouble with our right quadriceps. Ever since Day Two in the Smoky Mountains, a sharp, painful cramp has developed every afternoon in the same spot for both of us. We thought maybe it was because we went 28.5 miles that day, but is has been a recurring pain ever since. Mileage in the afternoon has been excruciating, but we have pushed on as best we could. So we are getting jobs in Hot Springs for a while...just kidding. However, we will drop mileage down below expected levels until we can figure something else out, as we are wary of taking another unplanned zero day. The Bluff Mountain Outfitters (in Hot Springs) was kind enough to let us use their computer to blog and check e-mail. We are planning to hit Erwin, Tennessee, on Thursday. More to come, hopefully some pictures soon. Thank you to everyone who has been commenting, posting, and reading the blog.

In the outfitter was the map of the entire Appalachian Trail. The exact same map I stared at before bed in my college apartment for a year-and-a-half. I wondered how I could ever complete such a task, and here I was doing it. It felt good – until I looked at where we were. We had made almost a pinky finger length on the over four-foot tall map. I do not know why I even looked at it with such a long way to go. Ben and I were not going to let it discourage us. We had a chuckle at how much work we had done the past few weeks and how many miles we still had to go. Instead of staring at millions of steps left taken on a piece of paper, we decided, it was time to take the few steps back to Elmer's.

At the convenience store in town on our way back, we acquired a bounty of Gatorades, snacks, and ice to do a little self-applied physical therapy. Lounging in the backyard of the hostel, Ben and I rested and enjoyed the remainder of the afternoon. Before we knew it, it was time for dinner. This time, the Smokey Mountain Diner would prove an excellent choice. A big salad, a choice influenced by our hostel stay, and a pizza were in order. No mound of veggies in a bowl nor cheese and crust stood a chance against our mountain man appetites.

I had a decent night's sleep that night at the hostel. Fortunately, I got the last bed available that night. Ben drew the short straw by bravely volunteering for the mattress available in the greenhouse at the back of the hostel. How bad could it be? I'm sure plenty of hikers have spent a night there before. However, in my defense, I shared a room with a somewhat odd character who I'm pretty sure spent half the night crying to a girlfriend, maybe boyfriend, on the phone. I tried not to listen too closely, but I knew where he was at, especially after my little experience fetching water the day before. I didn't think there was any way Ben was faring worse than I was.

For starters, there was a flood light shining through the greenhouse roof all night, giving the night vision effect. The light was strategically placed to be right in your eyes when you lay down. The mattress felt as if Andre the Giant had slept there every night previously, sending you rolling to the sunken midlle. Nature sounds were also among the ambiance as a fight broke out between stray cats off and on all night; at one point they were even fighting on the roof above him. Honestly, I don't know what he had to complain about.

The next morning we headed up and out of town. On our way back to the trail, on the sidewalk was a kiosk showing how many miles to Mt.

Katahdin in Maine, 1,869 miles. Remembered only by a picture, we tried to block it out of our parietal lobes as we pressed on. We opted out of visiting the actual hot springs of Hot Springs, North Carolina. Maybe it would have been a good idea to get another good soak with our cramps having been in a hot tub a couple nights ago while visiting with the Chappell's. Nevertheless, we marched on.

As we passed some crackhead-looking lady on our way up to Lover's Leap, where we neither loved, nor leaped, we got the feeling that our cramp had finally subsided. What a relief it would be to get rid of this ailment so we could get on with our journey worry-free. The rest of the day consisted of the typical ups and downs, seemingly pointless, that made up the Southern portion of the Appalachian Trail. Deciding to keep taking it a little easier on ourselves, figuring we could make up the mileage later, we stopped just 19 miles from Hot Springs at Little Laurel Shelter.

As we pulled into camp, which sits nicely on a ridge, waiting on us were three other hikers. Two girl hikers, who openly discussed weight loss being their reason for hiking, accompanied by a hiker who introduced himself as Lazy Bones. Just think of what a hiker who calls himself "Lazy Bones" would look like, and that's it. In casual conversation with the trio, they asked when we started. May 21st we replied. "What!" "Holy Shit, we started in April." We thought we might get this kind of reaction, but not this close to Springer. If you started April 1st, and it was now June 5th, that's 66 days to hike 290 miles. A whopping 4.3 miles a day, surely a few zero-days must be included. Not that there's anything wrong with taking so long, but I thought that was a little extreme.

Settling in to the shelter for the night, I was ready to redeem myself in my bear bag-hanging capabilities. Down the ridge from the open side of the shelter was a huge oak tree with a giant limb with tons of clearance to toss a line up and over it. It was an outrageous tree to pick for a bear bag, but I had to boost my self-esteem. However, if I failed, in front of this audience, it would have an even greater negative effect. Lazy Bones and crew were curious as to why we even hanging a bear bag: You guys actually do that? Nevertheless, I tied a rock to the end of the line, gave myself plenty of slack, and gave it the ol' heave ho. Trajectory, perfect. Distance, spot on. Manila rope fibers smoothly caught the limb of the tree, creating a soft whizzing sound as the weighted end to the rope pulled the line back down. The shelter erupted in applause. A sheepish grin was quickly plastered on my face as I strutted back to the shelter.

Epic bear bag hanging perfomed in front of Lazy Bones and Company

On the trail, it's the little things that you have to appreciate. Things like setting a bear bag line in the first toss on a tree some 30 feet in the air. Letting the good times roll, Ben and I also decided we were going to build a campfire for the first time on our trip. Gathering wood, constructing the initial structure as we learned in Boy Scouts. We wanted to build a fire to rival one Mr. Charville would orchestrate. We added some fire starter steroids, the denatured alcohol for our stoves, to ensure a good start. Lazy Bones and company continued to be impressed with our outdoorsmanship.

What Ben and I failed to notice was the intense summer thunderstorm brewing in the atmosphere. Sure enough, as soon as we got a comfortable-sized fire blazing, thunder came ever closer. Oddly enough, Lazy Bones and the two other girls decided they were going to hike on. It wasn't 5 minutes later that the absolute bottom fell out. Thunder and frighteningly close lightning strikes led us only to believe that we might find the threesome on the side of the trail somewhere tomorrow. With a valiant fight to stay ablaze, our fire stood no chance to the increasingly violent storm. All that hard work to get wood collected and getting a fire lit in anticipation of sharing it with the motley crew of Lazy Bones and the Chunky Gals, our efforts were in vain. Just as it's the little things that can bring you up, they can bring you right back down. Fortunately though, our spirits remained high. We had a shelter to ourselves, we were completely dry and out of the storm, and we had the joy of watching it as we hoped our fellow hikers rode it out safely.

"Socks that stand themselves up"

The next morning, just after we started hiking, we came to a fork in the trail. There were two options, both were the AT, but one was an alternate in case of severe weather. The other warned of exposed conditions and to consider the alternative if weather proved malicious. For a moment, I thought, "Oh, that's good, at least the three hikers we met the night before

Spencer McKay

had a somewhat safer route to take." Since the storm of the night before had long passed, we took the exposed ridge route. It was very rewarding with some of the best views on the trail yet. The section was referred to as the Blackstack Cliffs. From there, we were able to reach our fellow Troop 215 member, Drew Haley, who was planning to meet us in Erwin, Tennessee, the next day. Also, we had a promising voicemail left by Ben's mom. She revealed that an old neighbor lived in town and offered to host us at their home right next to the hostel in town. A little trail magic hook-up was in the making.

Around lunch time that day, we caught up with the two girls from the shelter the night before. They took the smart, safe choice of the alternate route during the storm that evening. Lazy Bones, on the other hand, perhaps chose the wrong time not to be lazy. Opting for the exposed ridge route, he must have been pounded by the storm. He was not with the two girls at the time either, which was worrisome. They said he was sleeping late, and we did recall passing a tent on the side of the trail right after we descended off the exposed ridge section of Blackstack Cliffs. Daylight was out as we finished our 21.5 miles into Hogback Ridge Shelter. That night we again took full advantage of a shelter all to ourselves by spreading out all our gear and not having to worry about sharing. By this point, we had developed a serious trail funk. Trail funk smells like hippie mixed with a high school locker room. It's not pleasant, but the fortunate thing for us was those who possess trail funk are immune to it. So surrounding yourself with other trail funk is not harmful. In the nightmare that is removing of the socks, foot funk rates among the most deadly of trail funk. Our socks literally could stand up by themselves, thus confirming our trail cred was officially intact.

The next morning we hiked through Sam's Gap. We vividly remembered this area as it was a starting point and ending point to a couple of our Troop 215 AT trips. In comfortable territory, we trod on. Ben and I began chatting about our hikes with the troop and how much fun they were. When Ben and I attended the summer AT outings with the troop, I had acquired the nickname "Warpzilla." There was no real reason behind it. We always gave each other nicknames; it was something to entertain ourselves while hiking.

"Warpzilla" had a nice ring to it. It doesn't require a vivid imagination for a mental snapshot. Some are less fortunate in their trail name and may go to great lengths to ensure one doesn't stick. For example, if someone that carried a little stuffed animal given to them by a family member before their trip was caught using it as a pillow, they could easy earn the name "Pillow Pup." Or, if someone had really nasty blisters and was having problems, someone might name them "Blister." When you earn your trail name, you have officially crossed over into the thru-hiker community. "Pillow Pup" is actually a friend of mine, Brandon Moore, who hiked the trail in 2011. He hated the name. So after being clear he would not easily respond to that name, no one would let him get off too easy. A hiker he was with suggested "Night Dog," but he did not like that either. Another hiker added a little Spanish twist, "El Perro Noche." Brandon accepted El Perro Noche, but I always encourage strangers to ask him how he got it.

As Ben and I ascended out of Sam's Gap in Tennessee, the incline seemed ridiculously steep. There were no attempts at building the trail in a switchback fashion that zig-zagged up the hill. Nope, it was take it or leave it. For some reason, a hovering cloud of gnats were buzzing all around me. An unfortunate circumstance that my trail funk could have been contributing to, the gnats did not seem to mind. Huffing and puffing up the hill, sweat dripping in my eyes, angered at the slope of the trail, all I needed was a gnat to fly in my mouth. Sure enough, right down the ol' windpipe. The gnat buzzed down the back of my throat, inducing a cough as I continued to drag myself up the trail. You alright? Ben asked. Yessss, I replied, aggravated. Bug flew in my mouth, I explained, in a less-than-thrilled tone. A few moments later, picking up the pace in anger and out of spite to get this climb behind us, another bug flew in. As it seemed to bounce off my dry, thirsty tongue, right down the hatch, the gnat quickly met his maker. Not without thoroughly pissing me off in the process.

After the quick ingestion, I tripped over a rock, which only angered me further. So much so, that I decided the next best thing to do was release into a fit of rage. I picked up that damn rock and threw it against a big-ass tree right beside me as hard as I could. A Godzilla-like roar erupted from my vocal chords while Ben stood frozen behind me. The rage quickly passed as the rock I threw slowly rolled back down the trail to Ben's feet. Warpzilla, it is, he said as we quietly continued on.

Fortunately, there were better things to look forward to in our immediate future than raging out, eating bugs, and throwing rocks like a 12-year-old. We were making our way to Erwin, Tennessee. Upon the approach to Erwin, we ran into a wiry old man hiking southbound with an old Army or Scout external frame pack. He introduced himself as simply Rambo Ron. After our brief conversation, Ben and I carried on down the trail. Now that my trail name had been confirmed, it was his turn. Ben appreciated the alliteration of Ron's trail name. Without too much thought, I blurted out, Bandanna Ben. I was hoping you'd say that, said Ben, who was, unbeknownst to me, luring me towards that answer. Ben didn't want to give himself his trail name, but as soon as I said it, I turned back to look at him and was grinning ear to ear.

Not only was Erwin a town we had visited before on one of our Troop AT trips, but we had a friend from our troop meeting us there. Better yet, we had arranged for some family friends of Ben to put us up for the night. As we strolled off the mountain onto blacktop, we looked for the house right next door to one of the hostels in town, Uncle Johnny's. It was here that the Honrath family lived and offered to host us. It was odd knocking on the door of someone you had never met. First, we hoped we had the right door; it would have been difficult explaining that mistake. However, as soon as the door was answered, any worry of having the wrong residence was diluted by the warm welcome we received. They knew exactly who we were.

The Honraths were extremely hospitable. They immediately gathered our dirty laundry, probably for their benefit as well as ours, and gave us clean clothes to change into so we could wash everything. Shortly after we arrived and introduced ourselves, our friend Drew Haley pulled up. Drew had brought our resupply box from Raleigh and was going to hang out for the night. While our laundry was starting up and dinner was being prepped by the Honraths, Ben and I had some business to tend to. We had somewhere to be: a place where the burgers are thick and the milkshakes hand spun, I'm talking about a little place called Hardee's. As Thickburgers were placed on trays with fries, a soda, and chocolate milkshake for each of us, we dove in mouth first to our feast. Drew did not miss a beat, ordering the same amount as our trail-starved stomachs. We travelled back to the Honraths after our meal, just in time for our second supper. Our second supper consisted of a giant spaghetti dinner and homemade chocolate chip cookie ice cream sandwiches. The only thing more amazing than the hospitality we were receiving and the amount of food that Ben and I just consumed was that Drew, too, consumed every bit as much as we did. If Drew ever thruhiked the trail, I believe he'd earn the trail name Hollow Legs 'cause who knows where all that food went.

While sharing some trail stories and enjoying some satellite television, we also managed to take a dip in the hot tub. It turned out to be an incredible day, minus the fit of rage earlier. With clean clothes, a bed to sleep in, and full bellies, we were very thankful for the Honraths. We did a little blogging that night, followed by phone calls back home to spread the word of the trail magic we were receiving.

Once again, the trail "enters woods and ascends" to no surprise by now. The first shelter we arrived at a couple miles after walking off the goodies from last night, we saw a younger guy taking a break. It appeared he might have been having some physical problems due to the number of bandages and wraps on his knees. Turns out, his name was "Royce" and he was actually from the same part of Florida that Ben was – the vast, widespread Jacksonville area. We chatted a bit but not for long as we had to get going.

Minutes later we came to a road crossing. For any other hikers, it would have been like any other of the hundreds of road crossings a thruhiker crosses over. A mere reminder of civilization left behind. Ben and I stopped in our tracks, staring at a guardrail. Any onlooker would have assumed us crazy, perhaps any thru-hiker, had they seen us, would have presumed us loco as well. At this very spot, six some odd years prior, we completed a section hike ending at Indian Grave Gap with our Scout Troop. I immediately recalled a photo taken of fellow Eagle Scout Jonathan Booton, Ben, Stephen, and myself. Younger, we rested on the guardrail with grins from ear to ear.

After contemplating the scene of the photo for a little bit, Royce caught up with us. We did something unusual for us and asked him if he would snap a photo of us on the guardrail for nostalgia's sake. He didn't think much of it; we thanked him and marched on. We were eager to continue the trail and had little to say each other for the next few hours. It's hard for anyone to lose someone so close. The trail reminds you in ways much more powerful than just seeing the same car a loved one drove, or their favorite restaurant. It's almost as if the trail had planned a memory.

And what good does taking a photo in the same spot even do for Ben and me. Is it some kind of reconnaissance through memory? A then and after, a cause and effect? What happened that allowed just Ben and me to be in that photograph? No Garrett. No Stephen. The picture itself is more about who is not there than who is. To anyone else, it's just a picture of two hikers, but for us, it remains a picture of one hiker. The one who is not there. Despite looking forward to sections of trail we had not previously hiked, we enjoyed reminiscing old memories throughout the southern portion. It was a constant motivator to see and recognize portions we had previously hiked. Even though some of our section hikes were southbound, stopping points and campsites would resurrect our perpetual déjà vu for the first 300 miles or so. Most of the time, it was a good thing. I say most of the time because it affected our judgment on how far away things were. Although we had a rough idea of where things were and because it's very hard to hike and read at the same time, we would go on instinct more often than not.

This came into play especially when approaching the shelter we planned to stay that night. Ben, the timely and itinerary-focused of the two of us, was the numbers guy. For some reason, he would ask me how far we always had. Probably an attempt to make up for how many times I asked him what time it was. I would try to take a quick look at my guidebook early on in the trip and shout out a distance of miles to go until we planned on stopping. If I was a few miles off, so what? More often than not, we got there faster than we were expecting because we were hiking much more quickly than when we were in scouts.

Meanwhile, amongst the constant recollection, we were approaching and climbing Roan High Knob. Roan rises above 6,000', an altitude the Appalachian Trail doesn't reach again until approaching the top of Mt. Washington, New Hampshire, about 1,471.3 miles away. In the cooler months of a typical thru-hike, I could see the weather getting nasty on the top of Roan, in fact, I've been accompanied there with a wintry mix, and it is not so pleasant. Due to our late Springer start date, we had just muddy trail to contend with. It was no light task getting up the steep sides of Roan Mountain, and with some disappointment, we crossed a parking lot at the top. A brief thought of "Damnit, I could have driven up here" quickly entered and left the brain as Ben and I decided to take advantage of a picnic table to plan the next few days.

I recall quickly realizing how close we actually were to Damascus, Virginia, and panicked a bit because we had not let my Dad know when to meet us there. His phone rang as I nervously awaited him to answer. I was losing touch with normal life. People can't just get up and leave town on a Wednesday. The joy of being exempt from the common man's duties for a while sank in as my Dad answered the phone. I hoped he would still be able to make the trip to Damascus. He had been keeping his schedule pretty clear, excited and ready to make the trip to see us. Garrett was also coming back to try and continue after resting his ankle at home for a couple of weeks.

With our first planned zero-day a few days down the trail, this was the first hard deadline we had in a couple of weeks. We were so anxious in fact that we hiked past the spot we picked that very afternoon to camp. With a beautiful descent into Carver's Gap, Tennessee, we waved good-bye to our home state of North Carolina. It was one-way, northbound traffic for the next 2 ½ months. The rest of the afternoon, we traversed the grassy, exposed ridge-line of Little Hump and Hump Mountains. It was a bluebird day, complete with wild ponies frolicking amongst us on Houston Ridge.

The unusually long span of above tree-line bliss ended, and we scrambled back down amongst the rhododendron and foliage. We burned past the ever-popular Overmountain Shelter to Apple Orchard Shelter. I had remembered reading that this shelter had burglar problems in the past due to its close proximity to US highway 19E. Hiking with my head up, looking optimistically for the shelter, I nearly stepped on a 5-foot black snake crossing the trail. One thing Ben enjoyed about hiking behind me was that I encountered most wildlife before he did, anything that could cause a problem at least. The worst part about hiking in front was, in the morning, I would always catch all the spider webs woven overnight across the trail. The song "Dreamweaver" usually played in my head during silk-heavy mornings. Although annoying, as long as the spiders were not in them, it was bearable.

Ashokan
Farewell

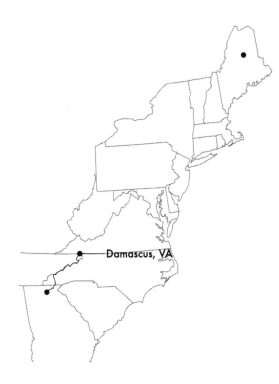

Damascus, VA

The night that we stayed at Apple Orchard Shelter, I encountered a problem. It was not a burglar nor a spider. I wish the black snake I almost stepped on were in the shelter to tell you the truth. Apple Orchard Shelter is one of the smaller shelters on the Appalachian Trail. It looks like an old shack, totally enclosed, except for a small doorway. The second it got dark, we were already down for the count, but with the excitement of Damascus, my Dad visiting, and Garrett coming back, I must have been a little restless. In the blink of an eye, the sun quickly took its last look at the Appalachians for the evening. A slight tapping sound grew into a frantic pattering. I could not for the life of me figure out what it was. I was not even sure if I was asleep or awake.

Precariously dancing the threshold of comatose and cognizant, the sound continued and began to drive me nuts. Finally, footsteps began to subside. Sighing brief relief, I closed my eyes and set my headlamp aside. All of about 10 seconds passed before I heard an unmistakable sound, a racket that can put fear into the most seasoned thru-hikers. It was the crinkling of a Snickers wrapper. Snicker bars themselves were not the disturbing part. Snickers are never disturbing. The sound of the empty wrapper of what used to be peanut, caramel-filled, nougaty, chocolate-covered energy and protein-packed snack was disturbing. I'm talking about the unspoken, four-legged foes of the trail. Some consider them a mammal that evokes more terror than that of a black bear or rattlesnake. Most encounter them in a science class in grade school, but out on the trail, these mice are wild.

They have no respect for a zipper, cotton, nylon, mesh, or fabric of any kind. And above all, they certainly have no respect for Snickers much less my beauty sleep. With our packs hanging almost directly above us, all I could think about was a Cirque de Mouse show above as they swung from pack to pack, taking inventory. Determined to end this furry little get together. I threw on my head lamp, jumped up (still in my sleeping bag), and frantically began searching for the guilty party. The raid of my pack came up empty. Keep in mind, I was trying to be courteous to Ben, as he had not been exposed to the terror at this point. I quietly laid back down, hoping the worst was over.

I puffed up my rain jacket, which doubled as my pillow, and tried to get comfy as my aggravation quelled. At the very moment I took my headlamp off, the crinkling continued. Since the sneak attack method failed the first time, I went for more of a Shock and Awe method the second go around. My arms swung like a plastic baseball bat crushing a piñata at a Quinceanera, and the curse words spewed out like little Ralphie finally getting the best of neighborhood bully, Scut Farkus. Yet as quickly as their footsteps were heard, they were gone. The only downside was that this time, Ben awoke in confusion, wondering what in the world was going on. I tried to explain what happened in a series of expletives strung together so nonsensically that it would have made a construction worker proud. Ben, however, was used to my outbursts by now. He just rolled over and told me to go back to bed. Little did he know the struggle I was fighting that night, but the noise must have scared the mice back across the state line to North Carolina and, for the rest of the night, the cease fire was upheld.

Another 20-plus mile day ensued after the long "house of mouse." When we awoke the next morning, Ben gazed off in a look of defeat. Victim of the aggravating varmint chewing through the zipper on the top of his pack, inside remained only a Sweet n' Salty Nature Valley wrapper. I tried to remind him that, if this were our biggest problem, we were sitting pretty.

Ben and I chose not to stop at Kinkora Hostel, a very popular hostel on the Appalachian Trail. We were making our way to Damascus with a serious head of steam. Before we stopped for the night, we came across Laurel Fork Falls, a very popular spot for thru-hikers, section hikers, and day hikers alike along the AT. As the summer's heat had begun, Ben decided to go for a dip. As the small waterfall cascaded down the rocks, I thought back to another Troop 215 trip when we visited this very spot. I remember the frantic excitement of the falls. I knew our shelter was just less than a mile away and was not too keen on having a swim.

A short hike along the river led us to where the shelter was supposed to be. Oddly, we began climbing. The prospect of an easy, riverside stroll to close out our day was quickly dashed as we ascended with the white blazes of the AT. Just as we began to really wonder if we passed our shelter somehow, we came to a directional sign, straight up. A validating sign can often be that little extra boost needed. Once again, the sun set daintily past the valley, as I hoped for a night much less eventful than the one before.

The next morning we awoke at dawn as the river continued rushing by below us. From Laurel Fork Shelter, we were only 2 hiking days away from Damascus, Virginia. We were giddy with excitement, at least for the first 5 minutes on the trail. As we followed the trail up a conspicuously unkempt portion, something did not seem quite right. On the AT, we were completely spoiled. As rugged and challenging as it may seem to hike from Georgia to Maine, the Appalachian Trail has been around for so long and has such an enormous backing of volunteers and trail groups, that it is literally nearly impossible to get lost. Granted, there may be a section here or there that is confusing, or you take a long break and forget which direction you came from; these are the main and avoidable ways to get "lost." In the grand scheme of things and comparative to its counterparts, the Pacific Crest Trail and Continental Divide Trail, the AT is a walk in the woods.

Simply unaware of just how good we had it, we were spoiled by the devoted volunteers and trail crews that dedicate many hours each year taking care of the trail. That is why our problem du jour was wondering if we were on the correct trail, because it was so unkept. There could have been a trail reroute, and we had taken the old AT. Also, we did not have topo maps of the entire trail. All we had was a guidebook with benchmark elevations for specific landmarks (i.e., peaks, valleys, roads, water sources.) All we knew was we were heading to Pond Flats. What we Southern Boys were thinking was that, usually, there's not a pond at the top of a mountain.

Stubbornly, we trekked on. It was like when you are driving, and you are 99% sure you missed your turn, but you keep driving anyway. All because of that 1% that says "if I turn around now, I will be turning around right before I figure out where I am." Finally, after false summit upon false summit, we reached the top of what had to be Pond Flats. The AT has a great irony about it. At the top, there was neither a pond, nor was it very flat. To hell with a cup of coffee to get you going, how about a 1300' climb in fewer than 4 miles to start the day off. Sometimes our nightly routine of reviewing the next day's hike did not happen. It would never be missed after this morning.

Next on the agenda was hiking down to and around the manmade Watauga Lake, a much more peaceful and routine endeavor than that of the previous few hours that morning. There was even a picnic area with indoor plumbing and running water at the Lake. It was as if the AT offered a subtle "sorry" for what we had just been through. Ben and I even contemplated camping there for the night – until the local Sheriff rolled through the picnic area. The good Samaritans and Scouts we were, we asked if we could camp there. Even though it would have cut the day extremely short, we felt we could make up the miles the next day. The Sheriff said no, so we begrudgingly marched on. It was an overcast day and nothing to write home about, so that made it a little easier to leave the lakeshore.

We were surprised that we had not seen many other hikers since we were in a popular section near Damascus. The two of us filled up with water for the night at a spring about half a mile from Iron Mountain Shelter. I wouldn't say that Ben and I grew weary of each other; that was never the case. However, there was a surplus of testosterone and an overwhelming lack of the opposite sex in the woods. Maybe that is why we were excited to spend a couple of days in Damascus, Virginia, where the chances of female interaction were much higher. Knots and curves of some trees were the closest thing we had to the reminder of some female anatomy. I won't even get started on the number of innuendos that hiking over Little Hump and Hump Mountain produced.

Approaching the shelter, we heard voices and hoped there was room for us. Then, lo and behold, an unmistakable sound made its way through the trees. It was that of the female species. An elusive creature, rarely found in the wild Appalachian Mountains. Ben and mine's ears perked up like a dog whose master was coming home. Slowly, as the shelter and the campsites around it came into view, it was clear that it was in fact a girl. Better yet, an extremely attractive girl. Attractive not only by "trail standards," but from what we could tell, in city life as well. "Trail standards" follow a similar principle as "beer goggles," (drinking until your decision-making abilities are hindered enough to pursue a coed below one's personal criteria). The only difference, of course, is being out in the wilderness so long that your judgment is altered rather than your level of intoxication.

Despite the rather foul smell we were wearing, Ben and I quickly struck up a conversation as we made our way into camp and began unpacking. We introduced ourselves with our trail names quickly followed by our real names, just to assure her that we were sane. Grace was her name, as I'm sure both Ben and I were thinking "yes...yes it is." Then quickly stepping out of the dark interior of the shelter were the father and grandfather of Grace. Our hopes of any attempt at "trail tail" were quickly dashed. Nevertheless, they were all excited to see thru-hikers in their natural habitat. By now, we had almost a quarter of it complete, and they actually believed we could make it.

The next day, I was a little surprised at how smitten Ben was by Grace. I don't think he was really enthralled with her specifically, but the idea of a girl who wanted to go out hiking and had her fun-loving personality. We spent the next few hours describing what we really wanted in a woman, like we really knew at the ages of 19 and 20. Of course, there is a song for every occasion, and in Ben's daydreaming of Grace, I ad-libbed a few lines from "You're Beautiful" by James Blount. Give me a break, it was one of 2007s Grammy nominees for song of the year. "She smiled at Ben at the shelter she was hiking with her dad. He won't lose any sleep that night 'cause Ben's got a plan." We had to keep it entertaining somehow, and we did. Girl talk subsided as the pace increased that day; we had camped 27 miles from Damascus the previous night and were very excited to get into town. So excited that we got into town at 2 o'clock in the afternoon. It took us just 7 hours, granted it was not the most daunting terrain we had faced yet, but we had a bed, burgers, beers, and showers on our minds. The first stop in town: Dairy King.

That's not a typo, Dairy King (now closed) was one of the finest establishments in Damascus, Virginia. Damascus is a place Ben and I had both travelled to multiple times during our scouting days not only because the AT runs right down main street but also because of the Virginia Creeper Trail. The Creeper Trail is an old railroad line retrofitted for hiking, cycling, and horseback riding. I had also been to Damascus growing up because Dad's girlfriend back in the day, Lisa, was from nearby Abingdon, Virginia.

It is a great little town and known across the board as the "Friendliest Town on the Trail." I don't think you'll find a hiker that disagrees with that. Once a year, there is an Appalachian Trail festival in May called "Trail Days." Ben and I were not able to experience the chaotic and crowded pilgrimage of hikers to Damascus for Trail Days because, well, it was happening when we were taking our first steps on the trail in Georgia. The festival is held in mid-May because that is the amount of time the average thru-hiker takes to start the trail in Georgia and arrive in Damascus. This meant that the average thru-hiker had a 459.5 mile head start on us.

Timing could not have worked out better. About 50 strides after leaving our Dairy King feast, my dad pulled his white Volvo to the side of the road right in front of us just as he was getting into town. We had not called or communicated with him since 3 days earlier when we told him what day we would be in town. I went in for a giant bear hug on Pops before my pungent odor got to his nose. It lasted about a second before he let out a "PEEYOU, you stink boy." It was almost becoming point of pride: the more I stunk, the more miles I was hiking. In tow with Dad was Garrett, who appeared rested and eager to get back on the trail.

Ben was not smelling any better as we packed our gear in my Dad's trunk and rode with windows down straight to the hotel where we were staying so we could take showers. After dad could smell again, and we got settled in, food was immediately on the mind. It's not like we just had a double cheeseburger with bacon, fries, and a milkshake at Dairy King. We were looking to fill the void that was our stomachs which had only been teased with Little Debbie's, Clif Bars, trail mix, and Bumble Bee chicken the past three days. Since Dad always knows where to eat, I get it honest, we drove to a steakhouse in Abingdon near our hotel. Not exactly dressed for the occasion, it was a little awkward at first. It probably looked like some guy and his son was buying two homeless guys a nice meal. I assumed that the AT was such a big part of the culture in the area that not too many people were worried. There was reason to remain worried though because it takes a couple of showers to really get all the trail funk off of you. You'll think you are fresh and clean until you bend down to tie your shoe and catch a whiff. Staying in Abingdon, we were the farthest away from the trail we had been since stepping off for the funeral. It felt weird and, as tough as it had been so far, I was already going through withdrawal. What in the heck was I going to do with an entire day off?

I was reintroduced to the exhilarating experience of driving a car as well. Even though we were hiking fast every day, going 20 miles an hour felt like a roller coaster. It seemed surreal to drive, more like playing a video game than anything. After dinner, we got back to the hotel and made plans to see the new Pirates of the Caribbean movie that night. Dad must have been tired from traveling, like we weren't, and we went without him. Ben had been talking about the new Pirate movie for weeks, and had gotten me excited about it too.

After getting used to waking up in the woods, to the rise of the sun, it was weird to wake up in a bed. The only thing that made it somewhat normal was that Dad was able to play the part of the snoring guy in the shelter. We slept in a few hours that morning as well while Dad had ventured across the parking lot to Huddle House. We quickly ordered pancakes, waffles, and coffee when we met him there. The rest of the day was spent relaxing, and enjoying the company of my father and our reunion with Garrett. To be honest, after a few weeks without Garrett, I was not sure how he would adjust to the pace of the trail. There was no doubt in my mind that he was more than capable of the journey, both physically and mentally. But Ben and I were in true hiking form, and we had been on a roll. That had me worried. I really wanted the 3 of us to do this thing together. However, for the majority of the time on the trip, that had not been the case. With so little room for error, everything had to go right.

As our zero day came to an end and my dad dropped us off at "the hostel" in the town of Damascus, we settled back in to our normal routine. There was still a good number of hikers and trail enthusiasts hanging around the hostel, as I imagine there usually are. Among them was Baltimore Jack, who I later learned is one of the biggest trail advocates out there. He told stories on the back porch. There was even a girl riding her bike across the US who stopped that night. Travelling with a violin, she was gladly accepting request as Jack inquired if she knew "Ashokan Farewell". It was absolutely beautiful, the perfect goodnight song. There wasn't a dry eye in the room.

Jack "Baltimore Jack" Tarlin
Appalachian Trail Legend 10/12/58-5/3/2016

Stepping out on the trail the next morning was harder than expected. We knew we had a tough day ahead; leaving a town on the AT always meant a climb was in our near future. We followed the Creeper Trail out of town and crossed the highway, entered the woods, and ascended once again. At least the trail maintenance crew was nice enough to provide a flight of stairs for the first 15 feet. After that, it was purely trail. Garrett seemed to be keeping up well; in fact, he took point. The trail had no intentions of letting us reminisce our time off in Damascus. It was demanding all of our energy as we veered off the Creeper trail and headed toward Mount Rogers (the highest point in Virginia) by way of White Top Mountain.

Before we exited the woods for an open bald climb to White Top and Thomas Knob Shelter near the top of Mount Rogers, we were passed by someone for the first time of the trip. Not another hiker though, it was a trail runner training for an ultra-marathon. We did not share much more words than a "hey, how you doing" the first time he passed us. But when he had turned around and came running back towards us, he was impressed at how far we had hiked since he turned around. If that wasn't a sign of a good pace, I don't know what is. Instead of taking in the view we had earned at the top of White Top, we were watching dark clouds moving rampantly towards us. From White Top to Thomas Knob Shelter was a completely exposed portion of the trail. This is not a section where you wanted to get caught in a summer thunderstorm. We were making excellent time, and I was impressed with Garrett's performance.

If we made it to Thomas Knob that would make a 28.5 mile day, our longest of the trip. Due to a 13- mile gap in shelters from Lost Mountain Shelter to Thomas Knob Shelter and the imposing weather, there was really only one choice: Thomas Knob or bust. Sure as shit, we started getting some precipitation about 3 miles away from Thomas Knob. We all knew quite well that a slow drizzle does not last for long before it becomes an all-out downpour during a summer thunderstorm in the Southeast. Just after we stopped for a moment to attach our pack covers, the first booms of thunder rolled in, and the bottom fell out.

Flashbacks of the "Whitewater hiking trip" played briefly in my mind as the trail quickly transformed from dirt and rock to mud puddle and a temporary stream. The rain was falling hard, and the temperature was dropping. Thunder became imminently louder and lightning struck around us. As we began to make a small descent on the ridge, we had to maneuver from a small amount of tree cover to the open. When I turned to pivot, my feet went straight out from under me. I thought I was down for the count, but the only thing that saved me was my trekking poles. I put so much weight on my poles in my reaction to keep from busting my ass that I ended up bending the left one. I found slight humor in the fact that the one piece of gear I was worried about holding in a lightning storm actually played a part in saving my freshly washed skivvies.

With some frighteningly close strikes, we finally saw the outline of the shelter through the storm. We began to frantically run and shout intermittently as if we were Phil and George. I don't think I've been so thankful to see a shelter in my life. Thomas Knob is a nice one, too; the only problem was it was a packed house. This particular shelter has a small upstairs portion accessible by a bunk bed type ladder. A couple of groups shuffled around and moved upstairs, which we were grateful for in these conditions. Pretty much everyone there had hiked out of Damascus.

It looked like a backpacker's yard sale in the shelter that night. Everyone had all of their gear spread out in attempt for it to dry. I pretty much knew none of it would dry because my sweaty clothes I wore each day did not even dry each night, and that was when it was in the 70s and 80s. Someone had a small thermometer on their pack: 36 DEGREES! I was sitting there thinking, Okay, 36 degrees outside and my sleeping bag is rated for 45, I'll be fine... Fortunately enough, we had boiled up some water to make ramen noodles. Typically, I drain the excess water, but not tonight, I needed all the warmth I could get. All the layers we had, we had on. We were fully expecting the summer heat wave to be in full effect at this time, not near freezing and soaking wet.

Despite the cold, we made it through the night. It took a little extra self-motivation to crawl out of the bag that morning. Clouds from the storm lingered the rest of the day while we entered Greyson Highlands, one of the most beautiful sections of the trail; at least when Mother Nature cooperates. On this day, it was not. With dense fog, open terrain, moss and rock, this place could have been the set for Lord of the Rings. Wild ponies are usually running about in the Highlands, but there were no sightings to be had. Even if they were out and about, we wouldn't have seen it because we could hardly see the trail.

I was still concerned about Garrett. It's one thing to do a 28.5-mile day, but it's a whole other story doing another one after that, then the day after that, and so on. While we were in Damascus, Garrett stopped in Mount

Rogers Outfitter. The store is notorious, much like Walasi-Yi store in Neel's Gap, for helping hikers work out the final kinks and perform repairs. After Garrett left the trail, he researched more into foot and ankle injuries. He had concluded that, although the shoes he wore at the beginning of the trail were light, they must not have offered the support and cushioning he needed. For the record, they were straight out of the box, but for a sneaker, that shouldn't be a big deal. When he hopped out of my Dad's car the day before, he was sporting some fresh new kicks. He had on a hybrid, high-top trail runner made by Montrail. They resembled the Montrail Hard Rock, which may be one of the greatest trail shoes of all time. At the outfitter in town, Garrett also purchased some SuperFeet inserts that one of the workers MacGuyvered into a Posturepedic by inserting cork into the arch. Flaunting a new pair of kicks every time we saw him, we couldn't help but start referring to him as Foot Locker.

Hopefully Garrett's problems had finally come to an end, and he could begin to enjoy his Journey. From Day 1, I was a bit concerned about Ben and Garrett's relationship. The last time they had seen each other was when they were in Cub Scouts. A lot can change from being fellow Cubs at the age of 7 to spending 24/7 together in the woods for a 3-month period. Garrett had just spent the previous summer at Philmont Scout Camp as a Ranger, hiking 20+ miles a day while leading young Scouts and Scoutmasters on their New Mexico Trek. Surely, someone who was more than capable of doing that could handle getting along with just one other person. Garrett was not afraid to tout his accomplishments of a successful Ranger at Philmont and bagging multiple 14,000-foot peaks in Colorado on his days off. Garrett just had that kind of personality, but if you gave him the time of day, you would see that it was less bragging and more of a want to share. When you do awesome things, there's no reason you can't talk about it.

Continuing to hike in the fog, I remained the buffer between Garrett and Ben while we hiked. Garrett was set on being the lead man. He talked of a recent trip to the AT with his family in the Greyson Highlands; unfortunately, he experienced the same gloomy weather as we were that day. Even though it was not raining, it might as well of been – everything was still wet from the night before and collecting condensation. It was just a nasty day to be hiking. Managing to make good time, zipping by shelter after shelter, we were excited for the next night's stay at Partnership Shelter. Rumors in trail journals revealed that you could order pizza from the shelter. If you haven't figured it out by now, food is one of a thru-hiker's greatest motivators. Yet, just as we began discussing the mountain of toppings, and perhaps a cheese stuffed crust on our pizza, booming thunder joined the conversation. Great, we thought, another storm to bear. At least we were hiking back below tree line at this point and not as exposed as yesterday. The problem was that we couldn't see the direction the storm was heading as we could the day before. At the rise of the ridge, a rare opening in the tree-formed canopy revealed its position. The black clouds were rolling up the valley, fast; we were not looking forward to this encounter.

Now, the itinerary Ben and I had made before the trip really seemed silly. This was not the kind of storm you wanted to hike through if at all possible. The only problem was, we did not really want to set up our tent and ride it out, and we were in between shelters to stop at for the night. Plan C it was. And what was "Plan C" exactly? Attempt our second hitch-hike of the trip into Troutdale, Virginia, with a storm bearing down on us. As the sky became darker and the storm closer, our thumbs were getting tired, and we were starting to wonder what Plan D was. Just as we were about to give up, an old white sedan pulled over to the side of the road. Y'all hiking the trail? the driver asked. The three of us responded with a collective "yep" to answer his obvious question. Man, I don't blame y'all for hitch-hiking into town. I just heard on the radio that there are tornado warnings and a nasty storm rolling through. That was our thought exactly. Ten seconds after we started rolling down the road, the bottom just completely fell out, and there was a unanimous joy that Plan C was the correct course of action. Rushing to make a decision on what to do, we did not really have time to consult our guidebook as to what was even in Troutdale, Virginia. I had a hunch that there was not much.

Our driver, who seemed like he might have picked up a hiker or two before knew right where to drop us off, but it wouldn't have taken a rocket science to figure out where to go. There was only one place to go: the Troutdale Trading Post. We weren't expecting much when we walked in, by which time our driver was long gone. Much to our surprise, the store was filled with hiker fare and a restaurant accented by a giant 50-inch TV. We were in heaven, and luckily enough, the PGA US Open was on, Tiger was reigning supreme, but Angel Cabrera ran away with the title. The elementary school lesson of "don't judge a book by its cover" had never paid off so well. It wasn't like we had much of a choice, but as the weather radar played as a picture-in-picture image on the screen, we became 100% confident in our choice. Once our bellies were full, we were directed by Jerry, the owner of the trading post, to head right up the street to the church. Matching the information in our guidebook, the Troutdale Baptist Church offered a hiker hostel.

As we headed to the small building behind the church, there was not a soul to be found. Someone had left directions explaining the showers were across the field and help ourselves to a towel and soap. The storm had passed through by now, and we cranked up the baseboard heater in the hiker shack as our clothes and gear finally got a chance to dry. Once the mud was washed off, we headed back down to Jerry's for a late dinner and the warm glow of the television before they closed for the evening. We were also able to Yogi a ride from Jerry the next morning. All was well in the world of the thru-hiker; it was as if the trail was apologizing for the potentially traumatic scramble to Thomas Knob Shelter. Everything was great until we walked back up the road to the church hostel. A dog came charging at us as we walked with Doritos and Gatorades. A Nacho Cheese decoy could have bought us some time, but I was willing to take my chances before I gave up my Big Grab bag. Two factors were working for us here: we were on the other side of the road, and for some reason, there was a decent amount of traffic to keep the dog from crossing; and there were 3 of us, and 1 of him. In my mother's constant fear of wildlife on the trail, the biggest threats to this point were Savage Mice and a Dog. No bears or snakes gave any kind of threat.

Garrett began struggling early on the next day. If he kind of dropped off to his own pace towards the end of the day, it was no big deal. No one ever said we all had to spend every waking moment together. Losing sight of him in the beginning of the day was much more worrisome. By no means was I expecting all three of us to march down the trail, single file, singing "we're the three best friends that anyone could have." But something was a little off for the first time since Garrett rejoined. He would fall back and yo-yo off our stride all day. After no sign of Foot Locker for an hour or so, Ben and I heard a galloping shuffle of sil-nylon, the undeniable squeak of rubber Crocs impacting the trail and the metal-on-rock "tink" of trekking poles. A red blur slowed and came into focus as Garrett caught up with us. It was a little spontaneous, but in true Garrett form. A light chuckle and a "c'mon, let's go" followed as we continued towards Partnership Shelter, where Garrett's Grandfather "Pops" and Dad were planning to pick Garrett up.

Perhaps that is why he was running: he knew he didn't have too far to go until the end of his day. We reached Partnership Shelter sometime after lunch and took a short break at the shelter while waiting for Garrett's family. We sat and read Curious George Goes Camping, which someone earlier had humorously left for the packs of thru-hikers that pushed through. I think we had it figured out at this point...I think. Once the Dixons had arrived, we made a plan to meet up with them in Atkins, Virginia, 10 miles up the trail. This particular section was not difficult and took us less than 3 hours. It always helped having an incentive of a hot meal and a motel room for the evening.

We strolled out of the tall grass waving with the wind to nothing more spectacular than an underpass for Interstate 81. Our focus was on the red barn-shaped building with "Restaurant" written on the side in big block letters. A restaurant so aptly named "The Barn" might have lacked creativity, but it didn't need any. We ate two dinners each, to Mr. Dixon's surprise. We really weren't embellishing the Blog Posts; we could put down some food, and it was becoming a bit of a bragging right. My Philly steak sandwich with fries was washed down with a Salisbury steak dinner, complete with mashed potatoes. Garrett revealed his plan to be shipped up trail to Pearisburg, Virginia, almost 100 miles up trail in an attempt to get his trail legs back so we could continue as a unit to Maine.

Czech Mate

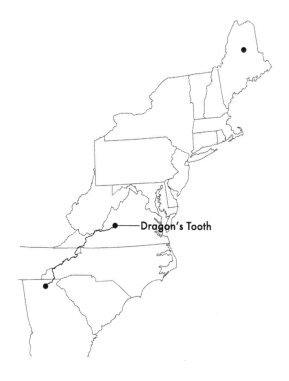

Dragon's Tooth

After saying goodbye to the Dixons, including Garrett, Ben and I got a room at the Relax Inn. Relaxing, if the sound of automobiles on the highway lulls you to sleep. It really wasn't all that bad though; all the amenities were there: air conditioning, beds, color TV, shower - the important things. I remember making some phone calls in the parking lot while sitting on the worn white picket fence along its border. Dessert was high on our list, so we each loaded up on some ice cream, in our continual preparation for the "Half-Gallon Challenge" that faced us in Pennsylvania at the halfway point. I went for the Ben and Jerry's. We selected pints due to their high richness of flavor, something we thought would be different than the bland flavors we suspected to be available at the half-way point. The ice cream was not only for training but is a known craved item among hikers. By the end of the journey, we would become Ben and Jerry's connoisseurs.

We dropped our room key in the box outside the office, old man Bandanna had to have a cup of coffee, and then we set out. It was a relatively tough day according to the guidebook, with a lot of climbing.

Anytime the trail brings you down to a highway or town, be prepared to climb out of it. We were excited about getting close to the end of our "Southern Virginia" section of our guidebooks. In preparation for the trail, hikers and trail enthusiasts talk about the Virginia Blues – a hiker mentality that it seems to take forever to hike the entire state. It's easy to see why, as the trail totals about 550 miles in Virginia, 25% of its entirety. The good part is, we were planning to average around 25 miles a day, taking it just 22 days. However, most thru-hikers, who take 5 months and average around 15 miles a day, would take around 36 days to complete the state. Fortunately for us and all the other hikers, Virginia is beautiful, and when you're done, you're nearly halfway!

The Appalachian Express, Ben and I, chugged along, nearing the shelter for the night. We were planning to stay at Chestnut Knob Shelter and were a little bit worried about no water source near the site. The elevation of the shelter is around 4,400 feet, a height we would not reach again until New Hampshire, unbeknownst to us at the time. We searched and searched until finally finding the water source called out a mile before the shelter in the guidebook. The weather had been relatively dry so far, and it was beginning to show in the quality of water sources. Ben and I drank all the motel water we still had in our packs and completely filled up. We even filled up a 3-liter water bladder we were carrying for times like this. This way, we could fix dinner, and make sure we had something to drink in the morning before we got going.

Finishing strong up the final climb, a stone building, fully enclosed, came into view. This section of the trail was a relatively untraveled one, unlike most of the miles we had already walked. Great, a fully enclosed shelter, I thought. Flashbacks to the mice attacks at Apple Orchard Shelter played in my head. Chestnut Knob Shelter was much larger though. Inside sat 2 hikers who did not appear to be together. There was a picnic table and bunks on each side. It was a nice little set-up and seemed relatively rodent-free. I'm sure that shelter has acted as a godsend much like Thomas Knob Shelter was for us. The two hikers inside were quiet. One was a girl who didn't seem very friendly, but I think she was just shy. The other was a section hiker who introduced himself as Jedi Birder. The Jedi part was clear;

he sounded exactly like Yoda – one of those voices that you have to really pay attention to what he was saying because you just focus on the sound of his voice. The Birder part was that he was passionate about bird-watching. He began to talk about trips he had gone on around the world for birds as Ben and I unpacked our things. I still remember the crescent moon that night in a clear, star-sprinkled sky.

The knob that the shelter sits on is relatively open and great for a little star-gazing. I briefly turned on the phone to check for signal. I had a few bars, so I called my Mom just to touch base. She was a worry-wart the entire time: her baby was out in the woods. I tried to call as much as I could, for her sanity, and less for mine. My aunt and uncle who lived in West Virginia were visiting her, so I was passed around the room. Support and praise continued from each family member I talked to. It felt good to be doing something so incredible and living completely in the moment.

The next morning we approached the buzzing of automobiles travelling another one of America's major Interstates, I-77. Shortly before passing underneath it, we walked along Virginia Backwoods Highway 615. As the trail dumped us on the gravel road, a Chrysler Minivan crept up behind us. We picked up the pace in a seemingly prey and predator situation. I wasn't trying to make the news. Any fears quickly subsided as the cheerful passengers of the van rolled down their windows and the husband/father yelled out excitedly, Have you guys seen the Appalachian Trail?! Ben and I laughingly looked at each other, Yep, you're on it! It was like opening that present on Christmas day, the one you wanted more than all the others, and it's the last one you're given. That was the look on the man's face as he shouted to his wife and daughters in the van, "Girls, this is it…Wow…we're on the Appalachian Trail!"

The husband proceeded to play 20 questions. Where did you start? Are you thru-hiking? When did you start? Finally he ended with, have you read A Walk in the Woods? Ben and I cringed on that last one. How many times were we going to be asked that question? One man's trail experience assumed by the general public to be the same journey as every other hiker.

I guess we excused his ignorance for his overall joy and amazement of the trail. If anything, Bill Bryson's book has made the trail more mainstream, for better or worse. Continuing to walk with the minivan slowly rolling and crunching the gravel alongside us, we approached a small picnic area. The convenience of it all was not overlooked by the family. Hey, do ya'll want to take a break? We have some grapes and bananas.

Now we're talking, I thought to myself. A little reward for our time.

Mom, Dad, and two pre-teen/teenage wiry, wavy-haired girls with braces smiles hopped out to join us for a trailside snack. One of the girls quietly whispered over to their mom, Ask them about the vest. Neither Ben nor I had on a vest, so we didn't know what she was talking about. As if taking a moment for the mother to process, she suddenly popped up from the picnic table. Oh yes! The vest! I was confused. She ran to the van retrieving a standard Polartec fleece, green, full-zipper vest from the trunk. The group then explained they were travelling to the Outer Banks of North Carolina from Ohio for an extended-family vacation. The vest's owner was the uncle of the two girls. He had left it at their home the prior holiday season. Since then, they were on a mission to get complete strangers to take a picture in it, along with the husband, mother and their two kids.

A nudge of my elbow to Bandanna's side propelled him towards the vest enough to make the mom believe he was standing up to put it on. She brought it over, begging me to get in the picture as well while Ben slipped the vest over his sweaty, dirty shirt. We then stood with the father and two daughters. The dad, who already thought this was the greatest thing ever, was grinning from ear to ear. The daughters, despite one of them suggesting it, were being subject to the embarrassment of their mother who held the camera. We were standing about as far apart as strangers in a photo would, but for momma bear, that wasn't good enough. "Get closer girls, come on!" The dad shoved himself between Ben and me, spread his arms out, and plopped one on both of us. The daughters, begrudgingly (and rightfully so, considering our stench) inched closer in front of us. Shortly after the photo, the family loaded up and headed on to the coast, leaving us a couple extra bananas and the bag of grapes. So potentially, in a forgetful uncle's photo album, or on his wall, there is a photograph of Ben and me with his family...classic.

Our next planned stop was Pearisburg, Virginia. Ben and I were in contact with our old scout troop who was starting their annual week-long backpacking trip on the AT that sparked our curiosity for the trail. We were hoping to catch up to them, and in an effort to do so, we hiked 33 miles, our longest day, from Chestnut Knob Shelter to Jenny Knob Shelter. That was followed by a 30-mile day into Pearisburg. Our troop had left Pearisburg to hike 50 miles north 3 days prior. We were pushing it as hard as we could to meet up with them before they finished.

On our long day into Pearisburg, our attention was caught by pink surveyor's tape hanging low in a tree directly above the trail, an unusual sight that we spotted from about 50 feet away. As we got closer and closer, we saw writing on the tape. It was the undeniable drafting script of Gary Mazur, former Scoutmaster and father of our friend Ryan. The tape labeled "Ben, Garrett, and Spencer" led us off trail about 30 yards to a 30- gallon black trash bag camouflaged with leaves from the forest floor. Inside sat 6 Orange Gatorades and assorted snacks that were typical of those given out in the food bags for the week-long troop trips that Ben and I were so familiar with. Carrying 3 extra Gatorades would have been heavy, so we decided to pound 2 of them right there. The snacks came in handy on the long day. Of course, we packed all the trash out.

Angel's Rest is a beautiful outcropping of scraggly rocks overlooking Pearisburg. It is followed by a less-than-desirable descent of almost 2000 feet in just 3 miles. Hiking steeply downhill is exhausting to say the least; I cannot imagine doing it without trekking poles. Trekking poles, however, odd they may look, are life savers. They are an important tool for the thru-hiker. Because of how many steps you are making on the trail, the trekking poles become an extension of your body. They can double as a tent stake, pole vault, and if push comes to shove, a weapon. I have saved myself from falling and possibly avoiding injury countless times when hiking with trekking poles. I never used them growing up but quickly fell in love with them. This descent was no different.

Northbound into Pearisburg creates a situation that divides the thru-hiker community. The trail crosses the first road into town but continues past it, roughly following the road, but on a trail. This sets up the purist vs. non-purist argument. Do you hike the trail, following the white blazes until the next road crossing closer to town? Or, do you try to hitch from there, ignoring the pointless, viewless, mundane blazes near a town that are seemingly insignificant. It may seem like a moot point to hike a section of trail that is not as pleasing to the eye as other portions. But some people take it pretty seriously and would claim that you did not hike the entire AT because you did not pass every single blaze.

For the simple fact of leaving no room for questioning, we hiked the small portion to the next road crossing. It's the Forest Gump mentality of "I've gone this far, might as well keep going." Besides, it was not a very good place to hitch from, and the road walk would have offered less shade. After the 2000' descent, a slight uphill was welcomed by the opposite group of muscles in our legs and gave us a chance to stretch out a stride again. We finished our 30-mile day strong as we checked in to the Plaza Motel. There were other motels and a hostel in Pearisburg, but they were clear across the spread-out town. When the woman at the office offered to do our laundry, we knew we had made the right decision. Ben and I were a little hesitant at first: who would volunteer for a task so vicious to one's sniffer? But we weren't complaining as we donned the always-undersized, ever-revealing bath towels as our garments. When laundry was finished, we headed down to the Hardee's. We had been awaiting an encore performance ever since Erwin, Tennessee. Two impressive trays began stacking up with item after item sliding down the stainless steel chutes accompanied by the whirring of a couple of chocolate shakes in the making.

Ben and I considered a pizza from Pizza Plus on the walk back but decided against it. That didn't stop Bandanna from a Blizzard at the DQ though. With fresh laundry and full bellies, we had successfully conquered yet another town on the AT. Unfortunately, because we got into town so late, the Post Office, in which waited our next round of supplies, had already closed. Typically, we tried to get out of town and on our way. This time, we were delayed because of the Post Office hours. We slept in a little, picked up our package from the PO and loaded up our bags for a 5-day, 148-mile stretch from Pearisburg to Glasgow, Virginia. This was a tall order, and we needed to average close to 30 miles a day so we could meet up with our former Scoutmaster Pete Haeseker and reunite once again with Garrett.

Knowing we were chasing our scout troop, desperately trying to meet up with them, our motors cranked. The unpleasant ascent out of Pearisburg, accompanied by toxic smells from some kind of chemical plant nearby made the late start difficult. We eventually reached Rice Field Shelter. This open field was just 1500' up our 2000' climb out of town. It was here we came across a hiker studying a very small sheet of paper, maybe 4"x6." He had scanned his entire guidebook and scaled it down to print very small, in effort to save weight. Ben and I found this quite peculiar. You hear about people going ultra-light, but it's different to actually see it. Come to find out, Andy was an actuarial statistician in the real world, which helped us comprehend his penchant for miniature guidebook pages.

I enjoyed the practicality and novelty of having a book that showed exactly where I had been and where I was going. I knew it would be a nice thing to have when I was done, so cutting out pages and throwing them away didn't seem like a reasonable thing to do. I still look back at the notes I wrote and liked having one entire piece of the trail in my hands. Andy's pack was not much larger than a CamelBak that you would see a mountain biker wearing. I had no idea how the guy was even surviving. Fortunately, we got to see him eat. He pulled out a big bottle of grape jelly, and a jar of peanut butter. The next item was a loaf of bread that looked like a bear had sat on. I guess calories are calories, no matter how smushed they are.

Ben and I ventured over to the shelter across Rice Field and saw that our Scoutmaster Gary Mazur had left us a note. It revealed that, if we were reading it, then we would not catch them. He wrote hopefully that we received the trail magic hidden off trail the day before. We nodded at each either as Ben read the journal entry aloud. It was a bummer that we did not get to see them, but they were there in spirit and we were honored to once again follow the footsteps of our fellow scouts. This section around Pearisburg made the farthest north our troop had ever travelled on the AT.

Our climbing finally brought us to our ending point of the day, Bailey Gap Shelter. For having such a late start, we sure made some serious miles. The shelter itself was quite impressive as well. A giant two-story shelter made out of at least 12x12 timbers. Walking up to it, I thought, How the hell did they even build this here? It is surrounded by giant pines. I suppose the materials were dropped in by helicopter, very impressive however it was constructed. There were a couple of hikers lounging around out front at the picnic tables. They were friendly and taken back a bit when we revealed our starting point for the day, a distance that these thru-hikers had taken 2 days to complete. It's not a point of bragging but certainly a point of pride.

Our favorite question on the trail was quickly becoming "Where'd ya'll hike from today?" Night time fell fast among the dense towering pine forest. Andy, however, was nowhere to be found. We thought, Damn, that kid is moving; we'll never see him again. And I'm sure he was thinking, I'll never see those guys again. Hoping for a quiet night, with no snorers or rodents scattering about, we cooked up a quick dinner of 3-cheese pasta. Our entrees that Bandanna and I prepared a month-and-a-half ago were becoming terribly bland and boring. Packets of Texas Pete and salt and pepper provided little counter for our taste buds. The two of us discussed Andy's approach. Obviously we were not interested in going quite as overboard, but it would be foolish to not even discuss some of his techniques. He was clearly hiking farther than we were, and the only difference was what we were carrying.

Spencer McKay

With our early starts, we were making excellent mileage in the morning, which gave us momentum heading into lunch time and the afternoon. Sure enough, 10 miles into our day when we stopped for water, we stumbled across Andy once again. He was purifying some water while meticulously attempting to un-crush a piece of bread for some surface area to apply some peanut butter and jelly on. It is almost as hard to reform a piece of bread as it is to put toothpaste back into the tube. To no avail, he raised up his bottle of jelly and squirted a few tablespoons into his mouth, followed by a sporkful of peanut butter and a bite of carbohydrates. It's all going to the same place.

The seemingly never-ending climb, broken up by our night's stay at Bailey Gap Shelter, had finally ended, followed only by a descent just as long. The Appalachian Trail tends to torture you like that. If you're going up, you're more than likely about to be hiking down. When you are hiking down, be prepared to ascend. The vertical distance travelled up and down on the AT can often correlate to the ups and downs of your emotions. Add in a little unexpected weather, and some thoughts of missing home and loved ones, and you've got yourself a concoction of AT doubt. I became extremely frustrated at one particular PUD (pointless up and down) as we approached Laurel Creek Shelter. With no attempt at even trying to switch back the trail up a 30-50% slope, Ben and I began slipping and losing traction in some muddy spots.

I'm sure Ben was expecting an outburst of sailor language and something to be thrown shortly. Ben muttered frustrating words a few steps behind me, but at least I knew we were both struggling up the slope that could have been easily made more bearable. When we arrived at the small shelter, we both just looked at each other as I quoted the late Chris Farley from Almost Heroes: "what in the hell was that all about." For whatever expletives I chose to leave out of the situation, an entry from the trail journal in the shelter by "Mowgli" more than made up for.

Just as I found a little pleasure in Ben being as frustrated as I was on the unthoughtful route to the shelter, we both enjoyed the damning nature of the entry. This was not the first time we noticed an entry from Mowgli. We pictured a small, tan boy running through the Appalachian Mountains with a red bandana as a loin cloth. His entries always seemed to be just a week or so ahead of us, so we must have been traveling at a similar pace. This began a sort of competition within the overall goal of hiking the entire trail. Operation "Catch Mowgli" was now full on.

A few hours later we made it to the Niday Shelter about 13 miles up the trail, hoping to find another post from Mowgli. Scanning the journal, we came across a post from Garrett, who had been hiking ahead of us. Judging by the date of his post, he was keeping his lead of 3 days ahead of us. That eased my mind about his future ability to keep up with Ben and me. We stayed in front of Andy, who had no trail name, until we reached the shelter. To say we had company at the shelter would be an understatement.

The unmistakable sound of human voices revealed the location of the nearby shelter. As we got closer, we still could not make out what was being said, despite its high decibel level. There were even a few barks resonating through the trees as we approached. The open side of the shelter faced away from the trail. We turned the corner to the elevated shelter with a small case of steps leading to its entry and instantly regretted that decision. Our inability to understand the loud voices from the trail was because they were in a different language. Ben and I must have not gotten the memo of the uber-casual dress at this particular shelter. Our evaluation of our bunk mates for the night was all too revealing: there stood a large Czech man in boxer briefs with a beer gut to be admired by even the heaviest of drinkers. If he had been alone, it would have been manageable. But this was a family outing. The family included the dad, whom we had met, two girls who didn't seem to have hiked at all judging by their energy levels, and the mother. In the darkness of the shelter, we spotted the producer of the barks heard down the trail. The K-9 was a big, black, hairy, labradoodle-ish creature that was quite protective.

Ben and I began to set our things in the shelter, and the dog went bonkers. Every word sounds like a curse word in Czech, but the dog's master must have been saying some terrible things as they were otherwise making an effort to be as hospitable as possible to share the shelter. Even though most thru-hikers despise hiking into a shelter swarming with a group of Boy Scouts, that would have been much preferable to this situation. From the moment the dog laid eyes on us, it would not stop barking. Mr. Boxer Brief, who was still in his boxer briefs, did not stop yelling back at the dog either. It was not until Ben and I moved our things 20 yards from the shelter that the dog finally settled down.

Andy had briefly hiked up to the shelter and quickly made a decision that Ben and I wished we had made: to hike on. "Dog tired" from our 27-mile day with our gear already unpacked, we were in it for the long haul. In our best efforts to continue a normal post-hiking routine, we gathered water for the next morning as foreign murmurs hovered. Sharing the picnic table outside the shelter, we cooked up our meals as they stared oddly at our alcohol stoves while peering over the metal wall of their classic, kelly-green Coleman stovetop. Wishful thinking of them serving up some kielbasa on hoagies was just that. They asked us short-ended questions, and our answers were respectful but brief. Between their questions and our answers they spoke quickly and intensely in native tongue. I communicated with Ben across the table with odd looks, wondering what kind of trash they were talking about us. Our expressions must have been obvious when Boxer Brief quickly interjected our silence, "Don't worry, we're not talking about you."

"Yeah, right" we thought to ourselves. To top it all off, the dad yelled to one of his daughters in the shelter. The tone of it sounded like an order as he slipped in an apology for the noise of the protective black beast hiding in the shadows of the shelter. A fancy little mesh fronted duffle bag was brought down the steps of the shelter to the picnic table. It was not a bag for clothes, nor one suited for the trail, and we had never seen anyone carry such an odd item. The girl smiled as she unzipped the bag to pull out a frisky feline. Chuckles commenced from Bandanna and me as we picked up the pace of making and eating dinner. There was no telling how far these people were traveling every day, but it could not have been far.

Darkness fell as the dog continued rustling around and barking with each zip of our backpack pockets and sleeping bags. In complete darkness, I realized the rookie mistake I had just made. During my effort to hurry up and get to sleep, I forgot to take a leak. I really did not want to break the peace and quiet, but an urge turned into an emergency while what seemed like an hour passed. I quietly yet hurriedly tried to exit my bag. I advanced the slider on my zipper past each chain width one by one until I was able to withdraw my right leg from the synthetic bag. Pivoting on my right ass cheek with my right leg in the air, I managed to sneak my left leg out as well. With no light (for fear of disturbing the dog), my hands fumbled around delicately for my Crocs. Both legs were now suspended in the air like the freeze-frame of a break dancer. Locating my camp shoes, I slipped them on, now in some kind of vulnerable yoga move.

The most delicate portion of the operation was next. Getting on my feet. I carefully stretched out so not to step on our crinkly ground cloth made of Tyvek. With dirt and rocks under my shoes, I was finally stepping away from the shelter. I needed to move quickly; this was getting close and exciting. Not quite as far from the shelter as I was hoping, I spotted a tree with a nice diameter to catch the clear and copious stream in an effort reduce the noise. Feeling as though I was on a mission, I was only halfway there. With a bit more clarity after "cashing the keg," I executed the mount back into my bag as swiftly, quietly, and delicately as my dismount. Pissing should never be this hard.

An early rise was in order after a mentally restless night. With nowhere near the deliberate silence of last night's movements, I packed up my things in an effort to get the hell out of Dodge. A single and low growl rumbled from the shelter as we passed the corner of the structure that revealed our Czech friends the afternoon before.

The morning's conversation focused on Dragon's Tooth, a climb we had only heard described by Steve's uncle, also named Steve.   During our pre-hike preparation while at the Harrington's house for a week, Uncle

Steve would stop by regularly to see how we were coming along. Uncle Steve had not spent a whole lot of time on the trail, but he spoke of a place called Dragon's Tooth. Ben and I, who had a decent number of miles under our belts, had never heard of it. Similar to the way in which Garrett always described Mt. Katahdin, Uncle Steve seemed to be exaggerating his story about how difficult the climb up Dragon's Tooth was. He described the giant outcropping of pointed rock at the top of a mountain, climbing by hand, pulling yourself up in multiple places. At first, Ben and I thought he was joking at how hard he thought it was. But through the tone of his voice, and his hand gestures, we could tell he was completely serious. He also sounded completely serious when he thought there was a chance we would not be able to climb it. It became a running joke throughout our planning that we might as well not plan past Dragon's Tooth because we would not be able to make it any farther. I guess we will just have to turn around and head back when we get there, Ben and I thought.

At this point, we were feeling pretty bullet-proof, and laughed back Uncle Steve's story. We began adding our own embellishments to what we thought Dragon's Tooth would be like. After checking our guidebooks multiple times, we were sure we must be getting close to the top of Dragon's Tooth. So far, the climb had been no different from any other typical climb on the Appalachian Trail. Uncle Steve was really pulling our leg, we thought as the climb flattened out and the trail nestled itself between large vertical rock formations. Then the trail disappeared and became all stone. We navigated the tall formations that were undoubtedly the Teeth of Dragon's Tooth. We enjoyed the unobstructed vista overlooking Catawba Valley.

Descending Dragon's Tooth, Uncle Steve's story began to gain validity. There were a few sketchy spots where we had to carefully stretch down. An injury could have easily occurred as we tried to keep a reasonable pace, which is hard on steep downhill. We had a certain comfort with the trail though; staring down at our feet was no longer a necessity. Our peripheral vision had been trained, and we were confident in our landing points like a professional snowboarder in a half pipe. In fact, the trail had become much more enjoyable over the past couple of weeks. Although our brains and eyes were constantly taking in the surroundings and the direct obstacles in our path, we were spotting roots and rocks much more easily. This accomplishment resulted in a technique that allowed a larger amount of intake of our surroundings. Of course, there were times when the surface beneath our feet required our undivided attention, like the descent of Dragon's Tooth. Our body's reactions and senses were becoming very attuned to nature and our direct environment. It was a sensation experienced nowhere else. Bandanna and Warpzilla were in the zone.

The descent from Uncle Steve's Dragon's Tooth led us towards the small town of Catawba, Virginia. When I say "small town," I mean a restaurant and a general store. Downside was, it was a mile walk to the store and restaurant. The restaurant in Catawba, according to Bandanna Ben's guidebook by "Wingfoot" (a 7-time thru-hiker legend) was called The Home Place and was the best place to eat on the trail. The Home Place offered a family-style buffet. The family-style buffet is for the true fat ass. You don't even have to get up; they bring dishes out to the table like Momma does at Christmas. Of course, we had read about The Home Place the night before as we dined with the Central Europeans. The dinner bell rang from miles away.

The mile-and-change walk down the highway to the Catawba General store ensured a mile of uphill the next morning, but we weren't contemplating that yet. The white wooden rural structure that was the General Store looked like a blast from the past. A friendly couple managed the store. Before getting too comfortable, we asked if we could camp in the yard behind the store. We suspected that this was not the first time anyone had asked, but it was better to get the go-ahead instead of our experience at Neel's Gap some 660 miles prior. Already laying out his minimal gear near the barn where the tractor was parked, sat Andy.

We were almost positive he had not read anything about The Home Place restaurant just a quarter-mile across the highway. Perhaps the text on his shrunken guidebook discouraged any extra reading. He gladly

Spencer McKay

accepted the invite, at no surprise to Ben and me. There's only so much jelly and peanut butter you can shove down your throat anyway. To my disappointment, we had missed Bar-b-que Night by one day. Fear not though, it was Fried Chicken Night at The Home Place. It was a Southern Boy's delight as we requested plate after plate of downright home cookin'. I'm not sure how they stayed in business with the number of thru-hikers that must come through there, but I was sure glad they did.

After a gallon of sweet tea, fried chicken (a whole fried chicken), heaping spoonsful of macaroni-and-cheese, accompanied by Southern-style green beans (for you, Momma), the three of us waddled back to our beds by the tractor. I had a sneaking suspicion that this would be a great place for a snake to hang out as I laid down my head. Camping 50' from the road proved quieter than the previous night's rest shared with the traveling Czech Family Circus. My skin itched briefly as the dirt, grime, and possible bug bites were irritated by the humid southern air. Another successful day on the trail, I thought to myself. This was going incredibly smooth.

The next morning, the Catawba General Store began hustling and bustling with a crowd much larger and much earlier than I expected. Ben and I thought, What in the world – this place is in the middle of nowhere. Then, we realized that it was Saturday. I cannot for the life of me, even now, remember the last time I was not even aware of the day of the week. It was a wonderful feeling. The civilized folk (although still country) were gearing up for a weekend of fishing and outdoor activities with their families. We hikers stuck out like a sore thumb, if not for our stench then for our lack of camo. The store itself is very well stocked and even served hot meals. I remember a heat lamp keeping freshly made breakfast biscuits warm towards the back of the store. As the hardwood floor creaked with each step towards it, I began to try to make out what was on the wrappers. BEL and SEL were a couple of options. "Bacon, Egg and L? What the _____ is L? Oh God, Liver? No thanks!" I thought this through my head and just went for a BE, Bacon and Egg.

Sitting outside enjoying our breakfast biscuits, Ben unwraps a bacon, egg and cheese biscuit. Of course, it was halfway through my biscuit that I realized what I thought was a "L" was a "C," just written hurriedly and at an angle. While eating our breakfast, another hiker whom we did not see the night before started chatting us up as we began packing our things. He noticed a bunch of red dots on my legs, particularly just above the knees. He thought I had psoriasis, even though it looked nothing like it. Come to think of it though, my legs had been itchy the past couple of nights. My legs appeared to have a bunch of little bug bites, like bed bugs or something.

On our mile-long walk up the road back to the trail, we dealt with the uphill that was yesterday's downhill. Once on the trail, we quickly climbed up to McAfee Knob. Perhaps the most photographed spot on the Appalachian Trail, a large rock overhangs the cliffs that drop into mature green forest. It is one of the first times on the trail, and to the grandest proportion thus far, that you can look out and literally see no signs of civilization. The dense, lush glow of the forest on that summer morning looked like a green blanket draped across the earth. It reminded me of how a snow storm covers everything to make it all appear smooth and even. Only hills could be made out of the undulating upper crust of our planet.

Sitting on the protruding rock was Andy, who remained surprised every time we caught up with him. What he didn't know was that we were about to make a giant push. However, while on a phone call from McAfee Knob, we had a voicemail from Mrs. Harrington. Uncle Steve – Dragon's Tooth Uncle Steve – had reserved us a hotel room that night in Daleville, Virginia. This put a little twist in our daily plans, as we were planning on hiking past there. After studying the guidebook, we realized it was right on the trail and our last opportunity for Bojangle's Famous Chicken N' Biscuits for the next 2 months. For a couple of Southern Boys, it was a temptation too great to forbear. I was already dreading the days above the Mason Dixon line where sweet tea was non-existent.

Weaving between highway crossings in the final half mile leading into town, the trail was lined with blackberry bushes and made for a nice palate cleanser to help our taste buds transfer from the nutty, earthy taste and texture of Clif Bars to the more processed and flavor enhanced goodness of fried chicken, seasoned fries, a fluffy buttery biscuit, and of course, sweet tea – a combination to make any vegan shiver, or at least shake their head at. The hike consisted of two major, juxtaposing diet plans: On-Trail and Off-Trail. On-Trail consisted of anything in bar form. Candy, Clif, Power, Lara, Luna – if it had a general rectangular form, we ate it and we ate a lot of it. Our diet on the trail was supplemented by more geometric shapes, mostly of the Little Debbie variety. We had our bases covered with circles of fudge rounds and oatmeal cream pies. An occasional cylinder Swiss roll was inhaled although the typically reliable structural shape rarely held up in a pack.

The Econo-Lodge welcomed us with open arms. Well, not really, but with all expenses paid, we felt like royalty. Out of our hotel room window, we could make out the unmistakable shadow of a roofline next door that could be only one of two things: a Pizza Hut, or what used to be a Pizza Hut. I was always a Domino's man myself, but there remains a warm, cheesy, gooey place in my heart for Stuffed Crust. Cheese in the crust is pure genius, a perfect matrimony of science and baking. It is food of the gods until you order an XL Mighty Meaty Stuffed Crust pizza. Then it's the food of thru-hikers. The interior of fake ivy and flowers couldn't hold a candle to the mountain laurel and rhododendron on the last 714 miles of trail. Our minds were in our stomach though, as we wasted not a thought on the forgery of flowers. Answering trivia cards placed on the tables of the track lit empty booths was hard enough. Our thoughts were doughed up by pizza where every bite is a perfect bite. We remained stumped on the question of "What is the name of the Boston-born, North Carolina-originating singer-songwriter with the hit song "Fire and _____." As we watched our trademark-ridden pie being pulled out of the oven and placed into its dark brown cardboard envelope of glory, my brain fart ceased as I replied "JT" while standing up to receive our order.

While making the rounds outside of our luxurious, single-night Econo-Lodge room, we added a destination on our route: the Exxon down the street. The fluorescent- illuminated contents on the interior of the convenient store would make our next search easy from the outside. The yellow and white standalone freezer with waist-high sliding glass doors on the top glowed with a more intense luminosity than all other objects in the store. Like a lactose treasure chest, it drew us in a bee-line straight to it, pizza in tow. We quickly scanned its contents from left to right, past the Drumsticks, Klondike, and Snickers ice cream bars – early choices that could have nearly derailed our mission. It was the final third of the freezer that stored what we were hunting. The Brooklyn Born Haagen-Dazs received a pass as we analyzed the flavors of two different New Yorkers with a Vermont quirk.

As stuffed crust was stuffed down our throats, root beer flowed like wine, and our Ben and Jerry's softened, we tuned in to "Braveheart" on the as-advertised color cable TV and HBO. We joined William Wallace in spirit, not to defeat the British Army but the XL Stuffed Crust Mighty Meaty that lay before us. Polishing off the final slices, we took a break to enjoy the "freedom speech." Ben and Jerry's soon followed. The plan for the past few town stops was to ensure we were well prepared for the half-gallon challenge in Pennsylvania. In doing so, we each ate a pint of our flavor du jour. As Bandanna Ben and I sat watching TV, Ben had an epiphany while rotating the container confirming the enormous amount of calories we were consuming.

Bandanna: Our ice cream training regiment has a small flaw.

Warpzilla: How so?"

Bandanna: What does Mr. Charville say about how much a pint weighs?

Warpzilla: A pint's a pound the world around.

Bandanna: Exactly!

Warpzilla: So what are you getting at?

Bandanna: How many pints are in a half gallon?

Warpzilla: Uhhhh.....two....wait.

Spencer McKay

Oh crap.

We had been completely misleading ourselves in our ability to annihilate the half-gallon of ice cream that waited just 400 miles ahead. We promised ourselves that, with an early end to the day before, we would give ourselves a kick in the ass the next morning. Despite a 20-mile day coming into Daleville, it felt like we had taken an entire day off. After ransacking the continental breakfast for everything it had, we slapped our plastic key cards on the reception desk, headed out the front door, took a left, and we were back on the trail.

Ten by Ten

Shenandoah
National Park

The trail is an ambiguous creature. It represents a life within Life. It did not take long to grasp that ideology. When good things come, you take them, and when times are bad, you trudge through the mud, the rain and the pain. Difficult pursuits in Life are represented in every square inch of the 2000-mile footpath. Every stumble or trip on a rock or root is a misspoken word, a lie, or a broken promise. Every summit topped is the core necessity of humanity in its most literal form. The proverbial climb is not one of a lifetime; it is stripped down into its simplest state. There is only one choice: keep climbing. When the climb ends, you will inevitably descend. Life guarantees the same circumstance. There is and always will be an up, and a down. Rarely are you not doing one or the other. The trail is forgiving, perhaps more so than Life in that the guarantee of the ending of the ascent or descent is, if not a visual one, then at least one of logic. Neither can you climb forever nor descend endlessly. Change is constant, and when think you've got it figured out, expect curveballs. There's no bullshit. You are 100% in the moment, all of the time. That is where life on the trail and the trail of life part ways. It's an unfortunately unavoidable fact.

Perhaps Hershey's has it all wrong – change is not bad. It's all too easy to get sucked into the vortex of an endless career. Hasn't anyone ever told you they love their job and you wanted to smack them in the face, or better yet yourself? They either: A.) Really do love their job; B.) You really hate yours; C.) They are lying to themselves, or D.) All of the Above. Select the best answer, but we all speak of deviation from our own status quo. For some, speaking of change is good enough. Others take it a step further and help people change. Yet the hardest thing to actually do is to change yourself. That being said, what better way to do so than put yourself in an environment like the trail where everything is constantly changing? The change in weather and terrain is much more acceptable and adaptable than that of raising mortgage and gasoline.

In the world of miles per gallon, we made damn good time out of Daleville. Running on fried chicken and pizza gets you only so far as it was quickly back to the "bar" food we were all too accustomed to. Our 10 x 10 philosophy, co-opted from "Statistician Andy," was a recipe for success. Ten miles in the bag by 10 in the morning. Ben and I were developing the habit of not only adapting such hiking techniques as (10x10), but elaborating on them as well, DER/T (Distance= Rate/Time) was the acronym of the day, every day. Unless of course we found ourselves in town, then it was AYCE. As important as "making miles" had become to the 2 of us, when a couple having a picnic on the side of the Blue Ridge Parkway from the tailgate of their Explorer asked us if we wanted a Coca-Cola, it was really hard to pass that up.

Bandanna and I were never guilty of aggressive yogi-ing. The couple was shell-shocked after we informed them we had walked as far as they had driven from Yankeeland. Because they were shocked but impressed, our egos were boosted a bit as we pounded our ice-cold Coca-Colas. We saddled back up and thanked the couple for the trail magic, which turned into a conversation of what trail magic was. With packs on, sternum straps snapped, and waist belts tightened, we nervously sipped from our water bladders as we awaited a pause in the dying conversation. Finally, we exchanged parting goodbyes and off we went into the woods.

Cruising past shelter after shelter, we finally reached our stopping point in that night at Bryant Ridge Shelter. With a steady climb for the latter end of the day, our shelter radar was tricking us. Typically you learn to feel when a shelter is around the corner, without ever pulling out the guidebook. Trail maintainers are pretty consistent on where they put shelters. There's typically a water source nearby, and it is located in a gentle curve of the trail to allow for easy access in and out. Pushing ourselves around each curve of a mountainside and hiking close together, we would recite "this would be a great place for a shelter," yet there was no shelter. Each little rise became more like a mountain as we pushed into another gear to pick up the pace. I was becoming a believer in the philosophy digging back to my cross-country days that, if you didn't like the terrain you were running on, or in this case hiking on, just speed up, and you'll have a change of environment soon. Hamstrings and shins tightened up on the way down, and calves and quads flexed on the way up our final paces.

As we turned the corner in a mature pine forest, the impact of our heavy steps were absorbed by the spring of layers of fallen needles. Our tired feet smiled at the extra-cushioned terrain late in the day. In the final hours of hiking, the trail becomes some kind of hallucinogenic drug. You try to make out a shelter in the distance, but no signs or side trail appears. As soon as you convince yourself that it's another mile or so, you swear you hear voices from other people that must be chatting and relaxing at the shelter. Sure enough, the voices in your head dissipate and you cannot hear a thing, not even your hiking partner. At a certain point, the brain just shuts down; your legs and feet keep motoring along. You start focusing on your stride. Stretching each step just a fraction farther than your previous one until you just cannot stretch any farther. Joints and muscles start to feel like Jell-O. You probably aren't stretching farther with each stride as you think you are, yet that's what it feels like. Just when you feel like you cannot take another step, "poof," like magic, there's your shelter. In the case of Bryant Ridge Shelter, it was well hidden down in a small valley from the trail, but as we approached it, we soon realized it was the biggest damn shelter we'd ever seen.

Built out of what appear to be 12x12 timber, this thing was no joke. There is a legit upstairs, and you begin to wonder how this thing was even built. It's 8 miles to the nearest road to the north and 4 miles to the nearest road to the south. There's no way this amount of timber was carried all the way up to its location. Ben and I were accompanied by two other hikers that night. I spent the rest of the evening dreaming of the tour de fast food Ben and I had planned the next day.

Early to rise and a greasy burger on the mind, Ben and I hoofed it 24 miles to the James River bridge crossing by early afternoon. With the punctuality of a Marine and the jokes of a comedian, one of our Scoutmasters, Mr. Haeseker (aka Pete) and his son/fellow scout Jay were waiting for us at VA 130 in their trusty, emerald green Honda van. How they ever kept the stench of Troop 215 scouts from Tenderfoot to Eagle fresh off backcountry weekends out of that thing I'll never know. In my more senior scouting days, I recall the opportunity to "DJ" and ride shotgun alongside Mr. H. Given the state Ben and I were in, it might have been enough smell to just drive that thing to Carmax the second they got back to Raleigh. No grudge against the closest town to the trail, Glasgow, Virginia, we ventured a little further off trail to the religious college town of Liberty University, Lynchburg, Virginia, for slightly better accommodations and more calorie options. Before even nailing down a place to lay our heads that night, our stomachs growled from the tan leather captain's chairs in the second row. The Haesekers had been following the blog, they knew what was up.

"Will Five Guys Burgers and Fries work?" Pete hollered from the driver's seat. Is the Pope Catholic? You're damn right: a double bacon cheeseburger all the way will work! As we polished off our meal, we climbed back in the van, just as we pulled out of the parking lot, Ben spotted a Chick-fil-a across the street. Boy, wouldn't a milkshake from there be nice he said. "Yes Ben, yes it would." As we were handed our frosty beverages through the window with the classic "my pleasure" from the attendant, I thought to myself, no, the pleasure, is all ours. I went for the new flavor of banana pudding while Ben stuck with the more classical chocolate, whipped cream and cherry on top to boot. Then, as if Jerry Falwell himself sent an angel down, on the horizon, I could not believe my eyes. Was it a mirage? It was the Spanish style arched and tiled building with bright colors and stucco exterior that we all know so well. Designed by no other than architect Robert McKay, I knew there was a reason it always felt like home. I had to support the family business, besides, they had just come out with their Taquitos. How could I resist? I leaned forward to request just one more stop before we find a place to sleep for the night. As the Tour de France was just gearing up in the middle of Lance Armstrong's reign of supremacy, I topped off my tour with crunchy chicken wrapped in a tortilla and fried to perfection with sour creamacy to dip. Worth every bite.

Checking in at Travelodge, we turned on the tube as the Haesekers encouraged each of us to please take a shower. It was at this time that Pete and Jay got a little lesson in Thru-Hiker Laundry 101. Today's lecture: "What to wear when everything you have is being washed." The simple answer: rain gear. Fortunately, for the Haesekers' sake, Travelodge was one of the rare motels that provided a bath towel that would actually fit around a normal-sized man. All of Ben's and my clothes combined into a medium-sized load. While waiting for our laundry, we began laying out and showing the Haesekers everything in our packs. It was at this point we began realizing how much we really did not need.

Pete and Jay watched as we set to the side everything we thought we could do without. First, it started with a Ziploc of Vitamin I (Ibuprofen). We felt confident they were no longer needed. Then, the Band-Aids and Neosporin got cut from the team. Then we both took a page out of the thru-hiker playbook that we had been discussing for a while. We decided the trustworthy ruggedness of our Nalgenes were simply not worth the weight. We would replace them with 32oz bottles that we bought at the store. This way, we could pack out a couple of Gatorades, and when we'd drunk it, boom, water bottle. If a hiker is really smart, they drink the Gatorade down until there's have about 4oz left and then fill it up with water. The watered-down Gatorade is a nice break from the monotony of regular water. A few items later, we both came to our lightweight alcohol stoves and titanium bowls and, in turn, our denatured alcohol for fuel. We began discussing what a shame it was that we used these items only once a day. Pete and Jay looked at each other, Are they seriously considering not cooking? Simultaneously Ben and I placed our cook sets, and fuel into the "send home" pile. Bandanna and I felt as though some weight had been lifted from our shoulders. We wouldn't have to waste time cooking one meal a day; we could just get to our shelter for the night, eat a few more snickers, maybe some prepackaged chicken or tuna, and call it a night.

When all was said and done, we each would send home a medium stuff sack of stuff that we did not need. As we handed them to Mr. Haeseker the next day as we packed up the van, he was shocked that we even had anything left in our bags. Not cooking is referred to as "going cold." The only downside was that we had wasted our time preparing countless pasta meals at the Harrington's home just a month ago. The upside, beyond carrying less and saving time so we could hike more, was that when we returned for college in the fall, we had an abundance of carefully prepared pasta dinners.

Randomly, just as we completed our "shake down" at 770 miles completed, my phone rang. It was Garrett; he had been picked up off the trail the day prior in the same spot as us. Excited to hear about his progress, I informed him we were in Lynchburg, Virginia and to come meet up with us at the hotel. I was excited to have Garrett back once again. Ben and I weren't exactly sure who he was with, but I believe it was a friend from school who didn't live too far away. When Garrett arrived that evening he was pretty impressed with our Tour de Fast Food, and slightly jealous I think.

Fully resupplied and our stomachs' growling briefly pardoned, we headed back to the trail. It was a short visit, but one of utmost encouragement. As we pulled back in to the parking lot where the Haesekers picked us up the day before, it was weird thinking Mr. H and Jay were not getting out to hike with us. On scout trips of the past, that was always the case. The Three Muskateers were once again all on the trail together. Garrett had come back for another return. We had not seen him in 10 days, since Atkins, Virginia. His entries in the trail journals were few and far between, and to be honest, we had begun to seriously worry about him. According to Garrett there was nothing to worry about; I probably trusted that statement more than Ben did. Garrett quickly began rattling off the wonderful time he was making. We were able to snap a picture of the three of us, all proud of our new trail shoes. They were all identical. The only difference between our shoes from Garrett's was that they were our second pair of shoes since Georgia, some 770 miles ago, and Garrett's 6th or 7th. As we said our goodbyes to the Haesekers,we threw our newly lightened packs on our back and began our "going cold" portion of the trip, with 1,400 miles to go.

When you're walking on the trail, it can be quite difficult to hear if the person in front of you is talking. This seemed more like a challenge for Garrett than a misunderstanding. Ben and I are both fairly quiet people. I do not consider myself the talker in most relationships, and I'd be willing to bet Ben doesn't either. Perhaps this was part of our success as trail partners the last 800 miles. It sets up an interesting combination once you add a talker into the mix. If I told you Garrett wanted to be a politician, you could talk to him for about 30 seconds and say "yeah, I can see that."

Amongst his rambling, Garrett was explaining what he had been up to since his Dad picked him up at Partnership Shelter in Southern Virginia. Somehow, he was able to keep the same pace Ben and I were hiking at, even with taking a few days off with some gal he knew at college. Suspicion ran high, as I'm sure Ben's would have been as well if he could hear him. Despite our doubts and with fluctuating elevation change over the next couple of days before we got to Shenandoah National Park, which hikers recognize as the "Shenandoah Sidewalk," Garrett kept up. Garrett's most revealing moment was as we took a rest at the Tye River after descending a mountain called The Priest.

Garrett had been complaining of some chafing on the descent to the Tye River, and we knew there was another big climb waiting for us up the trail. I could relate to Garrett's condition, as mentioned when I was a wee little boy scout. To Garrett's good fortune, a little something called Body Glide had been invented since my problematic experience. Body Glide comes in deodorant stick form and acts as a skin lubricant to prevent chafing. It is convenient for application -- no cream to rub on, no powder that goes everywhere. Garrett digs down in his pack and pulls out two different sticks of Body Glide. Why do you have two? Ben asked.

Well, Garrett said, this one is for my feet and arms for hot spots and my shoulder straps rubbing, and this one with the skull-and-cross bones drawn on it is for my crotch. A fair precaution, as Ben and I nodded in agreement. In disagreement, Garrett drops his shorts in front of us, fortunately it was the "moon side," and began applying his Body Glide to prevent said chafing.

After climbing our long ascent up the "Three Ridges," I was actually feeling proud of Garrett. I knew he was capable of hanging with us, just like in the first week, but I enjoyed when all of us were cranking out big mileage days. When we reached the top, Garrett ran into a hiker he had mentioned the day before. They were the rare hiking combo of mother and son. They cracked a few jokes, and he introduced us as "the dudes he was telling her about." Conversation was friendly as we spoke about the tough climb up "The Priest" and the "Three Ridges." I envied Garrett's gregariousness. Although he was not hiking with Ben and me, it put me at ease knowing Footlocker was enjoying the trail on his own accord.

There was never any intent for us to get split up in the first place. We were so obsessive about completing this trail for Steve that it never even crossed our minds. It is often said amongst fellow hikers that time spent with someone on the trail is quantified exponentially in comparison to spending time with someone in the "Real World." I think Garrett's persona is advantageous in regard to this theory. The fact that a mother and son were thru-hiking the trail was ridiculous enough, so it was no surprise to me Garrett was all over it. It was becoming clear that Garrett's goals and attitude about the trail and life on it was much different from mine and Ben's. As far as Bandanna and I were concerned, we had little time to make friends. In order to cover the mileage that we were, it was sun-up to sundown hiking. There are benefits to both the way Ben and I were hiking as well as to the experience that Garrett was now able to have.

I became elated that Garrett was with us, and nothing was really going wrong; it was the reason we had ever even began planning the trip in the first place. Ben and Garrett seemed to be getting along well enough. For the 2 of them, it was basically like pursuing an extreme three-month adventure with someone you had never even met. I actually thought the 3 of us might finish the entire trail together. Ben and I were "steady goes it," and Garrett had his trail legs under him. After the completion of 55 miles in 2 days, we had a "short" 20 miles into Rock Fish Gap/Waynesboro, Virginia. I was particularly excited for this town stop not only because we had heard such good things about easier terrain to come in the Shenandoahs, but also because my mom (Zoe) and stepdad (Randy) were coming to resupply us.

I'm convinced that my mother will be late to her own funeral, but she is the kindest, sweetest, most compassionate woman you'd ever meet. A true Southern Belle. Born and raised in Raleigh, North Carolina, where she still lives, and dang (she'll never curse) proud of it. Rather than say she was late to meet us, we'll just say we knocked out that 20 miles earlier than expected. When we stepped off the trail at Rock Fish Gap, there was a Visitor Center that had a list of Trail Angels that would come pick you up and take you to Waynesboro. We just couldn't resist another opportunity at a Hardee's Thickburger. I phoned my folks and told them we were at the Hardee's in town. My mother worried of course that we would spoil our appetites for all the "goodies" she had made us (that probably held them up leaving Raleigh on time). Don't worry, I reassured her, we'll take care of everything.

As soon as my mom pulled up, my smile was ear to ear. She was crucial to the ongoing logistics operation, coordinating when to mail items, making trips to REI for little things we needed in the next drop, and constantly talking with Ben's and Garrett's parents as well as the Harringtons. Of course, like most sons, I couldn't tell my mom absolutely everything. No need to harp on the total discomfort of putting my sweat-soaked clothes back on every morning, the "come to Jesus" moment Ben and I had with our leg cramps in the Smoky Mountains, or what was becoming apparent: my chiggers. Ever since that hiker inquired about the tons of red spots on my legs at Catawba General Store in Catawba, Virginia, a few days ago, the situation had gotten much worse. It even freaked me out a few times. On multiple occasions, I woke up during the night with the worst itching sensation from just above my knees to halfway up my thighs. Because we typically slept in shelters, with other people, I always tried to be courteous during my night-time terrors. I was not even sure what chiggers were. I assumed they were just bed bugs. This was the most painful, exasperating thing I had ever experienced. I suffered in the silence and darkness of night, sleeping next to complete strangers. If anyone ever saw me shoot up in the middle of the night, scratching at what felt like -- and literally was – something crawling under my skin, they would surely have written me off as insane. It was the most unbearable surge of pain, often for minutes at a time, with no warning. At least with a cramp, you can feel it coming on and stretch it out. But this was an invasion of my body.

After hugging Mom and saying our hellos, Mom looked directly at my legs (because moms just know): Oh my word, what is wrong with your legs? Mosquito bites?

No, I said, I think it's chiggers.

In a classic mom-response, she said, We have to get you a doctor, or, or an Urgent Care, or, oh my gosh, an emergency room! Randy, where is the closest doctor's office? Like he would know in a town he's never been to.

It's fine Mom," I said. I had a feeling that the only reason that the itching had not gotten absolutely terrible was because of the frequency we had been hitting towns,and I was able to get a shower and wash off the dirt and grime. I did think it would be nice to get some steroid pills or something for the pain, or a sleep aid. So we dropped off Ben, Garrett, and Randy at the hotel, and I went to the local Urgent Care with my Mom.

I really did not want to make this a big deal; I just wanted to spend time with my Mom, and 90% of the time, my legs felt fine. They never bothered me while I was walking, which was the only thing that mattered to me. It was the 10%, however, that mom was worried about. "Chiggers," also known as red bugs or harvest mites, are most prevalent in the Southeastern US in forests, grasslands, and near streams and rivers. Check, check, and check.

"In treatment of chiggers, there's no one method that works for everyone," the doctor said. Thanks Doc, I thought to myself. He rattled off some backwoods remedies such as painting the affected areas with nail polish remover.

Nope, haven't tried that, I responded.

Hot showers or baths often help to reduce the itch, have you been doing that? he asked.

I began with a laugh and explained my situation and how that was not exactly an option. He quickly whipped out the prescription pad as I explained the itching was only at night. The doctor prescribed me two different topical creams. One for daily use and the other to rub on during the night if I woke up to one of my "episodes" again.

My mother and I knew very little about chiggers. The doctor began explaining how they do not actually bite; they just dig down in your skin, creating a hole which is what creates the pimple-like bumps. He also added that affected areas are worse where exposed to sunlight. Which I was happy to hear, because I wasn't planning on hiking naked any time soon. It felt like I was 10 years old with my mother at the pediatrician's office. To my dismay, it was even worse, nearing 20 years and at Urgent Care with her instead. Nevertheless, Zoe had to take care of her baby boy.

Zoe "Zoezilla" McKay-Tucker aka Mom taking her first step on the Appalachian Trail

Finally, I got back to the hotel with Randy and the guys. My folks brought my computer, so I headed up the uploading of all the pictures we had not gotten the chance to, and we each spent the night talking to my parents and friends on the phone. I was enjoying the time with Mom and Randy. They were so instrumental in making this trip possible on every level. There was no talking-them-into-it stage; they completely supported it from Day One. For that, I am forever indebted. Everything was going swell as Randy arrived from getting pizzas. Two enormous pies were carried through the door. We gorged ourselves on the familiar trail favorite. Mom was astounded at the number of calories we were consuming. What growing boys, she said. Throughout her visit, mom kept saying, I just want to step on the trail! She had been sending my brother and me on backpacking trips for years through scouts, but had never once actually done it herself, much less seen the AT.

Zoe, aka Zoezilla, wasn't exactly keen on our idea on not cooking anymore. But, what do you mean? she protested, you're not going to cook a hot meal before you go to bed? Ben and I were completely ok with that "Yes, Mom", that's what we're doing, I responded, as any maturing male would say to his mother. She wants to baby me to this day, but the more you let her, the more she wants to. I can't fault her for that: a mother's love is a mother's love.

She finally calmed down about it and figured that, if we had made it this far, we knew what we were talking about it. I would have explained it to her in depth; that we got the idea from Andy, then we'd have to explain who Andy was, and that Andy was carrying just a CamelBak, which we would also have to explain what that was. Mom could go on about proper etiquette or manners, but when it came to the outdoors, there was little resistance.

The next morning, we got off to a late start. Moseying out of the comfy beds and snacking on morning pizza, we finally began packing up. Getting our things together typically took about 5-10 minutes in the morning. There was little dilly dallying around. But when you have an entire hotel room to spread out in, making sure you have everything is essential. Mom felt obliged to take care of the laundry portion during the resupply and was smart enough to bring a spare change of clothes so she could wash anything and everything we needed. Since we all had the same gear, just slightly different sizes we made sure we had a fresh change of underwear, not just a change of underwear, ie. I wasn't wearing Ben's, Ben wasn't wearing Garrett's and Garrett wasn't wearing mine. That would have been a change in underwear, for sure.

Packing the things into the trunk, we had convinced Mom and Randy to hike Dragon's Tooth on their way back home. I thought it would be a nice little day-hike for them as well as a good preparation for them when they met us at the end of the trail in Maine at Mt. Katahdin. Mom was dead-set on hiking up the end of the trail with us, and it was all she talked about. She had been training every day by skipping the elevator at work and taking the 7 flights of stairs to her desk instead. I was worried about my mom's concept of the trail, considering I had never seen her do athletics of any kind in her life. She claims, to this day, to be "the best darn cheerleader that Millbrook High School never had. "Which I can believe, because at every cross country or track event, or any of my brother's basketball games, she cheered us on, pom-poms and all

To be honest, I'm sure she had the pom-poms packed just in case she and Randy picked us up right off the trail, like when you're a little kid playing soccer and there's an arm tunnel made by all the parents that the kids run through with Capri Suns and Orange slices at the end. I know my Mom just wanted to spend more time with me, Ben, and Garrett; the last time we had seen each other was when she dropped me off at the Harringtons the morning we left for Springer Mountain in Georgia for the beginning of our trek. I think the only reason we got dropped off was so that she could actually see the trail. As we arrived at Rock Fish Gap on a slow and quiet car ride. Mom was, of course, concerned about me "going back out there" with my chiggers. I had made it this far; there was no concern in my mind.

As we strapped our bags on our backs, sipping delicious hotel tap water from our water bladders in our packs, it was time for good-byes. Not before, however, Mom was able to snap a pic of her beside an Appalachian Trail marker. During a lingering goodbye, I actually got a little teary-eyed. I did miss my Mom, Randy, family, and friends. We took one last picture together and then strolled across the road heading towards Shenandoah National Park. I began thinking at that moment, Do the people I know and love even understand what we are doing? As I worked through their answers, I thought, Absolutely not. All they can fathom is that it is indeed a great adventure. Hell, most of my friends have never even done anything like this, much less even thought about. I began thinking, I must be a complete weirdo to them. Suddenly, when I thought about how far I had already come, despite the hardship, pain, and struggle; that was all suddenly ok.

Despite the late start that day, we were shooting for Pinefield Hut that evening, a solid 30-mile performance. I'm not sure if it was the pace, his health, or my parents' visit making him homesick, but Garrett ended up lagging behind towards the end of the day. While Ben and I ate our cold dinners about a mile from where the shelter was, we waited for Garrett. Ben and I sat at the lovely Ivy Creek Overlook along Skyline Drive. Skyline is the northern sibling of the Blue Ridge Parkway. I thought for sure he would be right behind us, but we waited, and waited. Before we knew it, because of the late start, we had to get to camp because it was getting dark. The purplish-blue haze of sundown was upon us. Ben and I had managed to not have to night hike yet, and we weren't planning on starting now.

Shortly, we pulled into Pinefield Hut, right at darkness. The shelter was occupied, but we squeezed in. If sleeping next to strangers was not odd enough, sleeping next to strangers that were already asleep was even odder. As Bandanna and I set down our packs and slid our thermarests onto the cool, dusty, wood floor of the shelter, a small light through the trees appeared and flickered closer and closer. To our relief, it was Garrett. My angst over Foot Locker's ability to keep up with us that had been briefly subdued was now creeping back. Ben and I squeezed our sleeping pads closer together to make room.

Just as we were about to hit the hay and join the hikers already sawing logs, we recognized a familiar face amongst the moving shine of a few people's head lamps around the small fire outside the shelter. It was none other than Baltimore Jack, the fella' we had met at "The Hostel" in Damascus, Virginia. He accompanied us during the young girl's violin performance of Ashokan Farewell. She happened to be biking across the country, and just as unlikely as it was to cross her path, it was proportionately so to run into Jack again. We said our hellos and got on with the getting to bed thing.

In the morning, Garrett was slow to rise and told us to go ahead, that he would catch up, or at least meet us in Harpers Ferry. Ben and I looked a little shocked to hear this. Meet you at Harpers? I said to myself. It was like Garrett did not want to hike with us. Garrett's statement caught me off-guard. I was hoping the rest of the trip would continue per the last few days, like it was "supposed to be." The blame was on no one. It had already been a different trip than planned, so Garrett was letting it be just that. That is how I made peace with it at that moment. Before we scooted away, Baltimore Jack asked us to deliver a note to someone up the trail, figuring we would catch up with them in the next couple of days. The note was for "The Dude" – it wasn't out of our element. Not one bit.

We continued walking along the famed Shenandoah Sidewalk. With around one million visitors a year, the trail in Shenandoah is so well kept that it's a breeze to hike. Much of it is double-wide, which Ben and I enjoyed. The deer in SNP are so used to visitors you could literally go up and pet the damn things. There are signs telling you not to, but I don't think that stops people from doing it. We were moving pretty quickly, and hitting mileage above 30 miles a day, including the previous day. Early on, having done about 12 miles by 10AM, Bandanna and I decided that we should shoot for Rock Spring Hut, a smooth 32.1 miles from Pinefield Hut. Without having to really look down at our feet for rocks and roots and trail hazards, we were really able to stretch out the legs and keep our heads up. As wonderful as the condition of the trail was, so too was the scenery. You could tell the trail was engineered for people that were not hiking the entire Appalachian Trail as there were a decent number of day hikers. There were good views with little effort, and the terrain was not very difficult. Ben and I loved it, having walked 913 miles to get to the easy part.

That evening, as we strolled into Rock Spring Hut, we were expecting a crowded shelter, but just one lone hiker chick was there. She introduced herself as Stardust as we exchanged small talk. She became instantly awesome when she offered Ben and me one untouched turkey wrap from a lodge off of Skyline Drive that Ben and I had passed up. A hiker giving another hiker food? This was a new concept. I don't know if I'd ever give up food because I "wasn't hungry." So we ate our halves of the turkey wrap while watching the sunset through the trees. The night became unusually cold, a feeling we hadn't dealt with since the thunderstorm on top of Mt. Rogers at Thomas Knob Shelter. I actually slept like a friggin' baby as it was one of the first nights I was actually able to stay in my sleeping bag because I didn't wake up sweating. Ben recalls someone coming in to the shelter very late, but it didn't phase me.

When we woke up at 6:30 that morning, we made out a figure in the corner atop the cleverly-built bunk bed shelter. They had emptied out their entire pack, to use as a sleeping bag, and had a pack cover as a blanket. Sitting beside the sleeping hiker was half of a six-pack of Busch (not Busch Light, just Busch) with the remaining three still in its 6-ring plastic holder. Popping up from their uncomfortable-looking slumber as Ben and I strapped on our packs, to our surprise, was Foot Locker.

Whoa! What's up, man, I asked. He was excited to see us and quickly explained that the six-pack was for us to share when he arrived at the shelter, but that was much later than he intended. I was saddened as a cold brewski would have hit the spot with that turkey wrap. He offered me one, and we drank one right there. Busch for breakfast. Ben and I asked if he was coming and he just waved us on. This confirmed that we would see him next in Harper's Ferry, where we were taking a day off with the Harringtons for July 4th.

Talk
With
Jesus

Pine Grove Furnace
State Park

Who knew a Busch would get you going so fast in the morning? Ben and I "hopped" out to a quick start again and crushed a lot of miles before lunch. We had been hearing from other hikers and read in trail journals that the blackberry milkshakes at Elkwallow Wayside (right off Skyline Drive) were stellar. That might have fueled the fire to get our asses up the trail. 1:00PM rolled around, and we cruised up to the Wayside. We knew right where to go, as we could smell it from a mile away. The grill was serving up double cheeseburgers and the famed blackberry milkshakes. Purchases at the general store commenced with burgers, fries, milkshakes, and some extracurricular snacks including brown sugar and apple cinnamon Pop Tarts for breakfast the next day.

We hunted down a picnic table in the shade, and devoured our on-trail goodies. Technique was not lost on us as we were sure to dip a few fries in the milkshake, take a bite of burger, and then wash it down with more milkshake. After another episode of binge eating, we laid out on the picnic table. Momma always said not to go swimming until 30 minutes after eating, but we ate so much it felt like we were swimming. After a two-hour break, we decided to hit the trail once again. Don't discount the fact that we heaved ourselves 24 miles to get to this point. The only problem, if you want to call it that, was that our next 2 shelter options were 6 and 16 miles away. We could have stopped in an hour and a half at Gravel Springs Hut at 4:30 in the afternoon. That, however, just wasn't our style. So we decided to take the extra mile (or 10) to Tom Floyd Wayside.

Cruising by Gravel Springs Hut, we pushed daylight all the way to Tom Floyd. Just before sunset, like the night before, we rolled into a full shelter. Never the worry though, after 39 miles, there's not much stopping you from a good night's sleep. Because we came into camp so late, some hikers were interested in where we had started that day. After revealing our starting location to an older married couple, they were more than impressed. They had been hiking sections for some time, and were enthralled. Being the modest guys we are, Ben and I were proud but not boastful. They felt bad though when they saw us laying out our sleeping pads on the porch of the shelter. We were asleep before they had a chance to offer up their spots in the Hut. As quick as we were to sleep, we were also to rise.

What we had was a banner day awaiting us: the "Appalachian Roller Coaster," West Virginia-Virginia State Line, Harper's Ferry, and a day off with Garrett and the Harringtons. Apparently, the Appalachian Roller Coaster is a section in Northern Virginia that is a series of Pointless Ups and Downs (PUDs). Twelve to be exact, from what I've gathered; the section crosses the western side of a ridge line that is developed at the top. Therefore, to keep the trail a trail, it rides tightly up and down the side of this range of mountains. It's really just a matter of going up 100-600 ft and dropping right back down only to do it again. It gets a lot of hype for being really difficult, but it's really not much different than any other section of the AT.

Going up one of the last 12 PUDs, we met a couple sitting atop that was having dinner. They were no other than Stitch and Figgy. Figgy would later become famous as her picture was on the cover of the 2008 Appalachian Trail Thru Hiker's Companion. So yeah, we met her, no big deal. If I recall correctly she was vegan, and had Ben and I totally confused as to what exactly that was. Some hardcore vegetarian was all I could think. We exchanged blogs and chatted for a bit. Shortly, we were on our way to continue our quest of 30+ mile days in a row. Our destination for the night was Sam Moore Shelter, which would leave us an "easy" 23-mile day into Harper's Ferry. The next day we realized we were just 3 miles from Bear's Den Hostel, which is right on the trail, and made for a good breakfast spot.

Walking into Harper's Ferry was like going back in time. The town is rich with history of the Civil War. Knee-high stone walls line the undulating street as we naturally gravitated towards the outfitter in town. We couldn't resist going in. Lord knows we did not need anything though. In the tight, crowded shop we shuffled our way around other thru-hikers. The front porch of the shop was littered with dirty, grungy, sweat-stained packs. Instead of a bike rack, this place needed a pack rack. It felt good knowing we were seeing so many other hikers because we were catching those who started in Georgia nearly 2 months before we did.

Shuffling through the store packed shoulder-to-shoulder, which had a lingering haze of trail funk, an abrupt society-induced claustrophobia fell upon me. After being in the outdoors for so long, I found the small, crowded space nearly unbearable. My concept of space and scale was severely out of whack. Perhaps Ben's and my thinking was taking shape to our surroundings. It feels healthy to put yourself in such open environments, where the only enclosed area is the bag you sleep in.

Through the musk, untrimmed facial hair and outdoor gear, I spotted Foot Locker roaming through the store as we searched for the nearest exit. We stepped outside to catch up and ventured to the Comfort Inn in hope of getting a room despite the crowd of thru-hikers flooding the town. Fortunately, we were able to shack up in a double, non-smoking room. We were not sure how Garrett had gotten to Harper's, but it was not important. Once again, the three of us were together, just like it was "supposed" to be.

Garrett seemed only mildly impressed by the big mileage we pulled going through Shenandoah National Park. I thought for sure he would be ecstatic with our progress. However, his attitude was much the opposite. Walking around town, making our way to the headquarters of the ATC, he began suggesting we ought to consider skipping the entire state of Pennsylvania.

This was borderline blasphemous, and Ben took the adjuration with slightly more insult than perhaps intended. I understood Garrett's thinking. His concern that we would be unable to complete the entirety of the trail with just 45 days of hiking left was not all that unwarranted. An exponentially greater effort would have to be put forth compared to the challenge and struggle we had already endured. Bandanna and I undoubtedly had our blinders on, but rightfully so. The confidence of making it 1,000 miles into the journey, we had every reason to believe that the completion of the AT was inevitable. Barring any major setbacks, we thought we would finish. It would have to be a setback of such epic proportion that nothing short of death would stop us from achieving our goal. This, of course, was a realization we came to in our "come to Jesus" moment during the leg cramp days. Our level of commitment and sacrifice was elevated beyond the endurance of physical pain and suffering, and greater than mental depletion; it was becoming more spiritual than ever.

Visiting the unofficial halfway point of the trail, the Appalachian Trail Conservancy Headquarters, was an inspiring event. Garrett showed us to the area where they keep records of past and present thru hikers in a photo log. We had our pictures taken, wrote our names on them (real and trail) along with our hometowns and blog address. I was a little disappointed that Garrett had already been to the headquarters and through this process so that we would not all be on the same page of the book together. Our trips, in all reality, were two different experiences though. Each thru-hike is special and significant to the individual, much of the experience is from within. It is a collective experience yet incredibly singular. Even my hike was much different from Ben's hike. Every hiker is subject to their own thoughts while walking. And as much as it is similar to other hikers in physical surroundings and uncontrollable variables such as weather, no two thru-hikers can have the same thru-hike. Not even Ben and I, who spent every second together.

S p e n c e r M c K a y

After finishing our visit to the ATC, we roamed around town and made it back to the hotel in excitement for our first full day off in 600 miles of hiking and for a visit from the Harringtons for the first time since they dropped us off at the start on Springer Mountain. The pain of losing Steve was one that continued to linger even as we knew what his family must be going through and will perpetually go through was tenfold. A void never to be filled, an abyss you can stare into, but it's staring right back. I constantly reminded myself that what we were doing was a positive and honorable thing to do. The journey was a helpful tool for the three of us to grieve. Just like any tool, if you don't use it properly, it's not going to get the job done. We all grieved in our own separate ways. I reverently hoped, deep in my heart, to this day, and for the rest of my life, that what the 3 of us were attempting was not only good for us but good for the Harringtons.

Smiles and hugs were exchanged when we met Tim and Julie Harrington in Harper's Ferry the next morning; this put my doubt at ease. We relocated to a Hampton Inn along the Interstate. The day was filled with relaxation and catching the Harringtons up on all the shenanigans along the way. The blog was informative for followers back home, but with limited entries and censorship for our parents' peace of mind, we got to share the stories that did not make the blog. Our favorites included that of Tyvek Holy Shit, the fleece vest photo shoot, and the Czech family from Chicago with cat and dog in tow. On top of having a day off, it was also the 4th of July. In the spirit of Steve's pyrotechnic tendencies, we launched fireworks and ran around like dumbasses with sparklers and roman candles in the parking lot of the hotel. As good as the day off in Harper's Ferry, West Virginia felt, in the back of my mind I was worried that perhaps we ought to be hiking. Especially if a good friend and fellow hiker such as Foot Locker was concerned with our ability to complete the trail. Ben and I were well aware of the difficulty, but we owed it to the Harringtons and ourselves to enjoy a day off. Besides, they brought up a cake to celebrate Ben's and my birthday (2 days apart) early.

From Harper's Ferry onward, we would be in a completely unexplored part of the Appalachian Trail as well as farther and farther from home.

This meant no more uplifting resupplies from supportive family members and friends, and all trail magic would be solely based on random acts of kindness. With a rejuvenation and renewed sense of purpose that our hike was a positive reinforcement for the Harringtons (our Zero-day Heroes), our goodbyes on the edge of town were tear-jerking. Despite the emotion, there was a strong sense of moment. There was no other place in the world, and no other thing that I was supposed to be doing. Greater than the physical place though, was the place in the timeline of my life. With everything that I had ever done, there was no doubt: this is where I belonged and destined to be. Concurrently though, we would be doing the remaining portion of the trip as never expected. Two, instead of 3, Garrett had requested that the Harringtons take him farther up the trail, where he would hike for an indefinite period of time. So not only was this a goodbye to the Harringtons but to a friend and fellow hiker in Garrett as well.

"Was this hike, inspired and devoted to honoring a lost friend, able to have loss of its own? It certainly shook the foundations of the entire trip and what we had set out to do. Can it just be chalked up to unforeseen circumstances, or had I failed, had we failed?" My thoughts brought me to the realization that this (to be quite cliché) is life. However elementary it sounds, life is made up of mere losses and gains. It becomes an exercise of control. Not control over others or environment as much as control of self and the decisions you make. A simple idea yet intrinsically engrained with difficulty. Simplicity is what lies in the heart of man. In the moment, walking away with hand waving in the air, as Ben and I crossed a bridge to continue on the old C&O railroad path; we were leaving behind the warm, embracing hugs of the Harringtons and Garrett. What initially felt and started as a loss became a gain. A gain that the Harringtons, if only temporary, could experience joy in the darkness of their loss. Joy of knowing that Steve's bad decisions, which were minuscule in quantity and wildly disproportionate in consequence, would not be the lasting mark he would leave. The loss of his life would not be the unthreading of a woven cloth. Instead, we had been given the opportunity of his shortened life to be the catalyst. A shuttle in the loom, weaving the warp and the weft.

Heading north once again, Ben and I finally began talking after a quiet restart. Each mile walked felt like a dose of medicine for the soul. It was easy to have such thoughts of fulfillment due to the ease of terrain. We were not sure how long the trail would continue "easy" through Maryland and into Pennsylvania. The benchmark elevations associated with mile markers in our guidebooks looked promising. Pennsylvania on the trail is synonymous with one word to hikers: "rocks." One thru-hiker described it in a trail journal that it was as if all of the boulders on the entire AT had been collected, exploded into softball-sized pieces and dumped across the state of Pennsylvania. We were curious to see what the hype was all about. It was perceived to be a twisted ankle waiting to happen, further solidifying Garrett's expressed concern.

Before we crossed the Mason-Dixon Line, kissing our sweet tea goodbye, we came to a road crossing in the "land of pleasant living." There was a white pick-up truck right near the trail where we decided to take a quick snack break. The presumed driver of the truck was talking to a fellow hiker, but was out of sight, blocked by the cab. One of the voices sounded awfully familiar; as soon as we heard it, we both looked at each other. No words exchanged, but we were thinking the same thing. We wracked our brains trying to figure out how we knew that voice. As we packed up our gear, the voice came around the side of the truck to offer us some trail magic in the form of fresh fruit. As soon as he handed us some apples and oranges, it clicked. "Jedi Birder!" we said collectively. The fellow we had met at Chestnut Knob Shelter about 450 miles back. He was astonished and in disbelief at the ground we had covered in just 18 days. We visited with Jedi for a little longer, whose voice is a combination of Yoda and Kermit, so that explained the Yoda part; he was also a bird watcher (aka "birder"). His mantra was "southbound, always southbound," referring to the direction in which he hiked. From that point on, Ben and I always say, "northbound, always northbound" when asked about what direction we hike.

In 24 hours' time, Ben and I would be participating in one of the premiere challenges on the Appalachian Trail. There are a few unwritten challenges along the way that hikers attempt. One is the quad-state challenge, which is starting at the Virginia/West Virginia Line, going through West Virginia, past Harpers Ferry, giving yourself a few minutes to get in the thru-hiker log, and hiking all of the Maryland portion of the trail to the Pennsylvania border, thereby putting yourself in 4 states in a single day with 43 miles of hiking. Ben and I opted out of this one to spend a day with the Harrington's. We were fine without participating; we had already done a 39-mile day in a string of four 30-plus mile days through Northern Virginia. The challenge we were going to participate in was much more self-indulgent: the "half-gallon challenge." Journal entries in the shelters leading up to the Pine Grove Furnace State Park General Store, where the competition takes place, were filled with buzz of the half-gallon challenge. If Twitter had existed then, it would have been trending. The night before, we hiked until dusk. Unfortunately, because we had begun to catch up with the "bubble" of traditional start time thru-hikers, the shelter we arrived at was packed with hikers. Every square inch of the place was covered with some article of clothing, food, or gear. There was obviously no room in the shelter, so we didn't even bother.

Like outcasts amongst outcasts, Ben and I set down our packs and began eating our "cold" dinner. A couple of hikers came up to us and asked who we were in curiosity. When they began asking how far we had come from that day, our responses were taken with a sort of resentment since the fellow thru-hikers asking the questions had started about 2 months before we did, and we had just caught them. Bandanna and I are any- thing but pretentious, but it felt as though we came off that way. Truth was, we were simply hiking big miles. We were aware that we did not have the social experience that most thru-hikers do, but we were ok with that.

Given the amount of effort we exerted each day, getting to know other hikers whom that we would likely never see again seemed a bit of a waste of time. No one wanted to talk to a couple of young guys who just hiked in a month what took them 2 ½. We were still cordial in conversation and polite; hopefully our urgency was not taken the wrong way. We always had somewhere to be, and that somewhere was farther down the trail. Northbound, always northbound. It became apparent while eating our bagels with pepperoni and prepackaged chicken that our pace and overall itinerary greatly hindered what most hikers consider the best part of the trail. We had no one but each other to truly share our experience while a shelter packed of people were all buddy-buddy and carried on into the night.

With some 15-odd miles to get to the State Park that held our half gallons of ice cream, I had decided upon my plan of attack. After our realization in Daleville of how much ice cream a half-gallon really was, I knew we had to be smart about it if we were to complete it. Eating an entire half gallon of one single flavor seemed unwise. Ben and I decided that Neapolitan was the best approach. The trifecta: vanilla, chocolate and strawberry. Pretty smart, huh? We entered the general store and spotted the cooler filled with Hershey's brand half-gallon ice cream flavors. Sure enough, the pink cardboard container depicting a scoop of the ice cream inside on the top was cold to the touch with a thin layer of frost developing on its exterior as I removed it from the freezer. The cashier smirked as Ben and I were all smiles, purchasing our half gallons.

Either this was a brilliant scam developed by the General Store to sell absurd amounts of ice cream, or just a ridiculous tradition favorable to the store. Despite either scenario, we were all-in now. With ice cold Coca-Colas purchased to help wash down our snack, we tore open the packaging and dug out our bright orange sporks made of durable high strength plastic. Ben started the stopwatch on his watch as we cheered the first bite -- here goes nothing. It was difficult battling the brain freeze as it became apparent that this tradition was a race against the clock. Seeing as how it was in the 90's outside, one aspect of this epic feat of eating had not occurred to us until now: the rate at which our ice cream would melt. About 10 minutes had passed, and I had barely made a noticeable dent in each flavor of my Neapolitan carton.

I attempted to pick up the pace as the initial threat of brain freeze was wearing off. Slowly, as the minutes ticked by, our eyes started to glaze over. Every bite delivered to my mouth became a more begrudging one as the contents I was spooning never seemed to decrease. As the sweet cream continued to melt it became a luke warm milkshake in the bottom of the container. The pink-and-white flavors of strawberry and vanilla mixed with the dark brown chocolate color. Eventually, 40 minutes in, with a tiny island of solid ice cream left swimming in a pool of chocolate, I made one final push to slop in the last few bites. In pure professionalism, in order to complete, I turned the box up at a 45- degree angle so a corner of the now soggy box would more easily funnel the melted ice cream into my disgraceful face. One, two gulps of warm milkshake, and I was done. I rolled myself back into the store to show I had completed this once-exciting challenge. The damage was done. I showed the clerk my empty box as he handed me my wooden spoon, the kind you get with a school lunch single serving ice cream, with "Half Gallon Challenge Club" stamped on it in red.

In great pride, I stepped back outside to our table only to find Ben rubbing his stomach like a pregnant woman. I didn't want him to quit – he was so close, but there was no turning back; the white flag was already waving. There was nothing I could do to convince him to carry on. The threshold of still being able to eat his ice cream instead of drinking it had now surpassed. The brown milky pool that remained in his container was not appetizing. Bandanna was unable to complete the Half-Gallon Challenge.

In my ice cream coma, with enough sugar to induce Type II Diabetes, I mustered up enough energy to hobble over to the pay phone to share the good (relatively speaking) news of my great accomplishment back home. There was a man on the pay phone as I approached it, but he was speaking Spanish. It had been a few years since Spanish III in high school, so I wasn't exactly sure what he was saying. It was the stereotypical man-at-a-pay-phone scenario. He desperately attempted call after call, each one leading anticlimactically to voicemail after voicemail until the quarters ran out. Finally, after the last try, he gripped the sun-worn black-to- grey phone tightly, pressing it against his forehead. Its once shiny and glossy finish had become worn to a smooth matte. In the last shake of his head, when the receiving end of the headset clicked the switch hook down, the stranger

Spencer McKay

glanced at me. He apologetically asked if I needed to use the phone. He thanked me for my patience as I stood up to approach the phone.

I had my calling card ready to go, as I didn't have cell service in the area. I made a couple of quick calls, left a few messages as no one answered while they were at work. All the while, I couldn't help but notice the man on the phone before me lingering around the pay phone. He sat on the bench near the phone, head in his hands, elbows on his knees. I tried to think of more people to call, to buy some time, in hoping that this guy wouldn't solicit me for anything. I thought, "Come on Ben, where are you?" We hadn't spent 30 minutes apart this entire trip, now would be a great time to not let that happen.

Sure enough, it was time to face the music. As I hung up the phone for the last time, the Hispanic man rose from the bench and approached me. "Here we go," I said to myself. To my surprise, he introduced himself to me before asking for anything. Jesus, in a white tank top, long cut-off jean shorts, donned with fishing pole and tackle box must have been pretty desperate to approach a young white kid in running shorts and a sweaty Appalachian Trail t-shirt, carrying his cell phone, a debit card, calling card, and insurance card in a Ziploc baggie for advice. There was no going back now.

"Have you ever been in love?" asked Jesus. What an odd question to ask a complete stranger. The fact of the matter was, though, that I had, or at least thought I was. I just politely nodded and said yes, as I was not quite as ready to reveal my more private emotions to a complete stranger as Jesus was. He began asking me what he should do, and started giving me the lowdown on the situation. Jesus obviously needed someone to talk to, and I tried my best to listen to his dilemma. The mother of his children did not want anything to do with him, and she would rarely let them see him. He went into how he bought gifts for the kids, including a PlayStation 2, and how he "put a TV in every room of the house." Kind of an odd point of pride I thought to myself, considering I was currently deluged with thoughts of minimalism and how I didn't need a car, or a tv, or a computer.

As Jesus poured his heart out to me about how he loved this woman so much, the mother of his children, I couldn't help but think about the crossing of our paths. What could I possibly offer this distressed man. I figured the best thing I could do was just listen. During that conversation, I felt a great humility come over me. I genuinely wanted to help Jesus; I just had no idea how. Maybe he just needed someone to talk to, regardless of the temporary resolve that may have provided; it was clear he had to get it off his chest. Why then and there, at a state park in Pennsylvania, with a complete stranger. That I too did not know.

Jesus finally wound down a little bit, after showing me a picture of the mother of his children. Only True Love can drive a man that crazy, Even at 19 I knew that. I myself had been relieved of my duties in a 2 ½ year relationship before starting my hike. And up until that moment, I had managed block it out of my mind. I had not even talked to her since March. Yet when I heard Jesus mention love, it was like a trigger in my mind. Despite all the physical aspects that the trail demands of your body, your thoughts still wander. If anything, it helps keep your mind off what you're asking your body to do. On the other hand, although you are on the trail, removed from all things past life, you are still subject to previous experiences through thought. I was able to slip away from the conversation with the Hispanic man. As I came around the corner of the General Store, to a still comatose-looking Ben, his half glazed over eyes looked at me "Where have you been?" "Talking to Jesus" I said.

We finally packed up our things and headed out from the state park. Just before exiting the park, we hit the official halfway point of the Appalachian Trail. A sign marks the spot pointing 1,069 miles to Springer and 1,069 miles to Katahdin. This event called for a little self-reflection over the next 15 miles we were planning to hike the rest of the day, half gallon of ice cream and all. Looking back at our original trip itinerary that Ben and I had created in the Harrington's kitchen the week leading up to our trip, we had planned to be at this point on July 1st. In all reality, we were not too far off. The day we crossed the midpoint marker was July 7th. Not bad considering all the unforeseen conditions and 1,088 miles of walking. An 8' tall sign in the middle of a state park seemed like a small reward for having covered such a distance on foot.

The halfway point was an important crossing, and over the past few weeks, the trip had really changed. After confirming that our bodies were capable of high mileage; in the last 20 days (Damascus, Virginia, to Midpoint Marker) we averaged over 26 miles a day, including a zero day. The previous 23 days (Springer to Damascus) before that, we averaged just below 20 miles a day. It was always part of the plan to build up to the big mileage, which most thru-hikers know you can do in the central portion of the trail, typically from the Shennys aka the 'Doahs aka Shenandoah National Park to somewhere near the Massachusetts/Vermont Border. Although we were a few days off our original mark to hit the halfway point, our plan to slowly add more mileage stayed the same, and we were proud to have hiked this far.

In reality, once we arrived in Damascus, Virginia, we were confident in our physical ability to make it to Maine. At the halfway point, having stretches of 30-plus mile days in a row, we had no doubt we could physically do it. Ben and I had a confidence about ourselves that I had never really experienced before. During our time in Pennsylvania, where we passed the "bubble" of hikers that started at least a month before us, it was never our intent to be cocky about what we were accomplishing. Were we missing out on a huge part of the trail by ostracizing ourselves from the social scene? Absolutely. Yet as sad as that may sound, our lives simply did not allow any other time frame to hike the trail. Our sense of urgency was firmly planted by Steve's death. Yet the short time frame of our trip still took for granted a life we planned on continuing to live. The 3 of us were not planning on missing a beat: we were all from families where the course of expected action was high school -->college -->job -->wife -->house-->family.

Don't get me wrong – there's no problem with that, but it's always a bit boring to do what you're supposed to. The feeling we got from most people we met on the trail was that we were rushing it. Which may have been true, as we wasted hardly any time. Ben and I mused that we were just extremely efficient. The naysayers who proclaim we weren't even seeing the trail were judging under false pretense. How is it that we weren't "seeing the trail"? We were seeing more of the trail each day than most. I fell in love with that notion. I felt as though we were seeing more of the trail than most. Fewer towns visited, less time sitting in shelters, less time taking a break in one spot. We were perpetually moving, always taking in more and wanting more, too. It felt like my body was a sponge. I felt the earth with each step, the air with each breath, and the world with each sight. I woke up every morning wanting more, to experience more. Less was more, less town, less hitchhiking, less people, less talking. More trail, more walking, more wildlife, and more mountains.

As nice as going into town was – stuffing our face, relaxing and enjoying all the things we left behind in society - in reality, it is not difficult to ever get off the trail and go into town. Some take to temptation far too frequently for my liking. The reward of town becomes peripheral, nothing special, a common occurrence. Not to mention, the cost hiking the trail begins to skyrocket when you go into town. Motels and hotels, eating at restaurants, and buying snacks, beers and other treats adds up fast. Unfortunately, many hikers go home due to finances. Some hikers try to work along the way to keep funding their trip. For some, the goal is clear, to hike the entire trail, as for Ben and me. Others are pretty unsure on how to go about it. The discipline Bandanna and I were showing, our devotion to the completion of the trail, matched with our undying passion for it, was and remains extremely special to us. To experience more town than trail or to skip a section is only cheating yourself. Yes, the towns are nice; yes, they have a warm shower, food, TV, and a cozy bed. But that is not why Ben and I were out there.

Ben and I celebrated our birthdays, just two days apart with the Harrington's in Harper's Ferry, West Virginia. The giving, just never seemed to stop. The trail kept on giving, and we kept on taking. Through Ben's mom, we were able to hook up with the aunt and uncle of one of Ben's old friends from his brief time as an adolescent in New Hampshire. As luck would have it, they lived within walking distance from the trail. A hot lunch was a detour we just never could refuse. Once again we found ourselves ringing the doorbell of a welcoming home. Double-score as it was my birthday, and we had a chance to use their internet machine to upload pictures of the half-gallon challenge debauchery. Dan and Dianne Scaff opened their home to us and, along with a great meal, fed us all kinds of questions that we eagerly answered. Their curiosity and genuine excitement about the trail and our journey were refreshing and surprising considering they lived within walking distance. The skeptical coincidence of crossing the Mason-Dixon Line and the simultaneous prohibition of sweet tea began conjuring up the notion that the days of "Southern Hospitality" on the trail, all 1,059 miles of it, had stopped dead in its tracks.

Turns out, Pennsylvania was not the deprived barren wasteland of hosts and hostesses as my bias had sought it out to be. Hell, the way our time in Pennsylvania has gone so far, them folks were nothing but a couple sticks o' butter and a jar of mayonnaise short of kin. I can only recall one food from our meal with the Scaffs. This was not due to kitchen error or absence of flavor. Lord knows, Bandanna and I hadn't had anything green since we left Tennessee I don't think. Even then it was probably drowning in ranch, cooked with bacon, bacon placed on top of it, stuffed with bacon, wrapped with bacon or at least had something to do with a farm animal. When I caught eye of a green bean, it was like a blast from the past. Mom used to force those damn things down my gullet. Of course, my older brother took them like a champ. He was the Green Bean Machine. I shared my portion with to the four-legged friend below the dinner table. But lo and behold, slap yo' momma, you don't have to call me darlin', daddy needs a new pair of shoes – when that bowl of green beans gently slid into my reach across the table of the Scaff's home, you would have thought I had died and gone to heaven. This guy can walk over 1,600 miles but cannot eat a vegetable on his own?

What can I say, 20 never felt so good. Besides no pride shots taken, I had just eaten an entire half gallon of ice cream the day before. Any normal person would have one hand on a pink bottle of Bismol, and the other cupped to the side of his mouth calling for more TP. In addition to the green beans we had baked chicken, rice, homemade apple pie (with just a tad of ice cream). Then it was like everything the pulled out of the fridge and offered us to drink we couldn't say no.

"Orange Juice?"

"Ohh that sounds good."

"Milk?"

"Yes ma'am I'll have a glass"

"Gatorade?"

"Absolutely!"

Member - Half Gallon Challenge

Spencer McKay

The Last Place
You Check In
Before You
Check Out

Duncannon, PA

We said our thank-yous and goodbyes, and ventured back out to the neighborhood street, took a couple turns, and intersected with the trail once again. From the Scaff's, we hoofed it to the borough of Duncannon. A small town with a population of 2,000, Duncannon offered a promising evening of birthday celebration and relaxation as we had previously scoured over the map of the town in our guidebooks. Bandanna had even arranged for a friend, Justin, to travel from State College, Pennsylvania, and join us for dinner. We rolled into town mid-afternoon, crushing another 30-mile day (with a lunch stop) in the heat wave. It had been 4 days without a shower, and we were ready to freshen up and do some laundry once again. Accommodations for the evening were made at the dignified Doyle Hotel on Market Street.

Unbeknownst to us, the Doyle was legendary amongst the thru-hiker community. We were still encompassed within the populous "hiker bubble" (comprised of droves of hikers starting within the same time frame at the end of March to beginning of April), but Ben and I failed to get the memo.

The antiquated brick clad façade, wrap-around porch on the second level, and rotunda on the corner gives off an aura of brothel or speakeasy. I cannot be sure if we met the owners or not: the place was a mad house, an animal house. There was no second guessing our needs in the concierge's mind. Ben and I were another two weary, hungry, dirty hikers. The jukebox was bumping in the restaurant/bar while a continuous flow of hikers shuffled up and down the stairs to the room levels. I can only imagine if the century-plus old walls of the Doyle could talk. As the story goes the Doyle is "The last place you check in before you check out." Bandanna flipped the 30-buck bill for the double room, and we made our way up the winding wood stairs to the 2nd floor, every square inch of railing covered by a piece of hiker gear. Sleeping bags, socks, shirts and skibbies getting a good ol'- fashioned air dry. The line for getting some laundry done was about as ambiguous as a next-up beer pong list. You snooze, you lose. After inquiring amongst a few hikers for the next load in line, we figured that by the time Strider, Ranger, Doc, Happy, Turtle, Sunshine, Goat, and Moose finished up, we'd already be back on the trail.

The duct-taped door knob to our room led us to believe that the maintenance man was a thru-hiker at heart. After keying in, we found two beds, a single daybed and a double, sheeted at that. It was hot as hell; the Pennsylvania summer was bearing down hard, and the overall lack of A/C in the Mid-Atlantic seemed tragic. The Doyle had supplied the room with a fan, which made it bearable. Since laundry was out of the question, our next thought was we could at least run ourselves through a rinse cycle. Typical of most building's plumbing arrangements, the shower was near the laundry. The public restroom/showers could only pass as gently used if a used car salesman were handing out the towels. To a hiker though, if there's running water, they're going to use it. I never was a math major, so I spun the showerhead on, and it was already warm. Lucky me. With all the folks in this place, I figured the only thing left would be an ice bucket challenge. Then I stuck my hand into the stream, and it just kept getting hotter and hotter, close to boiling really. As much as I ate ramen noodles in college, I never wanted to be one. It all started adding up as the washing machine buzzer rang out across the hallway. This stay was turning into a wash, or lack thereof. Boiling hot showers, no A/C, no laundry, not the greatest, but a bed above ground, a real pillow, and some time to relax was premium.

On the way into town, I popped into the town post office to pick up a birthday package from Momma. Lord only knew what was inside the box; it had a good weight to it, for sure. My mother, aka "Zoezilla," is the most thoughtful person on earth. On the same hand, shes has the uncanny ability to embarrass her youngest son at the snap of a finger. The items that came out of her purse rivaled that of the home décor for the Banks family that appeared out of Mary Poppins' purse. It did not matter the place or the event. If we were at a restaurant for a birthday, confetti and a centerpiece were fished out and placed on the table along with a few presents. She has always wanted everyone around her to feel comfortable and cared for. So when her birthday boy was a 1000 miles away, with a 1000 more to go, the contents of the box could have been anything. True to form, Zoezilla packed the box with balloons, ribbons, and kazoos. After the fluff, we got down to brass tacks. Gatorades, IBC glass Root Beers, and snacks layered the rest of the box.

As we had settled into our room at the Doyle and unpacked the Birthday Box, Justin was arriving in town. We explored what there was in town and decided on a pizza shop for supper. Zeiderelli's pizza was well within walking distance from the Doyle. It was obnoxious really, but it was a luxury we just couldn't bear to pass up. So we did the sensible thing…and drove. A "Za" with all the fixings was ordered, and a foot-long grinder each, for good measure. Par for the course really. Yet another dinner companion impressed as Justin was in awe of our superhuman, calorie-cramming, pie-hole shoving abilities. I don't even know if it tasted good to be honest. The introduction of flavor-to-taste buds was so brief and frequent, it was like our taste buds attended a speed-dating event to find the perfect flavor, but by the end of the night, it couldn't remember a single seasoning. Filled up for the time being, we crashed in our room at the Doyle, hoping the night air would cool down a bit.

The next morning we woke up early, packed our things, and stepped out on the sidewalk. Metal tips of our trekking poles tinked the asphalt and concrete, syncing sporadically as our gaits differed. These were the solemn sounds of the sleepy Sunday Morning town. We tipped our hats to the

Doyle as we crossed the Susquehanna River. A few hours after Duncannon, Pennsylvania, is out of sight, hikers pass the Earl Shaffer Shelter on Peters Mountain. Earl is almost unanimously recognized as the very first thru-hiker of the Appalachian Trail when he walked its entire length in 1948. Shortly following Earl Shaffer's shelter is Peters Mountain Shelter, which is much more accommodating than the two-to-four maximum capacity of Earl's shelter. Ever since our little dehydration and cramping mishap in the Smoky Mountains, we had been taking on fluids like nobody's business. Yet with the quick getaway in Duncannon, we also failed to fill up our water supplies fully. Thus, when we made it to the shelter, 11 miles later, we were counting on some water. That's when we saw the discerning text in the guidebook. The water description starts out well: "Water source is in front of shelter." It goes downhill from there. Specifically, down 300 stone steps. Granted, it's a very well built side trail, but holy crap. Drop the pack and carry just your water bottles for this one, boys and girls. It's all good though, part of the gig. The closest shelter in our sights at the end of the day would be Rausch Gap Shelter; however, in anticipation that the shelter would be packed full of other thru-hikers by the time we rolled into camp, we posted up just shy of the shelter at Rausch Creek. The conclusion of another nearly 30-mile day is great prep work for some excellent sleep.

Unfortunately, the bumps on my legs, confirmed to be chiggers, were persistent in ruining the nightly dormance I had rightfully earned. Other aliases for a chigger include harvest mite, bed bug and Trombiculidae (in scientific circles). The chigger is a relentlessly annoying yet less fatal cousin to the tick. Red-headed step-children from the bowels of Satan is more like it. The area under distress ranged from knee to mid-thigh, thankfully leaving the family jewels out of it. From a hiking standpoint, the symptoms of a wickedly painful itch remained latent during walking hours. From a Goodnight Moon, Corduroy, nighty-night perspective, it was more like Where the Wild Things Are. After about a week of religiously applying the antihistamine creams per instructions of the urgent care Doctor in Waynesboro, Virginia, nights remained the only time when I had any symptoms other than a portion of my legs looking like a pimple- faced teenager. Of course, there's a million "treatments" and methods to get rid of chiggers. Top recommendations include laundering your clothes, and a hot shower or bath -- which I had ironically refused, for personal health and safety, at the Doyle.

Every night, I woke up in a terror of insane itchiness. Sleeping position seemed to have a lot do with the start of an itch. If my legs touched together in the chigger- populated regions, it would instantly cause a reaction. Avoiding an elementary catalyst as simple as not letting your legs touch would be a cinch if my legs, and the rest of my body, were not literally in a small, nylon, synthetic cocoon. It was all I could to do to not release a harrowing scream in the dead of night when an attack came on; it was almost worth doing just to see what Ben and other shelter dwellers would do. Instead, I took my torture with a side of silence each night and an un-scratchable itch burning below my skin. You see, what those little pricks do is insert their ugly, jackass feeding tube into your skin just to say "hello." As if coming over unannounced weren't enough, they proceed to inject you with cell-killing enzymes. Those enzymes then harden the damaged cells from the initial puncture, creating their very own straw straight to the good stuff. The only thing missing for these larvae's Happy Meal is a toy. Then they leave town as fast as they came after drinking all your beer and making a mess you have to deal with for days to come.

Despite the sleep interruptions, daytime activities continued as normal. The itching inconvenience was not going to deny me my thru-hike bid. The day prior, while we were at the Scaff's home, we got the chance to make some calls back home. Bandanna had organized yet another Trail Angel hook-up. We were feeling pretty spoiled at this point. My trail magic connections went no farther than Waynesboro, Virginia, when my folks came to see us at the beginning of Shenandoah National Park. As the mercury reached closer to 100 degrees, we crossed over PA 645 to find a '95 Dodge Sprint sitting in the lone shaded spot of a small gravel parking lot near the trail. "This is it!" Ben said as he approached the vehicle first. A jubilant older woman stepped out to greet us, Vera Coleman, at the youthful age of 79. Mrs. Coleman immediately gave you that grandma feel: short in stature, a full head of white hair and big round glasses. She was a wonderful, an unexpected dose of home. Ben's Mom's coworker's Mom was the connection. With 17 miles in the bag so far that day, we figured another hot lunch would serve us well and help us skip out on the hottest part of the day just after noon. It was not until after the all-you-can-eat buffet lunch at the Sholl Family Restaurant that we had even considered taking the rest of the day off. We felt about as useless as anyone does after a lunch buffet. Hiking or not, lunch buffets always make you feel the same way. Quick and easy going in, then you feel like a total slob afterwards. 'MURICA! Sweet Mrs. Coleman then proposed the idea that, if we wanted to do laundry and stay with her for the evening, she would be more than happy to have us. "Besides," she said, "I've already taken the day off from going to see my mother." "Your Mother?!" Ben and I thought. That's right, sweet Mrs. Coleman, 79 years old herself, took the day off from driving 30 miles each way to see her 95-year old mom, to take care of a 20- and 21-year-old instead. I nearly dared to ask which was more difficult. After all, it was Ben's 21st Birthday and I had been urging him to build up the courage and ask Mrs. Coleman if we could stop on the way to her house to grab some beers. The luck bucket was full enough, I suppose, as we were currently inhabiting a dry county, one of the world's remaining evils.

Bandanna quickly got his guidebook out and started crunching some numbers; it was turning into his thing. It was Tuesday, July 10 , and to stay on track we had to be in Delaware Water Gap, PA by Friday, July 13. It was just a cool 100.2 miles from Pine Grove, Pennsylvania. With a less-than-productive stay in Duncannon, as far as chores were concerned, we decided to enjoy the rest of our day and evening with Mrs. Coleman. I mentioned my chigger problem to Vera, and she tossed out the home remedy of putting finger nail polish remover over the bites. We stopped at the local drug store to pick some up along with some snacks for the evening. While our clothes churned in the washing machine, I sat in just my hiking shorts, applying nail polish remover to my body in Mrs. Coleman's Lay-z-boy. Ben took great humor in the home remedy of my parasitic misfortune. This home remedy removal was thought to "suffocate" the chiggers. Upon some post-hike research, I later discovered that chiggers were no longer on me at this point, the itch and bumps was just a side effect after the damage was done.

That evening, Mrs. Coleman provided excellent company. I'm sure taking care of a couple of young bucks in their roaring 20s was quite different than for her 90-year-old mother. Nevertheless, not a complaint to be had. I was a bit skeptical when she offered us milk to pour over our dessert bowl of strawberries, but after trying it, I don't think there's a better way to have them.

Bandanna Ben and Vera Coleman

Vera dropped Ben and me back off on the trail bright and squirrely the next morning. We had a little over a 100 miles to cover in 3 days and had to get back to it. Covering just over 23 miles by early afternoon, we found ourselves passing through Port Clinton, Pennsylvania, for a late lunch. According to some other hikers we met on the walk into town, hikers were allowed to camp in the town pavilion, which also had a privy nearby. Unfortunately, a few hikers decided to sneak into one of the local resident's hot tub for the evening and got caught, thus ruining a chance for a free place to stay for some. Ben and I were not planning on crashing anyway. The Port Clinton Hotel was our choice for lunch, and due to Bandanna's just having reached the current legal age for partaking of alcoholic beverages, a seat at the bar was an obvious choice.

Had it been my 21st birthday the day prior, I don't think I would have left the Port Clinton Hotel that evening. While we feasted over the menu options, I practically ordered Ben's first beer for him. I think I was more excited than he was. His Pops, Mike Burchardi, always drinks the original, Rocky Mountain-brewed, Banquet beer. Coors Original. Ben made no mistake in following suit with a big pour flowing over the rim of a frosty mug. It was just enough to make a young man's mouth water. Port Clinton Hotel also prides themselves on their large portions, a welcomed mission statement among hikers. Their variety of cheesesteaks made it hard to choose, but there was little opportunity to go wrong. When the suckers came out, it looked like an artillery shell. I was sure there would be fireworks to come after a monstrosity such as this. I was able to house mine, while Ben got the 2nd half of his to go.

I suffered the gut-bomb of a philly cheesesteak setting in my stomach for another 7 miles of hiking as we arrived at Windsor Furnace Shelter for the evening. We unpacked and set up for another night of shelter life. I drooled over Ben's 2nd half of sandwich like a dog stares at a T-bone; meanwhile I crammed another Clif bar and some prepackaged chicken down my throat. As he unpacked the sloppy, three-hour-old cheesesteak, the aroma alone would have brought any decent hiker to their knees. I think he let me have a bite just so I'd leave him alone.

Later the next day we found ourselves continuing to fumble through the boulder and rock fields of the stereotypical Pennsylvania terrain. Around the ascent to Bake Oven Knob, one of the finer viewpoints in Pennsylvania, we caught up with another thru-hiker named Unicycle Pirate. There was no desire to discover the nitty-gritty details about his trail name earnings. I optimistically thought he must have met up with Tyvek Holy Shit a while back. He appreciated the fast pace, but in our brief time with each other, commented of how I always hiked in front of Ben. "Do you always sit there and smell his butt sweat all day?" was the direct quote. "Never quite thought of it like that" Ben said nonchalantly. There was validity dwelling within Pirate's statement. It was not like fresh linen Febreeze was exhausting out of my muffler, but immunity to our funky fetor had long been achieved.

Undeterred by the dubious and craggy contours, we enjoyed exposed views for much of the day from cliff-walking and exposed outcroppings. We then descended Lehigh Gap to one of the lowest elevations on the entire trail, just 380 feet above sea level. There is significantly less glory in topping out a climb at 1500 feet rather than 5500 feet, but it's all relative. The truth was we had not been above 3000 feet since a brief period in Shenandoah National Park. Yes, we had become physically capable and confident in our hiking ability, what had to be done when we stopped, and how we refueled our bodies. Making miles became clockwork, extremely efficient and redundantly superfluous. Although an unbroken drive was required to get us to this point, there remained a parallel yearning for it to continue. A changing environment helped propel us through seemingly tedious and trite portions of trail. Where the trail lacked elevation, it gave us difficult trail conditions. When proximity to towns diminished, we faced uncertain water supply. Each step took us farther from home, while complete strangers continued opening their doors for us. The simple mathematic equation of Distance = Rate x Time is a representation just that: all too simple. Through our early struggle and triumph over the muscular cramping in the Smoky Mountains, no custody of doubt was ever held in believing we could not make it to the end.

We walked late into the evening. The lavender and periwinkle sky slowly retreated to gray. Our pace diminished like the end of a vinyl, harmonic melody of synchronized footsteps upon the gravel trail to a nearly unnoticeable stop in the music. There was a brief instance between the halt of footsteps and the purple hues of Earth's lid resigning that the infinity of time could be felt. Despite the spinning record of daylight ending, it was as if the music would reverberate forever, long after the needle had stopped. We camped among a small grove of pine trees under a set of power lines reveling in the twisted pleasure of fatigue and released endorphins at the end of a 38- mile day that made it the best place to stay yet. No need to push on to the next shelter; it was in reach only through nightlight and unwarranted exhaustion. It had no business being a beautiful section of trail, but it was.

Spencer McKay

The Mayor

Unionville, NY

High mileage continued in our effort to regain time reassigned to our stay with Grandma Coleman. Bandanna and I skipped our customary routine of discussing the upcoming town the night before our arrival. We were looking forward to the surprises it might bring. Since Pine Grove, Pennsylvania, we linked together three 30-mile-plus days to stay on track. The trail does not travel directly through Delaware Water Gap, Pennsylvania (DWG) but passes on the outskirts just a mile away. A small price to pay. This little town is good for a short-term resupply. Where the trail crosses PA 611/Main Street, most services are located on Broad Street. This is where one of the most irresistible aromas out of the more than 10,000 capable of identification ever came to tickle my cilia. Passing up on the Village Farmer & Bakery in Delaware Water Gap would have been an utter lapse in judgment and complete disregard for self. The quaint shop was slammed full of baked goods with every variety of pie under the sky. Signage in the shop announced the delicate pairing of a hot dog and slice of pie for the low-low price of $2.49. At such a price, any thru-hiker or "real worlder" alike would be foolish to deny such tantalizing temptation. Unless, of course, there was a baker's cart stacked slam full of golden brown, freshly baked pot pies releasing a scent and sight so grand that Colonel Sanders and the Doughboy would kneel in admiration.

Ben opted for the pumpkin pie as I devoured the chicken pot variety. It was then to the Pocono Inn to check in for the evening. The never-ending hallway lined with maroon carpet and beige walls felt more like an office building than a hotel. We were informed a recent renovation had just been completed after some flooding the year or so before. After passing room after room, left turns and right turns I was surprised we weren't back at the lobby. A "dirty hiker" reputation must have preceded us with quarantine to the far end of the building. Considering our scent and appearance, we would've had a hard time making a case otherwise.

We were awaiting the arrival of Chuck and Marybeth Harrington, who were making their way from the New York gridlock towards DWG. Children Tori, Kristen, Gavin, and Dylan joined as well. Chuck, who is Mr. Tim Harrington's 1st cousin once removed, and the gang took us out to a much nicer dinner than merited. Hopefully they weren't kidding when they said those four magic words – "Order whatever you want." I wouldn't advise saying that to a hungry hiker. So, as you could imagine, the black-on- white text describing the "Filet Mignon au Poivre" staring Ben and me down could not be ignored. Awaiting our peppercorn-crusted cow, Ben and I talked at great length of our journey thus far and explained what an honor it was to be hiking with Steve's ashes. Even this far into the trek, Steve remained our explicit motivation. The extended Harrington family was quite curious about the trail and how it is navigated. After dinner, we even took them to the edge of town where we got off the trail that afternoon to show them trail markings and give them a general sense as to what it was like.

People are amazed, even those who live within a few miles of the trail, at its existence. What is even more astonishing to me is how such a wonderful thing can go unnoticed. All too soon the evening of storytelling and fellowship with who were strangers just a couple of hours earlier came to a close. The Harringtons dropped us off at the Pocono Inn as we then mazed back to the Hiker Quarantine Area. For one of the first times, we did not rush out of town the next morning. The confidence of making it to yet another state border crossing, our 6th to be exact, had us feeling entitled. Entitled to one more visit to the Village Farmer & Bakery, of course. There I stood at the counter 9:30AM EST demanding a Chicken Pot Pie. Double fists slamming on the counter, chanting "CHICKEN POT PIE, CHICKEN POT PIE!" Okay, that's what I would have done, if the first batch of the day weren't just coming out of the oven. To my tastebud's delight, they would have one last rendezvous with their newest friend, subsequently followed by miles of daydreaming about their fluffy, creamy, tender, and buttery goodness.

It is a less than solitary walk across the border into New Jersey. Automotive traffic whizzes by as you cross the bridge of Interstate 80 over the Delaware River. I believe the trail now goes under the bridge in an effort to maintain hiker safety. Idiotically, Bandanna and I had assumed that the rock-infested, ankle-twisting terrain associated with the Pennsylvania portion of the trail would magically cease to exist, overcome by lush green pastures and pleasant gardens across Washington's Delaware River. Wrong. Fist-sized rocks littered the trail on the New Jersey side as well. My optimism had failed me again. Seven miles of trying to find a flat surface to place your foot upon, a chance finally presents itself as you come upon Sunfish Pond. It's one of the most magnificent places on the trail. Perhaps it's the lack of views over the past 300-400 miles that make this one so extraordinary. Maybe it was the memory of former Scout Master and lifetime mentor Gary Mazur mentioning this place on past outings from when he was a Scout himself. Whatever it was, it demanded our attention to reflect and enjoy the serenity.

Interrupting our peaceful moment before deciding to give Mr. Mazur a call, a startled couple out for the weekend approached Ben and me. Ben and I listened half-heartedly to their exclamation that they would not advise us to sit where we were because they had just seen a bear. The relatively open spot with a few other hikers around had us no reason to be alarmed. That didn't stop the city slickers from packing up their picnic blanket and sunscreen as fast as they could to get the hell out of Dodge. They were beside themselves and borderline offended when we nodded "Ok, thanks." Our previous experience with bear reports from the New Jersey stoner adolescents in the Smoky Mountains, sitting in the trail playing chess, hadn't given us a great impression of trail knowledge or wherewithal from those hanging their hats the Garden State.

From Sunfish Pond, the trail generally climbs with steep ascents and descents that our calves, quads, hammies and glutes had become accustomed to. With no scheduled trail magic for the day and the slow start out of town, we hoofed it about 25 miles to Brink Road Shelter. Trail Journals that night offered caution on an upcoming stop the next morning. At Culver Gap, US206 road crossing, stood a small restaurant "Joe To Go." The fare consisted of breakfast sandwiches, bagels, coffee and cold cuts for lunch. My expectations were low for receiving any southern hospitality during our stint in New Jersey as I subdued the stereotype of inferior hospitality. Posts consisted of everything from Joe denying hikers' access to fill up water bottles and even the denial of a little girl's urgent need for some good ol'-fashioned indoor plumbing. From what we could make of it, this guy was a real piece of work, to whom Ben and I planned on paying a visit the next morning, because he had bagels and we did not. Perhaps he remembered to take his medication, or at least took the right combination that day. We ate and filled up our water, no problem. One of the main complaints is that Joe sells "bottled water," but it's just milk jugs filled up from the spigot. Part of me wanted to bear witness to a flare-up of grumpy, crotchety 'ol Joe like the ones we had read so much about in the trail journal. It wasn't exactly all smiles, but maybe showering just 24 hours prior to our visit played in our favor.

Shuffling into the small town of Unionville, New York, that evening we were hoping to stumble upon a library or restaurant with internet access to post an update for everyone back home. In our wilderness wondering we often lost track in the days-of-the-week category. As luck would have it, on Sunday, the town was closed. In reconciliation of our current weekly position in the modern-day calendar, a note had been posted on the door of a local shop that gained our undivided attention. "HIKERS!" was a good start to any text. The note went on to apologize for the early shutdown, but the author of the memo left his phone number for rides and laundry that may be needed. So we called, and much to our surprise, it was the Mayor of Unionville, New York. Ok, the Mayor didn't answer; it was his sidekick Butch. Who sounded and then looked very much as you would imagine. Butch explained what was being offered up: come do laundry in the Mayor's house or just come in for a visit. It was made clear that no camping would be allowed on the official's premises. Just a short walk up the road from town center was the home. We were welcomed with smiles and open arms as Mayor Dick Ludwick showed us the lay of the land.

Mayor Dick Ludwig
1938 - 2015

Dick was a trail enthusiast to say the least and became a staple for a number of years for passing thru-hikers. In exchange for stories of our trials and tribulations on the trail, he told us stories of his time spent in Japan as a translator for the US Army. Dick was deeply interested in what drove people to hike and was fascinated by each story he heard. As we described the inspiration for our journey, he pushed up his sleeves and slid to the edge of his chair in his living room as we told him about the loss of our friend Steve. The Mayor's eyes teared up as if it were now his loss as well. We all shared a quick, frozen moment of mourning and empathy. Despite our short time with Mayor Ludwick, it was evident in his compassion that he must have experienced a similar situation on some level to have made such a connection. Without missing a beat, he quickly arose in a moment of revelation, and played what sounded like an Italian opera of Bocelli proportions. Caught up in the prior moment, I failed to retain the name of the song, but it was powerful.

As it was reiterated to Bandanna and me that we could not camp at the house, a Danish hiker named Alf, or Dain, or Nels, or some other single-syllable word that sounds like the substitute for a cuss word walked in the back door, having just completed pitching his tent. Dick begrudgingly admitted to the solitary exception to what seemed a hard-fast, no-camping rule. We traveled back down the hill from his house to inquire about a bunk that might be available at the local tavern, the Back Track Inn. A gray, stucco, exterior addition to the restaurant had a large rectangular sign with black lettering on white background reading "HOSTEL." Prior to inspecting the potential quarters for the evening, we entered for a burger and fries. Striking up a conversation with the waitress at the bar, our appearance once again blew our cover. She perked up at the confirmation of our current life status of thru-hiker. Proudly boasting of their new repurposed hostel on the side of the building, she offered up a free night's stay in exchange for good reviews on the trail. Unionville was certainly showing an affinity towards the hiker community.

Ben walked in to the bunk house right next door as I soaked in the view from the front porch overlooking the gravel parking lot. "Majesty!" I trumpeted and turned to follow Ben into the bunk house, but quickly stopped in my tracks. The "Hostel" was an old storage room of some kind, and the bunks, well, some canned food probably rested nicely on the shelves for a number of years. Standing room only as Ben and I unpacked our gear and attempted to settle in for the night. I felt like Gandalf in Bilbo's home hunkered down in our quaint shire for the evening. All we needed now was Thorin Oakenshield and his dwarfs to come filing in singing "Misty Mountains Cold" by candlelight while smoking their pipes. After tossing and turning for what felt like hours, I finally found a quasi-sleep worthy position. At least there was a fifty-fifty chance of the supports of the shelves, I mean bunks, keeping me from a midnight plunge to the concrete floor. The abrupt advance of Sunday-Funday voices leaving the bar approached the parking lot directly across the street from our Shire. Due to lack of funding, I presume, the only door on the place was a screen door. As the Chevys and Fords cranked up, our little home for the night turned center stage as headlights shined directly on us, totally ruining the moment.

We managed to guilt trip the Mayor into breakfast and a short ride back to the trail the next morning. The impromptu stay in Unionville was overall a nice one and not lacking on the entertainment front. In town, a former co-worker of Ben's dad reached out to us; she happened to live nearby. Ben was reeling in the magic like it was his job. The trail dances along the New Jersey/New York border similar to the North Carolina/ Tennessee section. About 10 miles north of Unionville, the trail crosses a magnificent suspension bridge followed by a 1-mile boardwalk over wetlands connecting the Pochuck and Wawayanda Mountains. The section required 24 years of planning, 7 years of construction, over $800,000 dollars to complete, and hands-down one of the most enjoyable 1-mile stretches of the AT scenically and strenuously as well. It offers an excellent respite between the PUDs and ankle-breaking rocks.

Six short miles after crossing our 7th state border, we popped out on to New York State Highway 17A. Less fortunate thru-hikers have just a westward .2 mile road walk to the Bellvale Creamery. Dianne Tarantino (no relation to Quentin) chauffeured us the required distance. We aren't above a .2 mile side trail, but when you ain't gotta, you ain't gonna. The original itinerary Ben and I resolutely crafted 2 ½ months ago had us staying at William Brien Shelter through this section. That had obviously shifted a bit due to earlier issues of Garrett's misfortune and our leg-cramping conundrum in the Smoky Mountains; we had fallen 10 days off our 84-

day complete thru-hike itinerary. In need of retribution from the previous night's shelfing, we would never be so rude as to refuse a proper bed by Ms. Dianne. What kind of gentlemen would we be to deny such hospitality? We entertained each other for the evening watching TV and ordering in pizza.

Another hard night on the Appalachian Trail behind us, we were looking forward to seeing what New York had to offer other than Thanksgiving Day Parades and New Year's Eves. Elevation through the state on the trail oscillates between 100' – 1,300' above sea-level. In addition, because you're not exactly in the middle of nowhere, to look at a topographic map would be disheartening to say the least. The trail snakes back and forth over and around as if a two-year-old took a crayon, placed it on the map, and didn't pick it up whilst running their hand up and down the paper. There's something extremely disconcerting when you realize you're hiking south when the clear objective is going from Georgia to Maine. In reality though, miles are miles, and we didn't give a damn which direction we were going, as long as it counted toward the final tally.

One of the more popular land features awaited us that afternoon, the "Lemon Squeezer," which, in essence, is true to its name. In this scenario, I had 56 days to lose enough weight to get my fat ass through the damn thing. If I wanted to get through now, I'd had better get a running start. Some Einstein thought it was a good idea to run the path of America's oldest National Scenic Trail directly through an 18- inch-wide crack between two massive rocks. Fortunately, thousands of people make it through each year, only mildly scathed, of course, by a mere flesh wound or two. In inclement weather, I could see it being a true obstacle.

Freshly squeezed, we made our way towards Bear Mountain State Park. For those lucky (or unlucky) enough to have avoided the Black Bear species on the AT thus far, the wait is over. An opportunity to face your fears is available at the Bear Mountain State Park Zoo, which, during park hours, the Trail goes right through. Upon ascending the treacherous, newly paved greenway to the top of Bear Mountain, hikers can see a marvelous view of the Hudson River and the New York Skyline. Ben and I, however, preferred the view to the west, which consisted of a sunset. Through another less-than- lengthy conversation, Ben and I decided cowboy camping on top of Bear Mountain, on the paved path, was the most brilliant of ideas. This act, of course, is frowned upon. But we were Leave No Trace capable; besides, man had left his trace in a fairly permanent fashion by paving the top of a mountain. We selfishly assumed the clouds rolling in that evening, giving our sunset dinner such depth, was for our sole enjoyment.

Meanwhile, tiny little frozen raindrops were beginning to rub together way up in those Karma Clouds. Just so happened, enough of those frigid 2 parts hydrogen 1 part oxygen droplets bounced off each other in that cloud that by around the time Oh-five-hundred came around, WHABLAAAAM! From the Poseidon of Zeus himself a lightning bolt struck down scaring whatever lemon I still had in me straight out. The ensuing bottom then fell out as we went from all our shit everywhere to all our shit stuffed quickly into our packs and ran for a nearby structure. Accompanying us under the refuge was a soda machine. We dug through our packs to find some lose change. All we had were a couple of golden US Dollars, when that was still a thing. Sacagawea sack-a-ja-screwed me as the little glimmer of hope I had in that golden dollar delivering me the sweet nectar of high fructose corn syrup, caramel color and other natural flavors faded abruptly as it clanked down in the coin return immediately following insertion.

Slowly but surely, as the rain continued, we donned our rain jackets, sorted out our packs the best we could, and started our walk for the day. I suppose that's what we got for our fortunate and recent run of trail magic. Much to our disappointment, but not to our surprise, the zoo was not yet open at 5:30AM. "Hey Bear, Hey Bear!" as we rerouted around the rest of the park to meet back up with the trail on the Bear Mountain bridge. With a heavy mist throughout the day, sightseeing was off the agenda. With such an early start, we were able to crank out 36.8 miles, our biggest day in a week, but our third longest day thus far.

Ididlyrod

Dalton, MA

Grin and bearing it another night in the woods, the following day we had the trail town of Kent, Connecticut, within striking distance and yes, yet another visit with some Trail Angels. The plan was to meet Christine and Ron Harrington, aunt and uncle of Stephen. Slowed in the early part of the day with continuing rain showers, it became evident we would not make it to the local outfitter in time to get the food drop that was mailed from Raleigh. Luckily, we got a cell phone signal, and the Harringtons were able to pick up our drop before they met us roadside so that we could avoid the .8 mile road walk into Kent proper. In our hunt for crossing our 8th border, we were also honing in on the trail's largest tree, the Dover Oak, estimated to be a sprightly 300-years-old and offering a girth of about 20'around. In accidental disrespect to the Dover Oak, we posed for pictures with what we thought was the largest tree on the Appalachian Trail, before we kept hiking and realized that although the first tree was a big'n, it won't no Dover Oak. Closest contender to the Dover in this heavyweight bout is the Keffer Oak, located just north of Pearisburg, Virginia, roughly 800 miles away.

Speaking of 800: from Kent, we had fewer than that many miles to Mt. Katahdin and the completion of our journey. Two-thirds of the way traversed across the Appalachian Trail. Ben and I stuck around town after Christine and Ron put us up in a quaint B&B known as the Fife & Drum. An unexpected luxury most thru-hikers probably do not splurge for, as the Inn was a little pricey along with most of the town. Although our intentions were to always get up and get going, and make miles, make miles, make miles, not many of the town's resources were available to us due to our late arrival. We treated ourselves to a proper breakfast, picked up some supplemental provisions from the grocer and ducked into the library to post pictures on our blog. As Ben crunched some data along with his bacon that morning, he shared with me the fact that since Harpers Ferry, West Virginia, we had averaged nearly 30 miles a day.

Have you ever noticed the narrow lane of vision while gazing across a landscape in a moving vehicle? Everything outside your focused lens is zipping past in a blur. Yet with eyes transfixed upon the horizon everything is slowed to a near halt. In perspective drawings, this is referred to as the vanishing point. It is the point that all lines lead back to or relate to in some form or fashion. It is this point, in conjunction with the horizon, that creates the true impetus of depth. Fair to say, I did worry about the speed of our trip. It was not ideal. It was not conducive to leisure. Many parts, a lot of parts, were painful. Entire days were miniscule in comparison to the scale of our objective. Each mile on average takes approximately 2,000 steps and the trail is 2,175 miles; the absolute minimum number of steps required is 4,350,000 (assuming you're an averaged-sized human being). Roughly, each single step is just 2 ten-millionths of a percent closer to the goal. To Kent, Connecticut, we had traveled 1,451 miles in 60 days or 1,220 hours. At a deafening speed of just over 1 mile an hour (including dormant hours of course), the ten-millionths were adding up.

The prior day's rain reminded us just how fortunate we had been. In fact, in our first day out of 60 days on our trip, it was the first day to actually rain all or most of the hours while we were hiking. I'm sure that pisses off a bunch of hikers out there. We were on the receiving end of a few summer afternoon thunderstorm deluges; other than that, extremely fortunate. In the old trail adage, "No Rain, No Pain, No Maine," we certainly had pain yet an uncalming deprivation in the rain department.

With 56 miles of trail in Connecticut, there's an added boost of morale when crossing yet another state-line, a true marker of progress. We were enjoying the scenery of New England. Connecticut has a Bear Mountain of its own. Early settlers along what is now the AT must have had limited imagination as many distinct geological features retain the same name. As we stopped for a break atop this Bear Mountain, a group of middle-aged men had just mounted the soaring 2,316 foot summit. I say that in jest, but let's give them the benefit of the doubt and say that they started that day at the road crossing that leads into Salisbury, Connecticut. If this were the case, it would have been a 6-mile climb of 1,596 feet to the top. Just cause for their huffing and puffing, but not enough restraint to hinder summit shouts as each one filed up to the rocky rest area on top. Nor did it prevent them from deciding upon a victory puff of the more herbal variety of tobacco, which may further explain their huff. We politely refused as we ended our break atop our highest point in quite some time.

Descending down a short hill we were closing in on The Hemlocks Lean-To (or Shelter) for the night. Laughter of the bellowing, bawling, and hollering type, all resonated with each humorous sound. Ben and I curiously approached the shelter in hope that our current streak of silence would be meeting its end.

As we approached, a couple of thru-hikers sitting at the picnic table greeted us from 20' away. "How y'all doin'?" "Good 'n you?" They were on the topic of a hiker who had made a name for himself as a beggar, thief and seemingly disingenuous stigma. Ben and I walked in on what we imagined to be quite a lengthy conversation. Any thru-hiker who takes on ruining the reputation of all the good hikers out there is nothing more than a nuisance. They paused their conversation to introduce themselves from the picnic table outside the shelter in a counterclockwise fashion. They rattled off their trail names. Alright was at the picnic table, on the edge of the shelter sitting on the wood floor was Wolf Taffy, across the shelter on the top left bunk was Lion and on the table beside Alright was Chop Stix, each of them friendly and within the same demographic as Ben and me. Alright's name right off the bat sparked some interest, almost jealousy. Why didn't I think of that? The others were oddly enough unique yet ubiquitously so. Alright had a vibe about him that was refreshingly optimistic. It's that nonchalant response to what could be a more revealing question, alright. How's your hike? Alright. Feeling any better today? Alright. Want to go walk 2,175 miles? Alright. Alright had planned to start out in Georgia with two of his friends. They were all going to name themselves "Alright", thus being "Alright, Alright, Alright". David Wooderson, eat your heart out. They even planned on sending McConaughey postcards along the way. Long story short, the other two dropped out, so it was just one "Alright".

Alright seemed genuinely alright. Like "that guy's alright." I suppose asking about his trail name triggered the stories we were about to hear, especially when Chopstix, Lion, and Wolf Taffy all collectively chimed in, "Tell em about JD!" It was in March when Alright was hiking through a chilly Georgia. He arrived at his shelter for the night with no other hikers around. This came as somewhat of a surprise to Alright, as he had seen many hikers that day. One of them, whom he had introduced himself, was JD. Normally, as most thru-hikers tend to discover, an empty shelter isn't necessarily a bad thing but a relieving solidarity. However, with the cold temperatures, he had been experiencing, a packed shelter with ample body heat would be far from disagreeable. Dinner and camp chores were wrapping up as the cold spring-sun was still setting low in the sky. As the night's chill was creeping in, a hootin' and hollerin' that I imagined to be similar to that of our buddies George and Phil came clamoring through the leafless trees. These cries were the chants of just one man though. One hiker, of large proportions, carrying nothing more than an over-packed daypack and dawning a pair of cut-off jeans and a white t-shirt emerged. The burly hiker approached the picnic table squinting through the spring dusk mountain air as he called out, "Is that you Alright?" (the two had met a couple days prior).

Humorously, as Ben and I listened to Alright tell the story, his voice changed to depict JD. It became very low as he revealed the other hiker's identity. It was a monster of a man nearly 6'7" pushing 300 pounds: JD. Of course the other hikers listening to Alright tell us the story chimed in saying the same thing "Is that you Alright?" in low, deep voices. Alright continued with his response in an oddly high pitched school boy voice characterizing himself, "yea, it's me, JD." JD plops down at the table, out of breath, "Hey man…we made it!" After a few minutes, JD began unpacking his ultralight, borderline ultra-dumb set-up. He crushed a few candy bars as he threw a tarp inside the shelter. Then it dawned on him that the evening's temperature could drop below hospitality settings and his standard issue blue plastic tarp can feature a drafty condition. While JD was hurriedly throwing handful upon handful of leaves onto his tarp, Alright asked what he was doing during the observance of a quite obvious lack of planning. Before JD even had time to answer, he had swan-dived himself onto his tarp and performed a burrito-style maneuver holding the far left end of the tarp rolling left to right. Leaves acting as insulation, JD was preparing himself for another cold night on the trail.

Alright, as you can imagine, was blown away by JD's actions. In an effort of humanity and humility, Alright offered him a spare long sleeve shirt. Keep in mind, of course, that Alright's toothpick frame was about 1/5 the size of JD's towering build. It was one of those offers that you don't really expect someone to take you up on. Nevertheless, JD responds "Hey…thanks man!" as he took the size medium shirt and turned it into a double-x. Alright must have assumed the desperation level of JD was pretty high at this point. Alright then started "Hey JD, if it gets really cold tonight, and you are really having a problem…we can share my sleeping bag." It was then that the rustling of the skin tight shirt, in his leaf and tarp burrito wrap sleeping system halted. He turned to Alright, "Ha-wha?, whoa man…I don't think it's gonna get that cold!" One can only imagine what JD must of thought when he heard that, much less what in the hell Alright was thinking to share a bag with a complete stranger.

That was the benchmark story we heard about JD. For all we know, this guy could be the next pioneer of ultralight. Step aside Ray Jardine and Andrew Skurka, there's a new kid in town. The leaf-tarp burrito sleeping system was just the first of groundbreaking inventions reported in these trail stories. You know how they call it a backpack because you wear it on your back? Well what about the front? The backpack makes things so uneven, balance is thrown all out of whack, and so much space is wasted. That's why trail reports from other hikers on the trail described JD's ingenuity once again. Your backpack, you see, carries the things you don't need while you are actualy hiking. But the front pack, ohhh, the front pack is for all the nondouble-jointed folks out there, the majority. Have you ever tried to get a snack, or your map (surely JD didn't have a map), or a sip of water, better yet a beer from your backpack while walking? You can forget it. That is, until you get another pack, and wear it "frontwards". Everything is right there. Alright, Chopstix, Lion and Wolf Taffy began describing that JD perhaps was making a name for himself on the trail. Taking advantage of trail magic, drinking entire cases of beer, and presumably taking money from donation boxes in hostels, JD soon had to start going by a number of different aliases including Iditarod and Ididdlyrod, as legend has it.

Judging by the ballpark age, these young men appeared to be of similar physical capabilities. Despite their early, slow start, it sounded like they were making decent mileage at this point. We had already passed the "bubble" of the majority of hikers, so anyone traveling faster than that was moving pretty good. Ben asked them if they knew who Mowgli was, as we were still tracking his entries in the trail journals. In the past couple weeks, we had made up some serious ground on our more or less one-way pen pal. We had been following his bread crumbs for a looooong time. "Who's Mowgli?" "Oh yeah, we've hiked with him for a bit." "He mentioned heading in to Boston from Dalton, Massachusetts, to see his girlfriend." Interesting, we thought to ourselves. We were two days away from Dalton. Then the thought struck us, that what if he gets to Dalton, heads in to Boston, and we zip right on through, and never even meet the guy?

The following night, we stayed at Upper Goose Pond Cabin. From Memorial Day to Labor Day, a volunteer caretaker oversees the large, two-story barn-like structure with large 2nd-level deck facing the pond. It's a most serene location and offers bunks, swimming, campsites, and water canoed in by the caretaker from a stream across the pond. An extensive effort in the saddle prompted another late arrival into camp for the evening. There was not ample time to visit with the other hikers and the caretaker, but we were enjoying the gradual drop in temperature during evening hours and expressed our gratitude for the fresh spring water.

Roaming land of inadequate cell phone coverage seemed to be a thing of the past as nearly every time we turned our devices on we had signal. To be on the safe side, we put a call in to the Shamrock Village Inn to secure a room for the night. With a final push into town, we checked in at the 'rock. During the process, I noticed a trail log for hikers at the concierge desk. Most recent check-out: Mowgli. We were hot on his trail after his return from Beantown. Unfortunately, Mowgli had never mentioned any kind of blog or website he was keeping to verify his whereabouts. We were tracking a ghost. Ben and I managed to snag a couple footlong subs from the local deli in time for a late lunch. Once again, the motivation of time off our feet and in a town drove us to knock out the 20.6 miles to Dalton in about 7 hours in the persistently dreary mist of New England.

That evening we had our first hankering for ice cream since the gluttonous, over-indulgent experience that was the half-gallon challenge. Three years prior to Ronald Reagan posting on Gorbachev's wall, he was signing important legislature to stamp July as National Ice Cream Month. From Breyer's to Dreyer's, we had now catapulted ourselves into Ben & Jerry's country. Every store with an anti-melting device sells the stuff, and we weren't mad about it. I went for a pint of Dave Matthews Band Magic Brownies Encore Edition, "Black Raspberry Ice Cream Swirled with Sweet Cream Ice Cream & Fudgy Brownies." I tried to savor it, but it was 86'ed before I knew it. DMB's Magic Brownies are now sadly in the Ben & Jerry's Flavor Graveyard, ranking 9th out of the Top 10 fallen soldiers.

To get from Dalton, Massachusetts, to Mt Katahdin, all we had to do was average 24.5 miles per day for the next 25 days. After 64 days on the trail, on 29 occasions we had averaged less than our remaining target average to complete the trail by August 17th. On almost half of our days on trail, we had not met what we needed to achieve every day for the next 25 days. Not to mention the final portion of a Northbound thru-hike is also the most difficult terrain on the entire trail. Not to mention we had not been above 3,000' in 610 miles. Not to mention our most remote sections of the trail remained. Our work was cut out for us.

Seventeen miles north of Dalton Mass. We ascended back to relatively higher elevation in the approach and summit of Mt. Greylock, Massachusetts' highest peak. Just before bagging the summit is an engraved rock with the quote of one of Massachusetts' most famous sons, Henry David Thoreau. Almost to the day, 162 years before, Thoreau set out to live in the woods in a self-built hut about 119 miles due east from where we stood reading his quote: "It were as well to be educated in the shadow of a mountain as in more classical shade. Some will remember, no doubt, not only that they went to college, but that they went to the mountain." The statement required little pondering. I fully recognize the good fortune of the life I was born in to. White, Male, American; many adversities lay at bay whilst knocking on others' doors.

As I was currently attending college, I found this quote quite powerful. I knew my education was important, but there are some aspects of life that a University provides a shortfall of nurturing and exposure to. In many ways, only life itself can administer such exposure. Yes, there's a chance that virtues such as self-awareness, integrity, and patience can all be experienced in a classroom or the post-grade school process. You can read and study them behind stacks of books; you can even feel them in some works such as Thoreau's. Tangibility of these virtues and many more is created by the mountains. Demand of patience was perceived early on in our trek as well as pain and fatigue. An all-encompassing fatigue where you are not just tired and heavy-eyed, but physically exhausted and mentally weary from having to convince your body day in and day out that you can do this, and that you are capable.

We camped that night at Sherman Brook, which has tent platforms available. Once again, we passed on the tenting process and slept under the stars as we had become well accustomed to. Just 2.5 miles into our day we crossed yet another state line, Massachusetts-Vermont. Vermont, the Green Mountain State. We were excited about the evergreens and the beautiful things to come. Shortly after snapping a few pictures at the State line, we ran across a park ranger. Said park ranger then informed us that Vermont had just received record rainfall totals throughout July and that all the hikers she had seen were calling it "Mudmont." We had become seasoned enough at this point to take trail news with a grain of salt. When you've hiked over 1,500 miles you tend to…I don't want to say disregard what other people have to say, but you disregard what other people have to say. A couple of miles in as we began crossing our first bog, it became clear that the trail had received a copious amount of rain.

Bogs, by definition, are "wet muddy ground too soft to support a heavy body." Well, my friends, I couldn't have said it better myself. Typically, what you will see throughout the trail in Vermont is a man-made raised trail for many short sections. A 4x4 post or repurposed log on its side with two 2x6 or 2x8 boards laid side by side on top of the posts from anywhere to just a few feet, to hundreds of feet in length. With increased rainfall, these "bog-walks" if you will, can easily become covered with just a few inches of standing water. Just another reason to carry trekking poles as they become your extended toes reaching out for the trail to identify the proper path. One wrong step to the left or the right, and you can easily sink down in mud above your knee. Fun stuff.

Bogging through Vermont, skipping plenty of opportunities to hitch-hike into town, due to our approaching deadline, we were pushing ourselves harder than ever. We took a short respite at Stratton Pond where we enjoyed the view and the summer breeze at its shores. Ben and I soon found ourselves deliberating whether or not to venture down in to Manchester Center, Vermont, for pizza, Ben & Jerry's, shower and bed. Yet just before the road crossing of VT11, there was a cooler of fresh fruit and Heineken. We crammed a few apples, oranges and beers into our pack and bypassed the tempting town stop. Summiting the wide grassy lanes up to Bromley

Mountain, I couldn't help but think how much this looked like a ski slope. As we crested the peak backlit by a purple, magenta, and tangerine sky, a ski lift surrounded by a large deck was in sight. A most opportune place take on our fresh fruit and hop water. Dusk quickly turned to dark as we began packing our things with that "we're good" mixed with "shit, it got really late" thought in our head. The next shelter was 8 miles away, and we had just zipped past Bromley Mountain Shelter on our way up. For the first time in over 1,600 miles, Ben and I were going to be hiking at night.

Night hiking can offer many different advantages with about tenfold more disadvantages. If it's a clear night, hiking by the stars and the moon can be fun with a romantic vibe. Not exactly what Bandanna and I had in mind. In the densely vegetated forests of the eastern United States, the light seldom finds its way through during the summer. Night hiking posed as more of a chore than a delight. We were used to moving fast, and during the day, finding the next place to plant your foot at 3 mph is not that difficult. When there are roughly 2,000 steps in a mile, moving at 3 mph, that's 6,000 steps or 100 steps a minute to figure out where you will be planting your next stride. At night, over certain terrain, the kind of terrain we were traversing, that feat was nearly impossible. We quickly became frustrated with our lack of pace. It took us nearly 2 hours to reach Mad Tom Notch, the first campsite with water.

On the bright side, we were able to quasi set up our tent for first – that's right – the first time on the entire trip. Well, that's not completely true, on night #2 of the trip waaaaaaay back in Georgia, Garrett, Ben, and I set up the 3-person tent we had been carrying. Since Garrett's departure, he was kind enough to let Ben and me borrow his MSR Twin Peaks tarp tent. A wonderful gesture indeed that would have been more exciting had we set it up before. Two trekking poles in the middle for the supports and stake down the sides, how hard could it be? After 31 miles working on a 15-hour day in the saddle, it made these two Eagle Scouts feel like Tenderfoots.

After the tent debacle, we still had to retrieve some water for the evening and the next morning. To our surprise, there was an old-school iron hand-pump well. We filled up our containers and fell asleep before our heads even hit the pillows. And by "pillow," I mean balled-up rain jacket placed on our shoes.

Mowgli

West Hartford, VT

In the morning, we shook off the cobwebs and did a few jumping jacks to get warm as the chill of an early Northeastern Fall was rearing its head. A pleasant day followed with tons of ponds and bogs to walk across. The evergreen country of Vermont is absolutely wonderful, a perpetual Christmas scene, even during the summer. With many of the lows experienced on the trail, one of two things can happen. It is either followed by another lower low, or a high. The trail gods must have ruled in our favor that day. We found ourselves standing at yet another road crossing. This time, Vermont State Highway 103. Just half a mile to the west stood the "Whistle Stop" Restaurant. There was no deep thought to make this decision. We were on our way after only a slight pause to check the guidebook.

As we had become accustomed to when entering a respectable place of business, we left our packs outside. The stench factor was off the charts these days. No more trail magic or random people meeting us. We were just flying by the seat of our pants from here on out. And what a sweet little nugget of a find this place was. The Whistle Stop had an array of appealing menu items. Soups and sandwiches with some Blue Plate specials. One item in particular sucked me in. It was called "The Gobbler." A turkey sandwich with no less than cranberry sauce, Swiss cheese, mashed potatoes, and gravy. Yes, all of that, on the sandwich. The turkey; moist, juicy, perfect. Cranberry, the perfect acidic balance to the rich melted Swiss. The mashed potatoes with gravy were just right for that creamy smooth finish after I crunched through the toasted marble rye.

A couple of hikers were finishing up an extended lunch stop when we walked up, talking somewhat nasty about the place, suggesting that the owners were not exactly hiker-friendly. Perhaps it was our boyish good looks, or just basic good manners, the staff was friendly and courteous. Once we completed our sandwich, we both ordered another, for good measure, and devoured every bite. "Don't act like you're not impressed," I thought as the sweet waitress came to get the clean plates, the second time. In continuing our conversation with the wait staff, we asked if there was camping around the back side of the building. The waitress leaned in real close and lowered her voice: "if you don't tell anyone, we'll let you sleep on the porch outside." You might as well have given us a key to the Biltmore.

Like Ratatouille in the kitchen, we had everything strewn out in seconds as soon as the staff locked up after the dinner "rush." The old caboose converted to restaurant with covered outdoor seating area was our Taj Mahal for the evening. For a second, we felt sorry for the guys who talked bad about this place, but only for a second. Still full from our double Thanksgiving lunch, a Snickers bar or two for dessert, and we were off to sleep.

A good night's rest led to another enjoyable day. The second highest mountain in Vermont soon lay under our feet, Killington. The "beast of the east" was no match for Ben and me. In a lack of judgment, mostly due to our Turkey Hangover, we opted out for the Killington Peak side trail. The side trail is not part of the AT, and is a .2 mile steep gut-buster from what I've heard. On top sits a snack bar and a gondola that could've taken us down into the Ski Village. Descending from (nearly) the top of Killington, hundreds of man-made rock stacks had been constructed. Mist and fog filled the air. Due to their sheer number, the rock towers proved more obstacle than sculpture. Evidence of people yet their absence was mysterious. With exponentially more people jumping on trail each year, not only on the Appalachian Trail, but all wilderness areas, we must remember the fundamental rules of Leave No Trace. Marking the trail with a cairn is one thing, but hundreds of rock towers....C'mon.

I understand that it's our nature to want to leave our mark, and no, I'm not aware of a #rockshortage. People and cultures have been staking their claim and posting their presence since the beginning of time. Do I believe creating these little sculptures is going to cause massive erosion issues on the mountain? No. Is it an unnecessary manifestation of the ego of humanity? Yes. Creating the 245th rock stack though, not necessary, excessive. In reality, you're not the next Andy Goldsworthy, and if you're trying to be, take a picture of your work, and think of it as a more temporary art installation, just as we are temporary installations on earth.

Shortly after shuffling down Killington, Ben and I took a break at US 4 Highway, which led to Rutland, Vermont. There was little interest in or need to go into town again, but as we scanned the miles ahead in the guidebook, trying to figure out our shelter for the evening, we came across Mountain Meadows Lodge listed in the guidebook as located "on A.T." Perfect. I mean, we were going right by it. Lo and behold, we whipped out the cell phone and had signal: it was meant to be. After a couple of rings, the owner, Bill, answered. We politely explained our situation and before I could even get it all out, "Thru-hikers? Really? Wow, there's just one problem." Soaring highs and low lows, I tell ya. "There's a wedding here this weekend, and the entire lodge is rented." "Oh man, ok, thanks anyway," I said. Just as I was about to hang up, Bill told me to hang on a second, "I'll go ask the bride and groom if they mind having you all here." Talk about some relocated Southern Hospitality! Much to our surprise, Bill came back on the phone after a few minutes and said, "Yes, come on, we'll see you soon!"

Dumbfounded by our luck once again, we arrived at Mountain Meadows Lodge in the early afternoon, narrowly avoiding a photo-bomb with the bride and groom on our way in. Bill met us at the front desk and got us settled in and showed us around. Bandanna and I graciously offered our most sincere appreciation time and time again. As if no worries, we were shown where all the amenities were, the computer with internet, laundry, and our room. Upon settling in our room, we ventured downstairs to throw up a blog post and some pictures. As we sat in the back of the room where the computer was, the rehearsal dinner was finishing up. In the same room. Family from the wedding came over and made sure to let us know we were welcome to any of the food in the buffet line. We accepted the offer and tried not to jump up immediately following their generous gesture.

Another unexpected stop, yet still a 21-mile-day in the books. Everything was routine at this point. With just 483 miles left to Big K (Mt. Katahdin). Despite our impromptu visit to Mountain Meadows Lodge, I had 3 weeks and 1 day before my butt was back in architecture studio seeing who could draw straightest line. Our current path consisted of 22 days, 456.8 miles, the most difficult terrain, and most unpredictable weather anywhere on the entire trail. The 20 miles a day we needed to average didn't scare us. The numbers were Bandanna-tested and Warpzilla- approved day after day. It was the violent Nor'easters, rock-and-root infested trail, elevations ranging from 400 to 6,288 feet. Our winning streak of good health lay in the balance. Our trail credentials and reputation was about to be tested like never before. Like the Tide every Saturday, a target was on our back, better yet, the soles of our feet, and the trail was about to bring it.

Waking up in a bed and packing up all our things in a hotel room and stepping right out onto the trail was the way to go. No worrying about hitchhiking back to the trail or lining up a shuttle. We were already there. The primo location allowed for an early start and the opportunity to crush the last little bit of Vermont. Geographically, about halfway up the state of Vermont, the trail takes a hard right, New Hampshire dead ahead. There was a decent amount of road walking through some quaint Vermont towns as we approached the Vermont and New Hampshire border, none more picturesque than the outskirts of West Hartford. We passed through fairly early in the morning, on a Monday. The town was only about 5 miles into our day.

As we passed houses and folks heading out on their workday commutes, one older man was working in his yard near the road. He initiated a conversation as we went through the typical 20 questions game you play when meeting a non-hiker on the trail. He knew enough to appreciate the pace we were holding. He followed that up with some very important information. Though we were moving fast, he began to tell us about a hiker he let camp on his front porch last night. "His name was Chris," he said, and asked if we knew him. Ben asked if he had a trail name, with the follow-up of "Was his trail name Mowgli?" The gentleman believed that's what it was. The hiker we had been tracking since Day One. Ben and I had read countless journal entries from this guy, and he was literally less than an hour away.

We politely and promptly ended our conversation after hastily laying out what was at stake here. The stranger hollered farewells as we clinched our trekking poles like Jimmy Johnson would his steering wheel and the pedal was to the metal. A mile-and-a-half up the trail, at the small water crossing of Podunk Brook, we stumbled upon a little bit of trail magic. Someone had tied up a bag of sodas and left them submerged in the ice cold brook. A unique way to keep your high-fructose corn syrup cool. Digging into the bag of liquid snacks, with his back to us, stood a young, tall, brawny man with jet-black hair bursting out from the edges of a red bandana. In true stalker fashion, as we rushed closer to him, we stopped right behind him and enunciated in unison, "Hello, Mowgli." Thinking back on it, "Hello, Mowgli" while standing creepily behind him? Really? That's the best we could do? It was like finally getting the courage to walk up and talk to a girl in middle school, she smiles and asks "What's Up?!" and all you can blurt out is "good." Hind sight 20/20 – we should have messed with him so much more.

Backtracking a bit to explain ourselves, I guess Mowgli accepted our awkwardness and the 3 of us hiked on from that point discussing the trials and tribulations of the trip thus far. Trading stories and seeing if we had met any of the same crazy people. Alright, Chop Stix, Tyvek Holy Shit, JD, and others. Before we knew it, it was lunch time, and we were making our second-to-last border crossing: from the Green Mountain State to The Granite State. It just so happens that the trail crosses the border on a bridge over the Connecticut River. Props to the trail creators and maintainers because just on the other side of the bridge lies Hanover, New Hampshire, a small college town and home of the Ivy League institution of Dartmouth. The Dartmouth Outing Club (DOC) offers tons of information for hikers passing through. Hopefully, no bad apples (even though there's one in every bunch) have ruined the generosity of the town and University since we passed through.

Travelling from Norwich, Vermont, over the river to Hanover, New Hampshire, the trail goes straight through town, a scenario typically seen in the southern portion of the trail, and a far less frequent happenstance north of the Mason-Dixon Line. All the college food categories are accounted for as you cross town: Pizza, bagels, sandwich shops, international cuisine, bars, and other college services. Number One on our list: Ben and Jerry's Phish Food: "Chocolate Ice Cream with Gooey Marshmallow Swirls, Caramel Swirls & Fudge Fish." Damn you, Ben Cohen and Jerry Greenfield, for making such unavoidable delicious treats when I still have 14 miles to hike. No matter what you snack on, the trail goes where it goes. Unfortunately for my lactose- coated stomach, the climb out of town goes from 490' just outside of town to 1,200' at Ledyard Spring past the Velvet Rocks in just over a mile.

Upon the climb, we caught up to a local college coed attempting 90 miles in 3 days – a feat we had managed only a handful of times and all we had been doing was walking for Seventy Days. Surely unhindered by binge eating, she scurried along up the trail. We enjoyed the view as she did so. I'm almost positive she had hairy legs, but even some trees were starting look attractive at this point.

As tempting as it was to stay at the Moose Mountain Shelter, an incredible handcrafted log cabin-style shelter assembled by the aforementioned DOC. The shelter was built with only hand tools and is of the highest quality. The Moose Mountain Shelter replaced the one previously farther south on the trail off Clark Pond Trail Loop. Interestingly enough, in 1968, Northeast Airline Flight 946 crashed into Moose Mountain with 42 souls on board. According to the National Transportation Safety Board post-crash report, the flight from Logan Airport to Montpelier, Vermont, was making a fuel stop in nearby Lebanon, New Hampshire, which sits in a valley. The plane was travelling at 600' below required altitude as the propellers on each side of the Fairchild Hiller 227 mowed itself into the side of the mountain killing 32 people. God bless them, their families and loved ones. Due to rescue and cleanup efforts, the summit was clear for a long time as vegetation is just now healing the scar. We yielded for only a break, but had we known of this incident at the time, would have shared a moment of silence and contemplation. We pushed on another hour to camp at Goose Pond Road, cowboy-style.

Midway through the next day we came upon Smarts Mountain, the Fire Warden's Cabin, and the fire tower. The history of the combo tower and cabin stretches back to 1915. The tower's responsibilities and caretakers have come and gone over the years. Its purpose ranged from watching for fires before topographic maps were available to radio repeater site. Smarts Fire Tower has eluded multiple scares of destruction due to weather, land ownership, and upkeep. However, due to the help of the ATC, DOC, and US Forest Service, the three have maintained its use since 1988, and for that, we are thankful. There is an incredible view from atop the 40' foot tower. Sadly, it was neither sunrise nor sunset, directly to the north stands Mt. Cube (7 soon-to-be-tackled trail miles away) and off to the northeast rises the White Mountains.

It was no secret the trail was ramping up its punishment. In the beginning, it was like speed dating – seeing what we liked, what worked and what didn't. "Don't worry, pal; you'll find the right one." Virginia Blues may get you thinking you aren't with the right one; maybe you need to be home.

Then, next thing you know, you've been seeing each other a couple months. No rough patches for a while through the Mid-Atlantic. Before you know it, you're meeting the parents, gradually requiring greater effort through the Berkshires of Massachusetts, then the Green Mountains of Vermont. This love affair was long past the stage of being coy and timid. I guess you could say this relationship status was in the shit-or-get-off-the-pot stage.

Mowgli, Bandanna, and I made it to the "Hikers Welcome Hostel at 6:45 PM" after the toughest day in a long time. New Hampshire was flexing its muscles early, and we had barely scratched the surface, great. In order to insure a spot at the hostel, we rushed directly there to make sure they could accommodate us. We took up a few cots that were available in a permanent scout camp-type tent. Without even thinking about it, we were unable to get to the Post Office in time to see if some of our warmer clothing had arrived via mail drop from back home. It would not have mattered too much as the PO closed at 5. At least we weren't looking at waiting for a package on Sunday scenario. Nevertheless, we figured we'd sort it out in the morning. The rest of the evening was spent showering, doing laundry, chowing down on some pay-as-you-eat freezer meals. I had about 3 of Marie Callender's Chicken Pot Pies (1,290 calories each), wishing each one were of the caliber of the ones served up at Village Market in Delaware Water Gap, Pennsylvania. We watched movies while waiting for laundry to finish and hit the hay anticipating an exciting day ascending into the White Mountains.

Mowgli

The French and Mooning

The White Mountains

With a couple extra layers of clothing from our package picked up the next morning along with some baked goods from Zoezilla, we made it out of town by 8AM. From Highway 25, where the hostel sat, heading north to the trailhead, the first major rise of the Whites soars above the highway on the horizon. The southern gateway into the White Mountains, Mt. Moosilauke, is 3,660' of elevation gain, in about 4 miles. The first 2 miles of the climb aren't that bad. It's all climbing; don't get me wrong. Skies were bluebird, and a slow burn churned in the calves and quads again. Gettin' nice on the pain gain. Around 2 miles in expectation of the summit, the trail turns from nice to naughty. Straight up as you can get while still walking. On a more eventful Jim Cantore kind of weather day, the trail would undoubtedly be less than lovely, like walking up a waterfall. Each step is a high knee while already going uphill, just to clear the exposed rocks that make up the trail. Not the rip-rap kind of stuff in Pennsylvania, but big rocks, little rocks, rocks at every angle. Navigation up the slope mandated undivided attention. Respect the mountain and it will respect you, except for when it just doesn't give a damn.

Finally atop the steepest section of the "Moos," the trees fizzled out to brush, grasses, low-lying mosses, and more rock. An encompassing 360° view is nearly captured as you make the final push to the rolling arch of the summit. Finally, atop its glory, the window into the Whites. The "Moos" delivered. Tell 'em I've graduated with honors, Cum Lawdhe Madeit. If this was the kind of scenery we were in for on our 5- day traverse of the Whites, we were in for a treat. Despite the maximum effort required to reach the top, there were quite a few hikers atop Mt. Moosilauke, some of them thru-hikers we had not met. The addition of Mowgli to our 2-man wolfpack, made us strong – a 3-man wolfpack.

In true Appalachian Trail fashion, the grandeur of ascension is immediately followed by the downfall of descent. I've got to give a shout-out to all the SOBO's out there because climbing "Moos" southbound seems absolutely absurd. Nevertheless, either way you choose to climb it, there's a large ascension succeeded with a devastating plunge. We headed straight, straight down, to Kinsman Notch, right back where we started at 1800' in 3.8 miles. In comparison to the south side of the mountain, the trail actually follows a stream as you come down Mt. Moosilauke. Let's pour some certainty on it though: you're probably envisioning a stream meandering and flowing. This water cascades down rock ledge after rock ledge much to the rhythm of one's feet crashing down the rock-laden trail along its edges. There's no doubt in my mind that, with a significant rain event or snowmelt, the "stream" and the trail are one and the same.

Over the past 26 days,we averaged over 28 miles a day. That streak took a drastic hit with our first day into the White Mountains, and we were ok with that. It would be foolish to overlook the sheer amount of strength and steadfastness required to climb up and down these mountains like a never-ending rollercoaster. That statement was proven to us as we achieved a gain of 17 miles our first day into the Whites. We stopped for the night at Eliza Brook Shelter, which for all you hikers thinking of hoofin' the AT on the cheap, is the last free shelter/campground through the White Mountains.

Throughout the White Mountains and beyond, the Appalachian Mountain Club (AMC) maintains trails, shelters, campsites, and the environment surrounding the trail. As noble as their dedication to preserve the majestic territory of this area, it can also be seen in a negative light among long-distance hikers, mainly because they represent some form of bureaucracy and structure. The dilemma is that, with the vast number of visitors entering the White Mountain National Forest every year, with no governing body or organization to oversee its use, it would be "loved to death." Without the AMC's efforts, in conjunction with the United States Forest Service, the White Mountains would be overrun, polluted, habitats destroyed and before you know it, nothing like the White Mountains we cherish today. Hats off to the service men and women that have worked for over a century to take care of this land.

There are 8 backcountry "huts" and 9 backcountry campsites along the AT in the White Mountains. Campsites run about $10 a night. The "huts" operate on 2 schedules: "Self-service" in the off months, and "Full Service" in the busy summer months. When the huts are in Self-Service, there is no full-time staff there. It's basically the freedom to use the Backcountry Inn for as low as $32 a night/person. During the Full-Service period, you can pay around $135 a night/person during the week and around $149 a night/person on the weekend. I understand the high price tag behind luxury of having dinner, breakfast and nightly entertainment whilst being miles from anywhere in the backcountry surrounded by one of the most beautiful landscapes in the world. I've got to ask the fundamental question though: is it necessary? Is this what the badass, the Rough Rider, Teddy Roosevelt, 26th President of the United States, had in mind?

Take a couple, a family, a group of scouts, outdoor enthusiasts or what have you. They go to the trouble of organizing a trip, plan it all out. Studying the maps, making an itinerary. Read all about the incredibly strenuous terrain, the difficulty of the climbs, the dangers of the descents. Find out it's all worth it because of the views. OHHHH the views, they make up for all of the effort (and they do). Arrive to a trailhead via bus, car, van, or what have you. Boots on the ground, we're climbing up a mountain! You forgot an extra pair of socks, "damnit", you'll deal with it. You're thirsty? Here, drink from this waterfall or babbling brook, or fresh spring. Down below you is the State whose motto is "Live Free or DIE" above you what is sure to be heaven or something close to it. Would not having a bed, dinner and breakfast cooked for you between one of the soaring 4,000 foot peaks along the way really be a deal breaker?

Fortunately, these high costs of camping and lodging can be skirted by thru-hikers. The ATC and AMC have been working together a long time and in their defense, thru-hikers are not subject to these high prices. Thru-hikers are subject to the same camping fees; however, if they wish to stay in a hut, they are given the option of a work to stay. This includes free lodging and meals in exchange for some simple chores assigned by the crew or "croo" staffing that particular hut. Tasks range somewhere in the sweeping and doing the dishes variety. Thru-hikers could even be asked to talk and tell stories about their hike thus far for the paying patron's nightly entertainment. Mowgli, Bandanna, and I were not planning to stay in any of the huts. What we did do though was to take full advantage of the huts each morning a little before lunch. Every day, right around lunch time, the huts offered all you can eat soup for $5. There were often leftover breakfast items that we devoured as well.

The first hut we approached was Lonesome Lake Hut, a hexagonal building on the way down to Franconia Notch. Hungarian Mushroom soup, five dolla', all you can eat. Sign us up. Gladly taking on some extra calories that we didn't have to carry, we studied our guidebooks of the massive elevation changes the next couple of days. Part of us wondered if the guidebook was correct: there were thousands of feet in elevation gain and loss over and over. Judging by the past couple of days, we were leaning more towards believing it despite telling ourselves "it could be off a little." The soup was so-so, but a warm lunch is always pleasing.

There is a massive network of trails all throughout the White Mountains, and the Appalachian Trail is just one of them. To make it a little more confusing, most of the signage does not say "Appalachian Trail." They often refer to the trail as the Franconia Ridge Trail. As we descended into Franconia Notch, elevation of 1,450', we began our climb straight back up towards Little Haystack Mountain at 4,800'. The trail continued to be insanely rocky with large steps required up and over positioning your plant foot just right to ensure positive gain with your next. Atop Little Haystack, you emerge from the treeline and become completely exposed. Looking back, you can see Lonesome Lake Hut, the Kinsman Mountains, and Mt. Moosilauke. It is a rewarding and nice change to not only see where we had been but where we were heading, too – a rare circumstance while hiking the Appalachian Trail, except for typically being able to see the next 100' in front of us.

As the tree line gives way, the trail manifests itself to open ridgeline walking with a clear path to Mt. Lincoln, which edged over us at 5,000'. This is the first time a northbound thru-hiker has been at this elevation since over 1300 miles ago on the climb out of Damascus, Virginia, up Mt. Rogers, and it is glorious! Two-and-a-half miles or so above treeline. We truly felt like a hiker ought to feel in the wild. Nothing but soaring rock peaks with greenery in between for as far as the eye can see. That evening, we skirted back below treeline and camped at Garfield Ridge Campsite.

Ben and I were no strangers to perspiration, but we were starting to wonder about Mowgli. The dude could sweat. I mean nearly immediately after he started to hike, we could've wrung out every piece of clothing he had on. Not really noticing this back at the Hikers Welcome Hostel in Glencliff, NH, we mistakenly did a load of laundry with his. We were by no means like roses, Ben and me. There was a noticeable change in funkitude the next few days of hiking. Another precaution hikers need to be aware of in the White Mountains is the unreliability of the water sources. Such is the problem with ridge walking as there is nowhere for water to actually collect because you are at the top and the whole gravity thing kind of takes it from there. Mowgli had quite the water purification technique as well. Here Ben and I were with our little MSR Miox which created a chlorine solution by sending an electric charge through unpurified water and rock salt, something straight out of "Popular Science." Mowgli, on the other hand, took a more one-ingredient method to his purification: household bleach. This was absolutely outrageous-sounding to us. The active ingredient in bleach is

Sodium Hydro chlorite, typically around the 6% range for most household bleach. Bleach is actually a common water purifier when in a pinch. The first thought is "Oh My God! Bleach?!" That was our reaction, but you only need between 2-5 drops per liter/quart. In hindsight, I realized that's almost precisely what our MSR Miox was producing.

"With current technology, we have been unable to identify these other compounds; therefore, we can claim only that we make a strong chlorine/hypochlorous acid solution."

Straight from MSR's website. We were basically making our own bleach while Mowgli was outsourcing his.

Another downfall to ridge walking is you always think you're closer to the next summit than you actually are. It's, as I like to call it, an obstacle illusion. With nothing blocking your view and being so used to not knowing where you're really heading on the AT, it's an odd sensation to finally see where you are heading. The illusion is that each rise you pass over is so steep that it blocks your view in front of you while its completely open to the left and right. Each rise that you crest presents itself as another false summit to the peak you're actually heading towards. The obstacle is that you begin to inaccurately judge how far you have gone and how far you have remaining. Typically, Ben and I were able to judge all of our water stops/breaks using an average of 3 miles an hour. But due to the terrain, that calculation was severely skewed. Everything just took longer and required greater effort. Thus, with the current set of circumstances, we were asking our bodies to do more and hydrating every chance we got. When we finally made the push over Mt. Lincoln and then Mt. Lafayette, we were slap out of water. For the first time, we had underestimated this crucial requirement.

Shuffling through our guide books, desperately searching for the next water source, we saw that the closest one was at Greenleaf Hut, which was a 1-mile side trail and over a 1000' descent and inevitable ascent from the AT. We weren't really interested in a detour of that nature. Yet we had put ourselves in a tight spot. Fortunately, we were all in the same boat. Reluctantly, we headed down the Greenleaf trail asking everyone coming up it if there was water, ANYWHERE, nearby. You would have thought we had not drank a drop in days. Suddenly the absence of water was a serious issue. We avoided this dilemma for nearly 2000 miles. Upset at ourselves for such a silly and basic mistake, we began to panic a bit. Stumbling upon a weekend warrior and assumed wife, we frantically asked, "Have you seen any water?" The hiker simply replied in a confused and stuttering manner…"I uhhh, I um, I dew not know, because-eh, I am French." So much for 4 years of Spanish in high school. I should've known. Asking a few more times, pointing to our water bottles, "Water. Have you seen any water?" "Ohh yes, uh just down the trail."

I don't know what kind of muck holes this guy had been drinking out of his entire life, what we found was a sight for sore eyes indeed. The saddest, murkiest excuse for a water source you'd ever seen. Dead bugs, clumps of moss; Hell, probably some bird excrement. We were in for a treat. This situation exposed the downside to not having a pump filter is situations like this. Chemical treatment of water often requires flowing water, or at least deep enough that you can just dunk your entire bottle down into the source. Neither were our current situation. We crafted a makeshift water scoop and filled up our containers, floaties and all. Zapping our MSR Miox a couple extra times we created what was sure to be enough chlorine solution to kill anything and everything. Our insides were sure to be clean, too.

Hydrated enough to make it down from Mt. Lafayette and the Franconia Ridge, we settled in to Garfield Ridge Campsite for the evening. Luckily, there was room in the Shelter that evening, and we did not have to set up any tents. Ben and I were astonished at the good fortune of the beautiful weather during our stint in the Whites thus far. I can easily see how inclement weather would make the traverse a million times more difficult. We forked over the $16 to camp at the shelter to the campsite "caretaker." On our way out the next morning, we observed what appeared to be the screens from a moldering privy. This ain't Pawpaw's outhouse. A moldering privy is slightly elevated and relies on the natural decomposition of "waste" using the introduction of air and microorganisms to break everything down. With each trip to the privy, the user throws in a handful or two of "duff" or mostly decomposed forest waste such as leaves, coarse sawdust, or wood shavings. Red worms are also typically introduced to help the process along as well. The compost concoction requires an occasional stir from a volunteer or "caretaker," and the screens are removed every so often and returned to the forest floor, away from trails, campsite and water sources of course.

Passing by Galehead Hut early that morning, we weren't quite there in time for the lunchtime soup option, and we were too early for breakfast leftovers to be up for the taking. Cruising on by with a slight respite of crazy climbs and descents, we made our way to Zealand Falls Hut. This portion of the trail, from Galehead to Zealand contains about the only little bit of flat that you'll find in the Whites. Although we had missed an opportunity for extra calories at Galehead, we hit the jackpot at Zealand Falls. Upon our arrival, a tray full of leftover pancakes was set out with "Free" written on a piece of cardboard right beside it. If you thought Mowgli, Ben and I were going to leave without making sure that sign could be thrown away, you'd be mistaken. Roughly 10 pancakes apiece, this hut system didn't seem so bad after all.

Zealand Falls Hut was about halfway down to Crawford Notch. Between Crawford and Pinkham Notch stands the Presidential Range. Its most notable peaks are named after, of course, some US Presidents and prominent US figures: Mt. Webster, Mt. Jackson, Mt. Pierce (Mt. Clinton), Mt. Franklin, and Mt. Washington. As we reached Crawford Notch, we had a bit of a treasure hunt to go on. The Paige Family, from BSA Troop 215 in Raleigh, was recently visiting the White Mountain area on a routine summer vacation. They were one of the vigorous followers of our blog back home, rooting us on the entire way. I had come to know their son, Spencer, on a few troop outings the past year or so. We had received instructions on accessing a little trail magic they had stashed for us on the northbound trail side of U.S. 302. Sure enough, about 80 paces up the trail and 45' off the trail, just out of view from the path, a black Hefty bag! Ahhh, but there was all treasure, no trash, in this Hefty. Orange Gatorades, an entire pack of

Oreos, and other snacks. We plopped on the ground right there and even shared our bounty with Mowgli. Every morsel in that bag was devoured. Despite our good fortune of pancake pandering earlier that morning, we were dead set on consuming the entire bit of magic. There was no way we were going to carry it on our backs either.

Fueled up for our ascent to Mt. Washington and the traverse of the Presidential Range, we headed up Webster Cliffs and Mount Webster. Back in Dalton, Massachusetts, I was in search for a body glide replacement. I had run out of the anti-chafing applicator a while back but figured it would be nice to have in the coming month. The only thing Ben and I could find was the Band-Aid brand "Friction Block" marketed for foot care. I assumed it was safe for full body usage and had applied some on my grundle. With the extra effort required and hiking mostly in sweat drenched shorts, I didn't think it would harm anything. Band-Aid's take on Body Glide seemed to work just as well. It was even scented, like a bouquet of flowers. As Mowgli hiked behind me stepping up and over large rock formations, I suppose he got a whiff. "Man! What is that smell? It smells like my girlfriend." I was pleased to inform him it was the Band-Aid anti-chafe stick, as Bandanna and I burst out laughing informing him of where the lovely scent was currently originating.

After a half an hour of laughing, we closed in on Nauman Tentsite. Camping here would put us in prime striking distance of Mt. Washington the next morning – home to the "Worst Weather in the World." Winters on Mt. Washington are especially brutal. The Summit records hurricane force winds about 110 days a year. In 1934 on April 12th, Mt. Washington became the Northern and Western Hemisphere record holder for highest surface wind speed at 231mph. Naturally, the weather station and historic buildings atop its peak are chained to the ground.

Over compensating for our lack of water transportation the day before, we were carrying a few extra pounds of H2O to ensure things went off without a hitch. If you decide to go to only one hut, I'd suggest the Lake of the Clouds Hut, not necessarily because it's such an awesome building (although it's pretty cool) but because of where it is. It often sees the weather much the same as the top of Washington. Unfortunately, the lake was not really visible, because we were, well, in a cloud. As you approach Washington, there's no telling what you're in for weather-wise. The Whites at this point yielded zero drops of rain and an abundance of sunshine to go around. At Lake of the Clouds Hut, we entered said visible collection of water particles, and visibility was severely tempered.

About half a mile before the Mt. Washington summit, the clouds began to break; rather, we were breaking out of the clouds. Atop the summit is a visitor's center, weather station and, most importantly, snack bar. The AT is just one way to the top. As we crested the final rise, we snapped a foggy photo with the summit sign and then promptly stepped off the trail across the parking lot and into the visitor's center. It may have not been the easiest way to the top, but it was definitely the most rewarding. In lieu of a car, you can also take the Mt. Washington Cog Train to the top. The Cog was the brainchild of New Hampshire's own Sylvester Marsh. After more than a decade of raising money and start date issues due to the Civil War, Marsh was laughed at by the New Hampshire Congress and called his idea the "Railway to the Moon" as it may as well of been a train to the moon as much a train to the summit of Mt. Washington. Marsh pressed on, and in 1869, rode atop Mt. Washington in his Cog with President Grant in tow.

The three of us hung around for a little bit out of the wind in the visitor center/snack bar, and even caught some good views. Just like I say about my home state of North Carolina, "If you don't like the weather, just wait a day." The same goes for Mt. Washington, except you only have to wait a minute. Feeling a bit like animals at the zoo as tourists began flooding in from the parking lot and cog station, we decided we ought to leave. There was rumor of thru-hiker tradition where the AT nears the cog's track. Whether in protest of the cog's "pollution" of the trail or just in good humor, Thru-hikers have been dropping their drawers and showing the conductor and passenger's their backside for years. "Mooning the Cog" seems to fall on the hilarious more than harmful side of things. Just like anything else this day and age though, one too many prudes disapproved and complained. Ben and I opted out, which we were thankful for. According to a New York Times article in November 2007, a "sting" operation was set up to bust hikers showing their ass. Undercover officers riding the cog ordered it to stop to give EIGHT hikers public nudity tickets in August and September of 2007. Due to Mt. Washington being in a National Forest, it is Federal Land, which means a federal offense. Really? Who's showing their ass now?

The remainder of the day was spent rounding off the Presidential Range. Rock hopping our way along, using every bit of balance we had as our packs acted as sails in the high wind conditions. A skillet with oil burning too hot is going to smoke. A similar glaze, if you will, is produced from overheated brake pads rubbing. That's the enjoyable smell we were subject to from the flock of tourists burning down the road from Mt. Washington's summit. Into the depths of Pinkham Notch we descended. Preferably, if a trail were to be completely rock laden, I'd rather have it on the up than the down. Unfortunately, it just doesn't work like that. There's no way to overstate the difficulty of navigating and maneuvering your way down these steep descents. In perfect weather, it was difficult. Even the slightest amount of dew, mist, rain, or, heaven forbid, ice makes a sojourn through the Whites an infinitely more problematic one. If there was only one section, one day to have trekking poles, today was that day. Finally, as we fully lowered ourselves down into Pinkham we entered, wouldn't ya know it, another Visitor's Center.

We were now running a little low on food, and had it not been for the soup at the Huts and little freebies along the way, it would have been more drastic. The Visitor's Center offered a $16 AYCE family-style dinner. You could say we got our money's worth. They even had breakfast items still available, and I'm pretty sure I spotted Mowgli putting heavy cream on his Fruit Loops for a little post-dinner dessert. You can't be completely anti-establishment all the time although that night we were not too interested in paying for a room and hiked up the trail a bit and ghost-camped off to the side for the evening. Mowgli had a tarp big enough to fit us all under and strung it up low to the ground to avoid being spotted through the thick brush on our relatively flat lie.

The Slowest Mile

Mahoosuc Notch

One of my college roommates at the time was Jason L'Heureux. Jason and the Chappell twins lived together. Jason is from Portland, Maine, not too far from where we were. Just before he was heading back to Charlotte for the school year, Jason made the two hour drive and visited Mowgli, Bandanna, and me in Gorham, New Hampshire. Our five-day stint through the White Mountains was nothing short of amazing. On the 100-mile stretch, we averaged 20 miles a day. Hats off to anyone crushing more miles than that in the Whites; you're a badass. We were extremely happy to have Jason along with us; after all, he had a car, and Gorham was pretty spread out.

Ben and I had finally wised up to whole mail drop game and confirmed back home to stop all mail. We were tired of the same ol' stuff. It was time to spice it up a little. At Walmart across town, we loaded up. Cosmic Brownie's, Chocolate Rounds, other Little Debbie delights, bagels, summer sausage, pepperoni's, peanut butter, and Nutella. Hell, I never even had the chocolate hazelnut spread. After checkout, we headed back to the parking lot to J's trusty ol' Camry. If you're ever perusing the Walmart parking lot, and you can't find the famed crazy people and behavior surely to be found in a Wally World sea of asphalt, then I got news for ya…it's you. Surely that was the appearance we must have had.

The next order of business was chow time. With around 14,000 of them in the United States, it occurred to us that we had not made a trail visit to the most popular, original, Big Mac Daddy of them all while on the trail: Mickey D's. Eero Saarinen had nothing on those Golden Arches as we abruptly requested Jason to pull in. Now it was time to show off for L'Heureux and give him a little Thru Hiker vs. Town Food show. Two double cheeseburgers, some nugs of course, those famous fries, a Big Mac with special sauce, and a McFlurry to wash it all down, each. It was a glorious sight indeed, seeing as how about 4 years earlier, the popular yet grotesque documentary "Super Size Me" had come out. In an effort for transparency, an effort still being called for today, Ronald had Nutrition Facts on the tray liner. What lacked transparency was all our food covering up the liner, until, of course, it was all in the digestive stage. Brilliant marketing, really, like showing you the trailer after you watched the movie. Fortunately, our daily intake was at a point where it didn't matter too much what we put in our bodies. Following some arithmetic, we tallied up our meals to see who the big winner was, as some of our "side" items were of different selection and size. Mowgli conquered the day with nearly 2000 calories, damn impressive.

As we helped Jason pick his jaw up off the floor after witnessing such glutton, we started searching for lodging that evening. We came across the Top Notch Inn, which was not listed in my "Thru-Hiker's Companion." Upon request of a room at the front desk, we were unfortunately turned down. Despite the hotel's not being in the guide book, the curious woman helping us seemed very familiar with the trail and the thru-hiker, which we were easily identified as. After being denied a standard room, she quickly perked up, "No regular rooms are available, BUUUUUUUT I think you'll like what we do have. It's called the Pinkham House; it's a two-story unit. Are you all too sore to walk up stairs? I hope not. There's three bedrooms: one king, one queen, and two singles with a pull-out couch. A full kitchen, living room and dining area. Do you think that would be enough?" We turned at each other in disbelief, wondering what in the world this would cost. "Since we're out of regular rooms, I'd be happy to just charge a regular room rate -- $95." "That'll work" as she swiped my Visa and handed us the keys to the castle. At today's going rates, that night should have cost about $230.

Did I mention the room had a washer and dryer? Well it did. We relaxed, did our laundry, cooked some "it's not delivery; it's DiGiorno" pizzas. All was right in the world. Thankful for Jason's chauffer services and company, I was happy to spend some time with him knowing in just 2 weeks' time and 300 miles later, we would be roommates for our junior year of college. It would be a tough row to hoe; completing the rest of the trail in the time we had, but we had made it this far. It was time to finish.

Although Gorham is the last town stop in New Hampshire, there's still a rugged, unforgiving 12 miles before entering "Vacationland" – the state of Maine. With our tanks topped off, we hungered for the final state-line crossing of the trip. In thru-hiker lore, the saying goes "No Rain, No Pain, No Maine." The pain part we had covered, but I suppose it was the time of year we started, and just luck of the draw, but there was a serious lack of rain. Without further ado, the often gloomy yet not always raining microclimate of the northeast opened up. The pop-pop of water splashing on semi-impermeable gear made of silnylon and ripstop fabric orchestrated with the dulling, sound-absorbing, miniscule thud of drops hitting the lush spruce and hemlock. In the crescendo of precipitation, our smiles and laughs quelled to a silent march of tired feet inching along the pine needle covered trail. The nearly waterlogged trail soaked into the cloth of our trail shoes. The pressure of each landing foot produced the effect of squeezing a sponge only to soak in just as much water as was released, just before the next foot was about to experience the same.

The sky had graded from blue to grey and darker still. A lone rumble of thunder progressed imminently closer. When it just did seem bearable, as though you can only get so wet, a chicken skin-producing chill swept across mountains and encompassed the trail in a nearly visible frosty breath of Mother Nature herself. Slips and stumbles occurred frequently as footing over the now root-laden and rocky surface. The days of joyously frolicking down the "Shenandoah Sidewalk" on a trail large enough to fit a car down were long behind us. Sky began to flash light, distributed through openings in the canopied trail above. It was hard to tell if I absolutely loved or unforgivingly hated it. It was 10 in the morning.

Not expecting these conditions, we should have probably watched a round or two of weather-on-the-8s instead of a repeating Sportscenter the night prior. Heavy and thunderous lightning was drawing full concern as we crossed over the top of Mt. Hayes and Cascade Mountain. Elevation had severely dropped from our time in the White Mountains, but being the tallest thing around in a storm on a mountaintop is still not the preferred situation, no matter what height you are. It was just after noon that we came upon Gentian Pond Shelter, a large log cabin-like structure with an upper bunk extending from the back wall about 1/3 of the way towards the open front. We settled in for a break, happy to be out of what was now a downpour. Upon rounding the corner of the shelter, which faced away from the trail and towards the storm, we shuffled up the steps, heads down and peripheral vision blocked by rain jacket hoods. Looking up from the final step into dry sanctuary sat a man on his tripod camping chair in the middle of the shelter. He donned a million-mile gaze, glasses pulled from his face in one hand and split open book in the other, staring off into the distance.

In startled discontent, he broke out of his trance and made room for the 3 of us as we shook off the residual moisture from our outermost layers. "My name is Colbert," he flamboyantly proclaimed in the tone and accent of the extremely unhelpful Frenchman on the Franconia Ridge when we were looking for water. "Great," I thought, give me one that can speaka-da-language when I've got to be stuck in a shelter with him. Despite his awkward introduction and the moment we caught him in, I couldn't help but chuckle at the thought of Stephen Colbert's character in the (at the time) new Colbert Report TV show. Prior to that moment, my closest connection to a Colbert was asking for an ice-cold beer, quickly.

As lightning now began striking visibly through the framed opening of the shelter, we quickly determined that today, literally, was a wash. Maine would have to wait 1 more day for our distinguished arrival. Able to retain our clean set of clothes for another 12 hours, we snacked and dipped heavily into our food supply out of boredom in the shelter. It was hard to sleep having hiked only 12 miles. Colbert's weirdness was masked by his silence, and as night fell early due to the lingering storm, a premium nature soundtrack of thunderclouds rolling away faded softly.

Excitement regenerated the next day as we trekked through the now even muddier, slippery root covered trail into Maine. Perhaps it was the indulgent McDonald's trip or irregular eating times of the days prior, but at the border crossing, I had a sudden urge for a bowel movement. The sneak attack kind that must be dealt with immediately. Zippers on a pack can never be more difficult as I fumbled for the pocket of my pack, which held some Charmin double-ply. Shuffling over and through brush to find a decent spot to crouch, my normal poop process was urgently interrupted as I released what could only be described as a demon.

With less thoughtfulness of where I went to do my business than normally taken, I returned to Mowgli and Bandanna. Like a carpet-dusting fart, the smell of this demon seemed to follow me back to the state line. Ben and Mowgli got a whiff in disgust and in jest "What did you eat?!" knowing full well what I ate because they were there with me and ate the same damn thing. We continued on into Maine, hiking out of the poo-pourri. As far as the location of the dirty deed, how was I supposed to know the trail was taking a sweeping left turn up ahead, looping us nearly right to the scene of the crime? I know they say everyone likes their own flavor, but that stench was downright wrong. A few up-tempo strides forced us out of the danger zone and we marched on excitedly towards the "Hardest Mile of the Trail."

The short Mahoosuc Mountain range spans about 30 miles in southeast Maine and does not have any peaks particularly impressive in height, but it does offer around 10,000 feet of elevation gain on the AT along with the fact that it is a much more remote section of the trail, less frequented by the metropolitan crowds of nearby cities. Reading through the next sequential landmark elevations listed in the guidebook invoked no fear: Mt. Carlo – 3,565', Goose Eye Mtn. (East Peak) – 3,790', Goose Eye Mtn. North Peak – 3,675'. The reality of the trail though was nothing to be trifled with. What exists are rock scrambles more difficult than anywhere experienced on the trail to this point. Dragon's Tooth a thousand times over, Uncle Steve would be Ubering for a helicopter. Manmade ladders of fir trunks assist in the most vertical sections along with rebar steps driven into the rock. The surrounding alpine landscape with added isolation make for some astounding views if you are fortunate enough to receive favorable weather. Ponds scatter the landscape far beneath your feet, reflecting the clouds above, revealing that perhaps the world is flat, with sky below and above. That theory is quickly erased as only low-lying brush and grasses atop these mountains hinder no view. Curve of the Earth is revealed as line of sight is unhindered and a visual of the Presidential Range of the White Mountains at your back.

Glaciers tearing through the area left huge boulders of schist in a granite valley which is formally known as the Mahoosuc Notch. It is on this one-mile stretch of trail that many a water bottle, knuckle and trekking pole go to die. As we approached the entrance to the notch, well-marked for being as in the middle of nowhere as it was, we began the "Hardest Mile" by basically crawling over a dead moose calf that had fallen into the notch and was obviously unable to get out. Maine didn't suck, but it sure stunk up to this point. As we breathed through our mouths to avoid the smell of the rotting carcass, we lowered ourselves into the jigsaw jungle-gym ravine that was sure to provide entertainment and challenge. Hopping from one giant rock to another was frequently required, planning each jump extremely carefully as the rock surfaces remain slick and rarely catch a glimmer of daylight.

Spencer McKay

Crawling and jamming ourselves through small cracks between boulders balanced on top of each other by some kind of magic felt more like caving than hiking. Between the laughing, cursing, what-the-hecking, and navigating through this maze, we could, in moments of quiet, hear the faint sound of water flowing. It was hard to tell if it was above, below or beside as the trickling flow echoed off each skewed metamorphic surface. There are some horror stories of people getting stuck, injured, and just taking for-EVER to get through the Mahoosuc Notch. For us, was it the most difficult mile? No, but it was undoubtedly the slowest. Nothing more than a few scraped knees and knuckles and an hour of our time, we were through the Notch. In an effort to make up for lost time the day before, when our time crunch was more serious than ever, we pushed on for a 25-mile day to Frye Notch lean-to.

Out of the Mahoosuc Notch, the trail continues as a slithery, cragged, gnarly bob and weave requiring agility and endurance. Our Salomon XA Pro 3D trail runners were taking a beating, our fourth and final pair allotted for the trip were going to have to do. We received our current pair just before the Whites in Glencliff, New Hampshire. At this point with the ruggedness of terrain, as I gazed down at my feet, it looked like I'd had the same pair on for the entire length of the trail, while it had actually been only 150 miles. Just a teenager in shoe years. Bogs reminiscent of Vermont required sensible foot placement as we meandered around ponds in the short moments between technical steep climbs up and down.

Feces
Hits the
Oscillator

Rangeley, ME

The calm of procrastination hovered over me, as if our little
adventure of hiking from Georgia to Maine was bubble-wrapped, safe, and
guaranteed to be delivered in 1 to 2 business days. It was now Wednesday,
August 8th. In 13 days, we had to cover 260 miles, 20 miles a day. The
slowest mile of the trail was behind us, the largest peaks as well. What did
remain was the most rugged isolated territory on the entire trail, my own
personal thoughts of perhaps actually completing this beast of an adventure,
and a river crossing that requires a canoe. This hump day was nothing short
of that. Moody Mountain and Old Blue Mountain are a serious kick in the
ass. As we began the steep summit up Old Blue, we stopped to fill up water
and have a snack to fuel up. There was a sign posted at the road crossing for
a new hostel down the road. They were offering all the thru-hiker amenities:
laundry, food, bed, shower, and with a nod to the younger population on
the trail, Xbox video games. This place was pulling at my heart strings.
Knowing we had to stay focused, we sat there on the edge of the trail and
snacked on what we had. We'd have to pass this one up.

Spencer McKay

I decided now was a good time to try out the Nutella I bought in Gorham. Twisting the white plastic top off and tearing through the paper and foil freshness seal across the top of the jar like a grizzly, I shoved my spork down in the creamy, dark, hazelnut spread. Nothing gradual about this taste test. In just enough time for my taste buds to signal to my brain, the same amount of time was used to spit every bit of it out. I couldn't stand it. I don't know what I thought it was going to taste like, more like peanut butter I guess. It was that odd sensation when you think you're picking up a sweet tea and take a big ol' sip only to find out it's unsweet. I secured the top back on in a profanity-laced tirade about how I had carried this disgusting item all the way from Gorham, New Hampshire, only to find out now how absolutely inedible it was. I shoved the pieces of the seal I had torn off back down into the jar and torqued the lid back. Palming the container in my hand, I cocked my arm back, considering a Katz-type throw of Spam off the side of the mountain, only to look right down in front of me to see it sitting on the ground under the hostel sign posting a trash can, in the middle of the woods. "Perfect." The full jar clanged and thudded against the interior of the bagless metal can as I slammed the top back on. Knowing my luck, I half expected it to bounce back out like one of those impossibly rigged games at the fair. I looked up at Ben and said, "Let's hike."

The day had turned misty as we ascended into the frequent low clouds that cover this pond-puddled landscape. Cloud juice dripped off our brows with a mixture of sweat as we made our final push amongst the low brush and tiny trees of Old Blue's rocky and rugged ascent. Wind gusts came across the top thrashing the cold, hardened skin of our legs. No need for a rain jacket though, we'd get just as wet from sweating with that thing on as we would just toughing it out and trucking along. A photo wasn't warranted either as no one would be able to make anything out. It was hard enough following the trail.

Clouds finally broke as we crested the Bemis Range. The sun was gradually sliding the hue tool of the sky from blue to purple. Mowgli snapped a photo of Ben and me in the foreground as the sun worked around us like a live window of Photoshop. Another 2 miles and we arrived at Bemis Mountain Lean to. A portion of the roof was a corrugated hard plastic or fiberglass, reminding me of something on a greenhouse. It was nicely placed as it let some light in during the remaining minutes we had of it. As the 3 of us set out our things in the shelter, making sure we did not intrude on the hikers who had already staked their claim, we shoved ourselves fairly close to each other. In common practice, we hung our packs along the front lintel on the open end of the shelter. Just in front of where we spread out our sleeping pads and bags for the night, there was an old external frame of a pack hanging right where Ben wanted to put his. You hear all kinds of stories of what hikers starting out in Georgia would leave behind in shelters; I guess the same was becoming true for people heading southbound, just beginning their journey.

Assuming that the pack was nothing more than garbage, Bandanna removed it from the nail it rested on and chucked it out of the shelter, and we watched it cling and clank the rocks on the ground just outside. About the time the cold, black metal frame released from Ben's hand as he flicked his wrist in follow through, "Hey man! What the Fuck!" from across the shelter. If this guy was trying to time up a distraction with a game-winning shot from the free throw line, he was way off. However, it was Ben who was way off. As the burly, young hiker, hopped up out of his sleeping bag and outside to grab his backpack frame, he grasped it and shook it in Ben's face. "Do you just throw other people's shit around man?" I suddenly wished I hadn't lost all the weight that I did; I didn't look too intimidating these days. Worst-case scenario, I thought Ben may have to take a free hit. Said owner of external frame continued on about how he had used that frame on his Pacific Crest Trail Thru-hike as well as his thru-hike across the Continental Divide trail. Those two trails, in conjunction with the Appalachian Trail make up the Triple Crown. Anyone who completes all 3 is Hiker Trash Royalty. So, here we were, Ben standing up in the shelter, shivering in his crocs, knowing he had really messed up. One pissed off, nearly triple-crowner, and Mowgli and I watching. Ben hopped on the apology train, "I'm sorry, I'm sorry, I'm sorry; I didn't mean to."

The next morning we watched curiously as the triple crowner packed up all his things. All Ben had thrown was literally an old external frame, nothing attached to it but the backpack straps. The hiker carefully lashed each once brightly colored stuff sack to the frame. It was quite the odd technique and Ben defends himself to this day – how was he supposed to know; "it looked like garbage." Shortly after watching ol' Triple Crown strap on his stuff sacks, Ben headed to the privy as I packed up my things, excited about heading to the 2nd-to-last resupply of the trip. I waited for Ben while sipping water, his bowel movement was taking much longer than usual. Bandanna comes shuffling back to the shelter with a halfway concerned, halfway proud look on his face. You know what I'm talking about gents, when you know you really dropped a good one. The pride quickly faded as Ben rubbed his stomach and said, "I don't know what that was, but let's hope that was the last of it."

We slung on our packs and headed down the trail, hoping to hitchhike into Rangeley, Maine, once we got to Highway 4. Mowgli took point as I hung back with Ben to make sure he was ok. I typically pooped once a day, during our first break, about 9 to 10 miles in; sometimes before we started hiking, sometimes around lunchtime, but generally, during our first break. When I felt the urge, 1 mile in, I knew it was coming and coming fast, keeping it "Close and Exciting." Well, close and exciting it was: no time for taking off the pack, grabbing my toilet paper and hand sanitizer; no waltzing through the woods look for the perfect spot. Personally, I prefer a smaller tree with enough girth that I can grab and support myself while properly adjusting my angle so as to not deploy excrement into my own drawers. There was no time for any of that pomp and circumstance. The thrust, the velocity – in all reality, I'm a little surprised I didn't get airborne. I made sure I didn't soil myself and walked back to the trail with a similarly discouraging look as Ben had given me at the lean-to.

Trying not to dwell on it too much, we continued on. A couple of nasty BM's, so what. Ain't the first and damn sure ain't the last. That's what we thought, until about 20 minutes later, I turn around to the shuffling of leaves and underbrush through the woods. Finally, maybe a moose I thought, and not a dead one like we saw in the Notch. Nope, just Ben darting his way through the woods, pack thrown off in the middle of the trail, I hadn't seen the man move this fast our entire trip. I waited for him to return so we could share this comical poop-excursion of a day. About 30 minutes went by, and then I Houdinied out of my pack and ran the 40 like Rich Eisen at the NFL combine, dropped my drawers, and you know the rest.

The same process occurred the entire way to Maine 4. I was just holding my toilet paper in my hand at this point. Fortunately, terrain-wise, it was the easiest day we'd had in a long time. If it were going to happen, we were extremely lucky on when it did. Imagine if this were just a day ago, in the Mahoosuc Notch, you know what, don't imagine, shit would be everywhere. Ben and I would have been known as the Splash Brothers. Mowgli hiked on ahead, and we didn't see him the rest of the day. Ben and I no longer stopped and waited for one another. Every once in a while I'd come across his pack on the side of the trail; then he'd come across mine. It was like clockwork, a rotating schedule, a series of strikes and counterstrikes. Somehow, by the grace of God, we made it 20 miles to the road. Completely out of toilet paper, water, hand sanitizer and energy, the comedy of it all had worn off. We were just thankful to get to the road, that beautiful road…, it was an amazing road. In added mercy, about 30 seconds after we got to the shoulder, a car approached us. With just enough time to stick a thumb out, the Ford Escape pulled over and within 45 seconds of reaching the road, we were in a car, and on our way to Rangeley, Maine.

Bandanna and I were quick to mention our current situation to the kind driver, a younger male knowledgeable about the AT's crossing where he picked us up. "No problem, just let me know if we need to pull over." As we entered the town limits, we quickly directed our driver to the Rangeley IGA, the local grocery. We thumbed past the nail care, the eye care, soaps, and deodorants. Our eyes were set on one thing, Imodium AD. We grabbed some Gatorade in the store and took   the maximum dose before even checking out. While we were there, we decided to resupply as well. Always thinking of maximizing time and effort. We bought everything we could think of that would be helpful to our current situation: yogurt, mashed potatoes, apple sauce, anything bland we could get our hands on. In an effort to not worry our parents, we figured we better try and take care of this with as little fuss as possible. I wouldn't put it past Zoezilla or Moonshine to hop on a flight or in a car and drive a 1,000 miles or more to get to us.

In the midst of shopping, Ben nudged me and pushed his basket of items towards me: "I gotta go, man." Thinking nothing of it by now, I took his basket, adhering to the "No Unpurchased Items Past This Point" sign. The small, local grocer had a single use, women's and men's restroom. With Bandanna's items, I figured I might as well stick close to the restroom and planned to use it directly after him. As he dealt with the issue, he took what felt like a leisure dump more than an emergency one. After waiting a few minutes that could have easily been just a few seconds, a dilemma of my own was brewing. I've got both baskets of goods, Ben's in the men's room with no sign of zipping up any time soon, and there's only a women's bathroom. Trying to be civil, I crossed my legs leaning up against the wall, held in every fart that was certainly not a fart, and tried my best to abide by the rules of civilization.

The demon inside me had a different plan. He wanted out, NOW! I checked my Southern Proper ways, left the baskets on the ground, and darted into the women's room. I always thought that the women's room would be cleaner. Boy, was I wrong. Anyway, that's an argument for another day. As soon as entering the threshold, there was no going back. Assisting the door closed once in the room, I fumbled with the slide lock, but it was clearly broken. It was a race against the clock now. All I could think was the poor woman who might walk in to see a homeless man having some serious issues. The ejection process complete; I was on to the more delicate stage of cleanup. God help me if the opposite sex walks in now. Hurriedly taking care of business, shuffling to pull up my britches, just as I was about to turn around to wash my hands, a large grey-headed woman with glasses opened the door. She let out a shriek, and all I could get out was a grunt. Missing the show by a split-second, I was not looking forward to facing her outside.

I slung my pack back on and slowly opened the door to find Ben hysterically laughing. At least the woman was nowhere in sight.

Upon checkout from the IGA, which I'm sure was glad to see us go, we phoned a hostel listed in the guidebook, the Gull Pond Lodge. After a few rings, a man answered, "Gulllll Pond Lodge." We asked if there was any room in the inn, and he obliged. He even offered up a ride to come get us from the IGA. Loaded up on sports drinks, ginger ale, safe and soothing foods, we headed to the lodge. The man on the phone was Bob O'Brien, a quintessential old guy with instant grandpa vibes. I cannot say enough good things about this man: he was warming, kind, funny, and at that point in our lives, a godsend. He showed us around the hostel, his home, as we grabbed a set of bunk beds in a room that had two sets in it. Ben boldly and unselfishly took the top, perhaps in feeling some guilt due to my women's room adventure. Informing Bob of our current situation, he took pity on us; we hoped it would be a one-night stay and back to the trail, but just in case, Mr. O'Brien offered up a ride to the clinic the next day if we didn't feel any better. A very low-key night ensued with the some TV in the living room downstairs, conveniently located next to the bathroom, the only bathroom in the hostel, mind you.

Staying on top of the recommended maximum dosage for Imodium AD over the next 12 hours was important. We thought at worst we'd get a late start the next day. Making it through the night without needing to buy Bob a new set of sheets was a positive. On the other hand, we had been sleeping, so was the beast inside us. I woke up with an urge at about 5 o'clock in the morning. As I crept down the stairs, daybreak was peaking its head outside. Just as I rounded the corner to the bathroom, the door shuts, fan and light combo switched on, and the shower cranked up. One of the other hikers staying at the hostel had beat me to it. I knocked anyway knowing this would be a longer endeavor than I could stand, "Occupied." I did the childish bathroom dance for a few seconds right outside the door, wracking my brain for other options. Trail life and civilization were clashing some-kinda bad the past 24 hours.

I shuffled up the stairs as quickly and quietly as I could to snag a roll of TP; we loaded up on that at IGA too, trying to be as courteous to the other hikers staying there as possible. I snuck back down the creaking wood steps and out the back door. I at least made my way off Bob's backyard lawn before having to drop trough. Sorry, Bob. All this before the sun was even up; what a wonderful day this was becoming. I muddled my way back into the house and upstairs to my bottom bunk, knowing full well I just lost a little piece of pride out there. Ben slept another hour or so as I lay there unable to fall back asleep. I was curious to see how he was feeling. At least Ben was able to have a more civil bowel experience when he woke up. We reconvened in the bunk room for a plan of attack. It was obvious this was not your average case of diarrhea. One of our greatest fears was coming true: the only thing that was going to stop us from finishing was either a significant illness and/or death at this point. The phone rang off the hook all morning at Gull Pond Lodge; each time Bob let it ring, and always picked up in the pause between two rings. Without fail, each time he answered, he bellowed out long and low "Gullll Pond Lodge." Bob's day was getting busier by the second, including a hiker that needed a shuttle about 30 miles away. We were able to catch a ride from him to the local clinic on his way out of town.

The doctor's office is the last place you want to be on a thru-hike. Their hours are seemingly impossible, and if something were to happen on a weekend, you are SOL, unless there happens to be a 24-hour urgent care or Hospital nearby, which is rarely the case. In our situation, it was Friday August 10th. Fortunately, being the small town that Rangeley is, we were able to be assisted right away. Talking with the nurses, we soon realized that some testing would be required, stool testing that is. The staff was less than thrilled, but it was not difficult producing a sample, that was being served up round the clock.

A stool sample usually takes about 2-3 days, and as I mentioned, it was Friday, so it wasn't looking like we'd be getting any confirmation until Monday at the earliest. Through conversation with the nurses and doctor, we were pretty convinced that this could only be one thing, the dirty G, Giardia. In good faith, the doctor wrote a prescription despite not having the test results. We walked back over to the pharmacy at the good ol' IGA. My picture wasn't posted in the front window to my relief. After the pharmacist handed over the prescriptions that were already filled, we immediately started the recommended dosage. The pharmacist noticed the drug and inquired to what was ailing us. In sympathy, he told us to come back if we had any issues.

Running on empty, we decided to have lunch in town and enjoy our ever-lengthening stay as much as possible. I finally said, "screw it" – this wasn't anything mashed potatoes, apple sauce, and yogurt was going to fix. I decided I was going to eat whatever I wanted. Ben was easily indoctrinated into that philosophy as well. So why not? A couple of pizzas it is at the local Italian joint, The Red Onion. They have a nice assortment of pies with lots of flavor options. As hungry as we thought we were, we had a hard time getting it all down, but we were at least hoping this would solidify some things if you know what I mean.

Arriving back at the hostel, we informed Bob this would be a more extended stay than originally thought. He drove a hard bargain, but we talked him down a little in price, probably out of his pity for us more than anything. Sitting in the living room when we returned to the Lodge was a hiker by the name of Teutonic Knight. He was a funny older guy who had just rented the first Jason Bourne movie, The Bourne Identity. Naturally, we asked him how he got the name and he replied, "Because that's all you need, Two tonics a night". We were thinking crusades, not alcohol. This guy was obsessed with the Jason Bourne movies, all available at the local, family-owned entertainment rental shop in town. I mean, they had pretty much any VHS you could think of. Having only seen the first one, we rented Bourne Supremacy the next day. Two Tonics was planning on leaving the next day but decided to stick around to watch the next one with us. It was nice being able to share some comraderie with some other hikers, something we did not do very often.

Between watching and re-watching the first two Bourne movies, I was struggling with the reality of the entire situation. Each day that went by not hiking was bumping up what we needed to average per day to finish the trail in time to make it back to school. When we got to Rangeley on the 9th of August, to finish, we would need to hike 20 miles a day for me to arrive on time, which included getting back to an airport after Katahdin and have my butt in a seat on August 20th. The 11th was 22, the 12th was 24, and the 13th was 27 1/2. If there was any positive to take away from all of this, it's that we were both suffering. Had only one of us been sick, it would have created a dynamic that I don't even feel comfortable thinking about. All that time, all the miles, the hardships, the joys, and the pain stopped us dead in our tracks just 220 miles from finishing the entire Appalachian Trail.

The pressure was unbearable. We both bit the bullet and called home. We had put it off a couple of days hoping we would get better, but even with the prescription, no improvements. I had always been told I was full of shit, never knew I really was. In some difficult phone calls back home, the worried mother effect kicked in. Zoezilla wanted to come pull me off the trail. She and Randy were trying to plan flights and rental car with Mr. Harrington and Ben's mom so they could meet us at the end. Not knowing when we would get better made that task impossible. My sweet mother was so worried about us, calling constantly, I made it clear to her that there was no way on God's green earth that I was coming home just to go back to school. Yet in the back of my mind, negative thoughts of leaving kept creeping in.

I had done the end of the trail, I did it with Garrett and Steve, just 2 years ago. So what if I didn't finish? Maybe that was the way it was supposed to be. Garrett wasn't able to summit again, why should I? Steve doesn't get the chance, why should I? I was lucky as hell to make it this far. We had pushed past the early days with everyone we met saying "No way you will make it" or "How ambitious" in a conceding tone. We busted our asses through Georgia, North Carolina, Tennessee, and Virginia fighting through the difficulty of Garrett stepping off. We caught and passed the bubble of hikers that started a week, 2 weeks, a month, even 2 and 3 months before us in the mid-Atlantic states of West Virginia, Maryland, Pennsylvania, New Jersey, and New York. We rose back into the highlands through Connecticut and Massachusetts. We stormed through the Green Mountains of Vermont and fought our way tooth and nail through the Whites of New Hampshire. Southern Maine threw us a couple low blows and still we pushed on. It was now, in the heart of Maine, the feces were hitting the oscillator.

On top of all of this, we had a only a full day's dosage left of our medication on Sunday, the 12th, and we were not feeling the slightest bit better. Beyond getting better in the immediate future, I was wondering how messed up we really were. Why did this happen? How? Then it hit me, that damn night, 2 weeks ago. The only time we night hiked because we stayed too late enjoying a sunset on the top of Bromley Mountain in Vermont. Ben and I couldn't believe it; that had to be it. It was the only water we did not purify on the entire trail. What are the odds? Pretty damn good I'd say. The well at Mad Not Tom Notch we pulled water from late that evening. In the midst of hangrily setting up our tent for the first time, in the dark, we slipped up, assumed everything would be fine as we nonchalantly dismissed the idea of purifying the water from that well. How stupid, how incredibly stupid. One act, one thing, one tiny little iota of a detail. I've heard of people not purifying water the entire way. Why us? Why now? I couldn't get it out of my head.

With our evening dose of the prescription, all that was left, we marched back up to the pharmacy, hoping the same guy was working that Sunday. Fortunately, he was. We told him the medicine was not working, not in the slightest. He pulled up the order in his system, "Giardia, right? Let me see here. No, no, no, no, this can't be right." He swung his screen around and showed us the prescribed dosage. "See that? That dosage is about a tenth of what you need." All this time, all the pain, the raw rear ends, and you tell me we've only had a tenth of what we needed. Ben and I were beyond livid, and I'm sure the pharmacist took the brunt of that disappointment. Thankfully, he was able to get a hold of the doctor on the phone, and refill our prescription to the proper amount. Popping the meds immediately afterwards, we headed back to the Red Onion for a celebratory pizza, feeling confident this was it, this was the answer.

We stuck around Rangeley on Monday as well. Poor Bob, he must have been getting sick of us. At this point, he would leave to go snag some hikers off the trail or shuttle them back and just put us in charge. Ben and I tried to do our best "Gullll Pond Lodge" impression when answering the phone, between rings, of course. Hikers would show up on foot, and we'd show them around, making sure Bob took their money when he returned. Two-Tonic Night finally parted ways with us; he wished us the best and made sure we were going to see the newly released Bourne Ultimatum the first chance we could. Thankful to have the dosage mix-up resolved, I still had a serious problem. It was Monday, August 13th. We were sticking around another day in Rangeley just to make sure the medicine took, making our return to the trail Tuesday the 14th. Ben and I would have to Average THIRTY SIX miles a day to finish on Sunday the 19th, leaving nothing short of a logistical nightmare to get back to school by Monday the 20th.

Then there was Ben. He was holding out on me.

Ben: "Why don't you call the Dean of the College of Architecture? See if you can miss a week. It's just drop/add week anyway right?"

Me: "Brilliant! … But I don't hardly know the Dean."

Ben: "So what? What's the worst that could happen?"

I mustered up enough courage to call Ken Lambla, Dean of the College of Architecture at UNC-Charlotte. I was a nervous wreck; I didn't know what to say. Getting into the College of Architecture was a privilege in itself; I made decent-enough grades, but hardly the performance to gain the attention of the Dean. If he didn't know who I was before, I was sure he'd know now. One thing I had going for me was a pretty darn good excuse. I was just days from finishing the Appalachian Trail, THE APPALCHIAN TRAIL. I had walked from Georgia to Maine. The more I thought about it, the more I was sure that there was absolutely no way he would say no. It may have been the most insignificant phone call he has ever received, but the most important to me. The future of the trip balanced on the other end of the line. I halfway wanted to say "Gulll Pond Lodge" when he answered, but decided against it. I explained my situation to Dean Lambla; he was familiar with the trail and, thank goodness, he was understanding. He gave me his blessing that I could miss the first week during Drop/Add but that I had better be sure to return on Monday, August 27th.

Back to
the Start

Mt. Katahdin

Springer Mt.

Bandanna's suggestion had bought us the time we needed. I was jacked up; this was the best news. I was ready to hop back on the trail immediately! Ben and I had to remind ourselves how to pack our bags again the next morning. With two last phone calls back home, we told our parents to be at Katahdin Stream Campground on Wednesday, August 22nd. That date gave us 9 days to cover just over 24 miles a day to get to the base of Mount Katahdin. We were feeling better, and the race was on. It wouldn't have been right if anyone else took us back to the trailhead, so Bob gave us a ride out of town; we snapped a photo with him after thanking him time and time again.

A few of the problems with Metronidazole, the drug we were prescribed, were the side effects: Side Effects May (did) include numbness and tingling in your hands and feet, trouble concentrating, dizziness or loss of balance, and dry mouth or unpleasant metallic taste. Needless to say, the hit-the-ground-running mentality we started with was shut down immediately. Walking around in town was fine, but the second we got back out on that trail, it was a totally different ballgame. With the numbness and dizzy spells on top of that awful metallic taste in our mouths, it was all we could do to walk a whopping 1.8 miles to the Piazza Rock Lean-To. It was all a numbers game now, and in the 9 days we had to get to Katahdin Stream Campground, we had completely botched the first day.

The next day that awful metallic taste was finally wearing off, but we had a hellacious climb up the igneous Saddleback Mountain. When there is hardly any vegetation, climbing becomes an entirely different experience. You must pay close attention to cairns and blazes on the rock or you can easily get turned around. In general, always go up, because the trail always does, until you can't go up any more. Along the route with our enjoyable view, we made out a couple of hikers in the distance. Mowgli had continued on without us out of Rangeley; he didn't even spend the night. He too was in the rush to return to classes. Too bad he didn't have a special pass from the Dean. We slowly gained on the figures that were irrefutably Chopsticks and Alright. As soon as they realized we were right behind them, they were struck with confusion, wondering how they got ahead of us. Hiking 1.8 miles in 5 days, that's how. Bummed for our unfortunate circumstance, we were still glad to see a familiar face, especially since Mowgli was most likely long gone by now. Our odds to catch him at this point were about the same for the Browns to win the Super Bowl...ever.

It's amazing how these massive rock formations soar out of the lake and pond-filled landscape. Traversing the crystalline feldspar ridge, formed by magma slowly cooling over hundreds of millions of years, the trail flexed its powerful, humbling muscles once again. We were back to our old ways, hiking from sun up to sun down. Chops and Alright confirmed they had heard Mowgli was closing in on Katahdin fast. Shortly after passing over Saddleback and the Saddleback Horn, we stopped to witness one of the famed shelters on the trail, Poplar Ridge Lean-To. I can only imagine the fear in hikers' eyes when they arrive, wet and tired, at this shelter. I envision no beauty rest being acquired whilst attempting a visit with the Sandman. In lieu of the traditional flat shelter floor or sleeping surface, the Poplar Ridge Lean-To offers the "baseball bat" flooring technique, one you will not

Spencer McKay

find on Aisle 27 in the back of your local Lowe's Home Improvement. My theory is the technique may have something to do with the namesake of the next mountain, which just so happens to be Spaulding Mtn. Shortly after the 4,000' peak of Spaulding Mountain, we descended for our camp spot for the night, Crocker Cirque. No, there weren't any trail bunnies swinging from ribbons hung high in the trees. A cirque is a large cupped opening or hollow carved out by a glacier with three extremely steep sides collecting ice and glacier debris. Through the creep of the glacier and freezing and thawing, the three steep sides are carved deeper and create a bowl shape, pushing everything out the open end – a natural feature rarely found, proving better to sleep on than a row of Louisville Sluggers.

Regaining our balance and agility by the minute, we were now in our last day of medication. It was just one more thing to add to the routine, trying to adhere to the prescription directions as much as possible. Take 1 to 2 hours prior to eating, check. Avoidance of heavy physical activity, not so much. Things were certainly cooling off even in August. The average low temp in nearby Stratton, Maine, is 73 and an average low of 49. Chiggers were a thing of the past, and sleeping was much more comfortable. Despite Mt. Katahdin soaring over its surrounding landscape, Big K wasn't the only milestone we had remaining.

The Bigelow Mountain Range spans a short yet rugged 17 miles, offering up the trademark rock and root scrambling required to hike through Maine. Despite our nearly 2,000- mile warm-up hike to get to this point, each slipping step on a wet, exposed tree root and every pack-weighted hop up and over boulders too small to be conquered with a step, the trail perpetually reminded us of who was boss. Bigelow Mountain rocks out in its own self-titled album of a mountain ridge. Named after Timothy Bigelow, Ol' Big Time Timmy Jim, one of Benedict Arnold's scouts who explored the area for the original stars and bars, the Continental Army. "Join or Die." What had happened was Benedict, aka Benny-D, was putting together an attack on the British forces in Quebec. Benedict was in cahoots with forces under Richard Montgomery at Fort Ticonderoga in New York while Benedict's troops headed out from Cambridge, Massachusetts; the two were planning to meet for the Battle of Quebec to open up a can of the newly invented U-S of A Premium Whoop-Ass. Turns out, what would later become the Appalachian Trail whooped the troops' butts. All we wanted to do was befriend the Canadians, show them that the Brits were garbage and to help us send them packing across the pond. The Battle of Quebec was a disaster: Arnold got caught by a Yankee Pea (musketball) and Montgomery got straight up whacked. Without Arnold's ambition, who knows when the next crazy man would have thought it a good idea to trek through Maine, during the winter, mind you.

Back to the Bigelows.... if I could hike only one section of the trail, ever again, it would be a toss-up between Franconia Ridge and the Bigelow Range. Maybe even a slight nod to the "Bigs" due to the favorable absence of weekend warriors and touristy crowds; ridgeline walking with dips and twists; and the random respite of pine needle-covered soil providing an added cushioned spring in our steps. Miles and miles of untamed wild stretches as far as the eye can see. Neither a vacant off season ski slope nor a perfume-laced day-hiker was within sight or scent. Our deadline didn't loom; the act of hiking absorbed our every thought and movement.

Virginia may take the cake for the state with most Appalachian Trail miles (550), but Maine is the runner-up in that contest (281). Yet if we were judging on a quality of mile basis in categories of difficulty, overall experience, and reward, there's no contest. On the Pacific Crest Trail (PCT), you'll frequently find the work of a crafty hiker who has made milestone mileage markers out of the trails natural resources. For example, upon reaching the a significant mileage total, the number "700" spelled out with giant pinecones as you approach the Sierra Nevada Range, or the number "300" spelled out with a 3 drawn in the dirt with 2 strategically placed cow pies placed beside it. A slight bit of hiker humor went a long way for morale. With the PCT, which travels through just 3 states, California, Oregon, and Washington, there's not as many morale boosters worth celebrating like the comparatively frequent border crossings of the AT. After our night at Little Bigelow lean-to though, we hit it: our 2,000- mile mark. That's a long damn way, and that was no shocker to Ben and me as we snapped a photo on the next road crossing with "2,000" painted on it.

Our adventure du jour was timing up our arrival to the bank of the Kennebec River. In the current hiker season, we had 2 opportunities to cross the Kennebec, the largest unbridged river on the trail. The Appalachian Trail Conservancy and the Maine Appalachian Trail Club join efforts every year to provide a canoe shuttle across the wide river. It is heavily encouraged to not attempt a ford, and I'd have to concur. Besides, the shuttle is part of the experience. We had from either 9 – 11 am to get across or from 2 – 4 pm. Seeing as how we had 21 miles to hike from the shelter to the Kennebec's bank, the morning window was out of the question. With time to spare, we awaited the canoe captain to paddle across and get us. The relatively short canoe ride propelled by the solo paddlers' forward-and-draw strokes achieved landfall on the opposite bank in about 10 minutes' time. I enjoyed letting someone else do all the work for a brief stint.

On the east bank, we were dropped off at the intersection of Main Street and Highway 201 in Caratunk, Maine. Having time to peruse our guidebook whilst waiting on the ferry, we noticed a restaurant was just 2 miles down the road on the other side of the river. Ben was able to Yogi a ride, and we headed to Northern Outdoors Resort. The giant cabin structure with a full-on restaurant and all kinds of activities and sports games in progress on the tube; it was like stepping off the ski slopes into the lodge. We were in heaven and knew this was going to be a hard place to leave. On top of the atmosphere, the food was out of bounds. I had a delicious quesadilla, a delicacy not enjoyed during my trail time. Bandanna and I were most thrilled to use our first porcelain throne since returning to the trail outside Rangeley. Have you ever had that nighttime, sniffling, sneezing, aching, coughing, stuffy-head fever that you just can't kick? Then all of a sudden you yack and hock up a loogie that seemingly carried the entire cold, leaving you instantly well again. I don't think my head spun all the way around, and there was no priest shouting "The power of Christ compels you," but it was a full-on exorcist of the demon that had haunted the success of our journey. I was ecstatic to flush that bad boy down. Let's be honest: double flush. Bandanna noticed an extra spring in my step as I returned to the dining area. I was pleased to inform him I was back to normal and suggested he attempt the same.

Ferry crossing and all, we were able to sneak in a 27-mile day and rested our heads at Pleasant Pond Lean-To for the evening. The trail leading into Monson, Maine, the last town with any remote proximity to the trail, descends off the Bigelows and carries hikers past Moxie Pond. In late August, the blackfly season is typically complete in this region. The swarming blood-suckers, of which there are 40+ species, can have a prolonged existence into late summer depending on the timing of spring and snowmelt. The females, the ones that bite, lay their eggs by the hundreds in fast-moving streams and rivers. Bumps similar to that of a mosquito bite can cover an unprepared hiker in no time. Resistance to these nasty, ruthless creatures can be achieved in a few ways, most importantly, DEET, and a lot of it. Black flies are attracted to carbon dioxide, which is why they always seem to buzz around the face, proving the usefulness of a head net. Wearing lighter colors also seems to help; almost all the animals they feed off of are dark, so this way, they won't confuse you with a moose.

Excited to reach Monson, we had read in trail journals and guidebooks about Shaw's Lodging. A hostel of epic reputation. The relatively easy trail conditions compared to that of what we had experienced in Maine thus far allowed for a day of 31 miles. With some struggle of hitching a ride, an older woman finally picked us up a few hours before sunset. There was no problem settling in at Shaw's, which is an old house with bedrooms, tents out back, and a full-on industrial kitchen. I was able to phone home and check in with Mom. She informed Ben and me that one of the principle architects of the firm I worked for the previous summer had been so kind as to leave his credit card number with the folks at The Lakeshore House restaurant down the street. Dinner was on Tom Wells tonight. Tom has been a tireless leader in the Boy Scouts across Raleigh and North Carolina for many years as well as a loyal follower of our blog. There was really no decision to be made after reviewing the menu – lobster rolls were the obvious choice. Everyone loves lobster, the most sophisticated way to eat butter. Ben and I watched the newly released show "Burn Notice" through the scratchy reception of the old tube television in our room as we drifted off into yet another trail-town food coma.

There are 150 compounds in bacon that all react when you drop it on the griddle. The process of cooking, or browning, that bacon is called the Maillard reaction. It is this reaction, specifically the nitrogen compounds including pyridine along with hydrocarbons, and aldehydes that produce that mind-numbing, saliva-inducing aroma when bacon is cooked. These scents traveled throughout the house as we exited hypnagogia, that delicate stage between awake and rest. As we shuffled our way downstairs like groggy elementary school kids, each step closer to the kitchen widened our eyes and messaged our insatiable appetites. Shaw's "breakfeast" offers a multitude of options and combinations. There are a few different categories. The building block of breakfast, eggs, cooked any way you want 'em, and then waffle or pancakes, sausage or bacon, homefries or hashbrowns. The deal is, when you order, then they ask how many eggs you want. Be careful, because that's the coinciding servings that you'll get of each of your other options. I ordered four eggs, over easy, the only way. Thus in return I received 4 eggs over easy, 4 strips of bacon, 4 pancakes and 4 heaping scoops of hash browns. Ben went with a slightly more reserved 3.

Knowing full well we were at the southern edge of the 100-Mile Wilderness, a famed stretch of the trail where hikers are warned via signage to "Beware." Once hikers enter the isolated stretch of trail, there are no opportunities for resupply. I suppose this is intimidating for a novice hiker, and even in our newly gained experience, just thinking about hiking 100 miles without any opportunity to refuel except for what we had on our backs suddenly seemed daunting. Thoughts of being stuck in the woods with nothing to eat, I figured I ought to go ahead and order 3 more eggs and everything that came along with it. Ben added an additional 2-egg order.

Not having time the night before to resupply one last time before our final push to Big K, we hopped into Tim's General Store to scrape together enough food to get us to Katahdin Stream Campground. Not having learned much from my Nutella incident, I decided to try what I understood to be a local soft drink called Moxie. Moxie, meaning vigor, courage, and aggressiveness, is exactly what you would need to drink an entire one of these. Flavoring of the drink comes from the gentian root extract and has an awfully bitter, some say licorice, some say bubble gum, flavor. It's more comparable to an aperitif than anything. Much like the Nutella, it met the bottom of a garbage can not long after its opening.

Dilly-dallying around with an enormous breakfast, packing up, and resupplying in the morning set us back in the day a little bit. Finding a ride back out of town was also an issue. With no luck outside the general store, we just started walking towards the trail with our thumbs out. Shortly, a young man appearing to be an outdoor enthusiast, judging by the stickers on his back windshield pulled over and hopped out of his car to confront of us, "You guys need a ride?" as he had already popped the trunk. Taken aback by his aggressive hiker services, all Ben and I could do was stare at his car. There was no physical damage – it was more of a size issue. Of course, we weren't going to turn down a ride in a Mustang. Only able to fit one pack in the trunk, I headed to the passenger side to find the guy's girlfriend sitting there. This debacle just got a lot more interesting. I'm pretty sure we each had a leg out the window and made a human pretzel while also holding Ben's pack in the backseat. Nevertheless, we made it back to the trailhead.

"There are no places to obtain supplies or get help until 100 miles north. Do not attempt this section unless you have a minimum of 10 days supplies and are fully equipped. This is the longest wilderness section of the entire A.T. and its difficulty should not be underestimated. Good Hiking! M.A.T.C."

That is how the sign reads when entering the 100-Mile Wilderness.

Ben and I nearly scoffed at it, then each thought, Well, I wonder if they're for real. They wouldn't put a sign up like this if they weren't serious. If I needed 10 days of food, my ass would be grass. I'd be late to school and would have to wait another year to make up the classes that I missed due to the way the curriculum worked. Either that sign didn't apply to us, or I was about to be in serious trouble.

Taking a break at a shelter, catching up on some trail journal entries, trying to catch a beat on Mowgli, we spotted a group of male hikers walking up. One of them instantly noticed us, which was weird because neither Ben nor I noticed him. "Gah, y'all look familiar." Well, the "y'all" was a clue. We got a southern fella' on our hands. "Don't I know you? I know y'all from somewhere?" "The article," one of the other men piped up. "That's it, y'all are the ones from the *News and Observer* article." The N&O is the Raleigh/Durham, North Carolina, newspaper. Just outside Damascus, Virginia, and once again in Pennsylvania at Vera "Grandma" Coleman's house, we had a couple of phone interviews with Ruth Sheehan, who was then a reporter and metro columnist for the newspaper. Unbeknownst to Bandanna and me, the article was released in the Sunday paper on August 12. Funny, 'cause at that point, the entire trip was in the balance of possibly not being completed. Turns out the guy was from Raleigh, my same high school even. Although a good 10 years older than me, he played 20 questions with some of the teachers he had, some of whom were still grinding along when I was there.

Ben and I continued on as the group of men headed south, and we headed north. The phenomenon of that encounter, like many of the encounters we had on our journey, was surreal. I contemplated the likelihood of that brush with fate for the remainder of the day. As mentioned, with the late start out of town, despite our cruise in the Mustang back to the trail, we only had about half a day worth of hiking before settling in for the night. Perhaps we should have considered the warning sign after all.

Since the descent from the top of Bigelow Mountain, the trail doesn't reach over 4,000' again until Katahdin. It barely reaches above 3,000' except for a 5-mile stretch that bags West Peak, Hay Mountain, and White Cap Mountain. Due to the pancake flat terrain, don't worry; the trail itself is still a rock- and root-infested muddy mess; any slight rise rewarding a view of your surroundings can reveal a silhouette of the final destination, Mount Katahdin. Just another mountain on our long journey. Except it's not. In clear weather, you can see Big K from up to 3 days away. It's a boastful shape confounding to gaze upon in the horizon. The 5,682' peak overwhelms even the most seasoned hikers. The next 3 days we would catch a glimpse of its glory ever so slightly; it waited still. It was at this point, that we knew without any shadow of doubt that we were going to complete the trail.

As lollipops and cotton candy as it may seem, with Katahdin in sight, we still had over 60 miles to go. Thoughts flipped through the rolodex of my mind. This incredible adventure was coming to an end. Every successful thru-hiker experiences it, yet none of them have the words to describe it. Sure, you can throw out some hogwash like "I can't put it into words" or "It's not the destination; it's the journey," both of which I say regularly when asked about my hike. For whatever reason, "The Scientist" by Coldplay resonated and played on repeat for both Bandanna and me. Reveling in the fact the lead singer of Coldplay's name is Chris Martin, which also happens to be the name on Mowgli's birth certificate, it just seemed to fit. We began singing the song when Ben made this connection one day in the Whites. For me, for Ben, it's about a journey, more specifically, the one we were currently on. If the song is meant to be about a relationship, well, I certainly believe that it is. Every detail of the trip started racing through my head.

Starting out, setting forth. The knowns, the unknowns. The weather, our bodies, our minds. How we missed Steve, how we'd give anything to bring him back. We wanted to bring joy to the Harringtons lives. Did we even achieve that? Tyvek Holy Shit, holy shit. That damn French guy in the Whites. Not Colbert, he was just quiet and weird. Alright's story about JD. Alright and Chops. Can't forget Mowgli; he was an awesome addition through New Hampshire and Southern Maine. I ate an entire half gallon of ice cream. The food, holy crap, the food. Nothing but Snickers, Clif Bars and Bumble Bee Chicken on the trail, then stuffing our fat faces with any kind of pizza, burger, or ice cream we could find in town. We should have been sponsored. Nah, too much work to line all that crap up. We had a hard enough time meeting our own deadline. I couldn't imagine having to report to someone else on my thru-hike. Life at 3-4 miles an hour was damn good. Crushing huge days. That was the best feeling. "Making miles, man, making miles." Ben got sick of my saying that. It was true though; we had to. It was the race within the journey. The vest family, I can't believe that damn family with the vest.

Speaking of families, that one with the big-ass black dog that wouldn't shut up. And a cat in a bag – they were hiking with a cat in a bag. Some pieces of gear recall memories as well. My bent all-to-hell trekking pole from almost wiping out in a thunderstorm trying to get to Thomas Knob Shelter. Shredded pockets on Ben and my hip belts from the shelter mice. The help, all the help, from everyone. Yeah, we did the walking, but that's about all we had to do. My parents, Ben's parents, the Harringtons, the Dixons, support from Troop 215, Pete and Jay Haeseker. Mr. Charville for even letting us get this crazy seed of an idea planted in our minds with exposure to the trail as adolescents. That time Drew Haley met us in Tennessee, then proceeded to eat everything we ate. I felt I had failed in one regard: keeping the crew together. Maybe we could have done more to hang with Garrett. Maybe we should have been more careful in the early days. It seemed all we could do to make up for those short days though. My legs, my legs looked like cannons. I was the skinniest I had ever been in my life. I might have needed a haircut and to shave this poor excuse for a beard off my face, but I looked good, damn good.

Even with the excruciating leg cramps, the discomfort of waking up and putting on my clothes, still completely saturated from sweat the day before back on. Ugh, pulling those damp, moist, funkadelic boxer briefs back on. Sliding that sweaty shirt back on as it gets caught on my shoulder and elbow. Overcoming the lack of indoor plumbing in my life for over 90 days. Busting my ass more times than I can remember. Those God-awful chigger bites. I don't wish that on anyone. Not having a traditional time frame to make this journey. Feeling rushed at times. The serenity was in the walking itself, the solitude. The simplest of tasks, putting one foot in front of another. I guess if you do one really easy thing millions and millions of times, it can turn out to be an amazing thing. And I must say, it really is an amazing thing.

People set out to hike the trail for every reason imaginable. Convicts hit the trail for redemption. Addicts for peace. Retirees because they've earned it. Young people because they don't know any damn better. For some it's a rite of passage, others just a passage of time. Each and every thru-hike is unique. The only common thread is the trail itself, that's it. Even the trail can morph in different weather conditions. Two different hikers could recall the exact same spot in complete opposites depending on when they were there.

We were unlucky sometimes and lucky a lot. It was a privilege to even attempt it. I started thinking a lot about hiking with Steve and Garrett in the Maine woods the evening before we summited Katahdin the next day in 2005. I swear I kept seeing his figure slipping just behind a tree as the trail twisted and turned up ahead. I had to do a lot of double-takes shortly after his death. I felt him around me, I thought I saw him in the frozen pizza aisle at Harris Teeter. How I wished it was all just a misunderstanding. Steve was fine, he's right here, see! He wasn't, he was gone. We had him with us though, his remains and his spirit. He was our X-factor, the catalyst, the inspiration. At each state border, we swapped who got to carry Steve. The small Nalgene bottle exchanged hands 13 times. I think it was at the New Jersey-New York Border where I realized he would end up with me for the final state of Maine. Since New Jersey was such a short portion of the trail, I convinced Ben that I should carry him through New York too. This would make it so Ben ended up with him at the end.

All those thoughts and more churned through my head all day. The next thing I knew, we had hiked our second-to-farthest day on the entire trip. Just .3 miles shy of our longest day. It was our last night on the trail. The next day we would meet my mom, Randy, Mr. Harrington, and Ben's mom at Katahdin Stream Campground. It was unreal. I started wondering how my mom would fare hiking up Katahdin. She assured me she had been walking up to her office on the 7th floor multiple times daily, and I even had her do a warm-up on the dreaded Dragon's Tooth. She'll be fine.

In the final shelter we would pass on the trail, we rested before the final push to the campground. Thirteen miles to the campground and 5 more to the top of Mt. Katahdin, we sat in silence on the dirt-covered wood floor of the lean-to. Ben thumbed through the trail journal as I sipped some water and had a snack. Eighteen miles from finishing, as Ben read through the journal, a news article fell out from between 2 pages. Bandanna read it aloud; it was all about the Pacific Crest Trail and its entirely different challenges compared to the Appalachian Trail. This was some sort of sick joke. Who would plant such information for thru-hikers to read a day before finishing the granddaddy of them all, the Appalachian Trail? I was exhausted, I couldn't fathom attempting something such as the PCT, as I

S p e n c e r   M c K a y

sat there doing the very thing that it would entail for the past 94 days. Ben looked at me, "So you want to hike the PCT?" "Hell NO!" I said.

Naturally, we arrived to Katahdin Stream Campground ahead of our company. Like I've said, Mom will be late to her own funeral. Ben and I claimed a campsite to accommodate multiple tents and a parking spot. We then proceeded to do what we had become profoundly efficient at, Yogi-ing food of other campers in a group nearby. It really didn't take much effort as it was obvious what we were there for. The group cooking up steaks and potatoes was quite familiar with the significance of our situation. Seeming like a fun, unfiltered group, they were happy to trade some grub for the more vulgar and raunchy stories of our adventure. Not long after, our folks finally arrived. I had never seen my mom so happy. One proud Momma! By the time we all greeted and hugged each other, it was dark. I proceeded to help Ben set up all the tents. "Not setting up in the dark again," we said to each other jokingly. Zoezilla was hilarious. She couldn't get over how "fun" it was going to be for me and Randy to sleep in the tent with her. Like she was taking her little boy camping. Having communicated with her the entire trip more than anyone other than Ben, she was the gopher, the secretary, the bank, provider of anything I needed while away. She is the most important of the many people I am forever indebted to. From the earliest conception of this grand journey, not one peep of negativity. Full support from start to finish. Except that time in Rangeley where she tried to convince me to come home, but we'll just chalk that up to Mom being worried about her baby boy. Besides, she came bearing gifts: foot-long subs, fresh fruit, desserts, Gatorade, you name it.

It was late to bed but early to rise as I had warned the group that Katahdin was no walk in the park. You never know what the weather is going to do, and if it were to rain, it'd be a slippery, dangerous mess. It was serious déjà vu. Two short years ago, I had walked up the same gravel path to the register to sign in on a summit attempt. I put all our names down, and nearly the identical start time as the July morning with Garrett and Steve, 6:30. The stone path allows for a group of 4-wide to travel for the first few hundred feet. Then it quickly narrows over some footbridges and turns to single-track before reaching Katahdin Stream Falls. Ben and I had agreed to empty our packs except for the essentials and some extra food and water for the parentals. No need for a sleeping bag, thermarest, our one spare set of clothes, a tent and some other miscellaneous items.

After the falls, it was becoming increasingly apparent that my mother was struggling. Of course, having become accustomed to hiking in front, I was in the lead and was going then stopping and waiting for the group time and time again. Randy made it clear to me that mom was pretty scared and on the verge of becoming upset. I dropped to the back, and Mr. Harrington, Malinda, and Ben took the lead. In the words of Ben "You were a mess that day; you were like a gazelle moving up and down and back and forth all over that mountain." It's true, I was jacked up, and emotions were full throttle. I couldn't believe this was it, we were here.

There was some comedy in it, mom's 5'-3 ½" frame trying to take giant steps over roots, boulders, and the rocky trail. She blamed it all on her short little legs, and I can see her point. I had taken for granted my height and stride. I tried my best to encourage her and patiently help her ascend. The thing about Katahdin though is it's relentless. Katahdin Stream Campground sits at just over 1,000' above sea level, and the trail rises up Katahdin to over 5,000' in just 5.2 miles. That's about 439 flights of stairs. So even though mom was walking up her stairs to the 7th floor at least 4 times a day, every day of the week, it would have taken her 15 days to reach the elevation gain of Katahdin. I did not enjoy seeing my mother struggle with something she wanted to do so passionately. The humor quickly wore off as we had been hiking for nearly 3 hours and were hardly halfway up the mountain, not to mention we had to get back down.

I knew getting above tree line was a big milestone we had to reach. Randy and I tried to encourage her, but nothing seemed to help. There are some intimidating maneuvers required, especially to someone not familiar with the strenuous nature of more extreme hiking and mountaineering. Some sections up Katahdin are so vertical, it feels as if you're just rock climbing as you cannot even see the top of the mountain. Just as we surfaced past a technical section, and positioned ourselves on the main ridge that leads you to the summit, Zoezilla was not only concerned about making it up but making it back down. The fear that mom was not going to make it up the climb had come to fruition. Through tears of sadness, we all hugged as I tried to explain I didn't need to go up, I wanted all of us to celebrate at the top together. It was already after noon, and I knew I had to get going with close to 2 miles left to the top. Mom, Randy, and I all embraced as they agreed it was best that they start making their way down and for me to get on my way. I was devastated but relieved. I don't think my mom's first helicopter ride needed to be an emergency one from the top of Mt. Katahdin. Perhaps I should have been carrying that Thermarest and sleeping bag.

I remained animated, hiking alone, trying to catch up with Ben, his mother, and Tim. Some tears were whisked away by the howling gusts across the mountain's ridge, others combining quickly with sweat as they rolled down my face into my splotchy beard. I spotted the threesome I was in search of, specks in the distance at this point. Turning on the jets, I went into overdrive pushing as hard as I possibly could up Katahdin. I knew it flattened out shortly at the approach to Thoreau Spring, an unreliable water source a mile from the summit. I felt the power of my stride, the flex of each muscle as I attempted stretching the length of each step a little bit more. I had never hiked so fast, like a man on fire. Less than a mile from the summit, I finally caught up. Seeing that they were confused and troubled that Randy and Mom were not with me, I broke the news that they couldn't make it. Malinda was a trouper for making it. Tim too, who was battling recovery from heart issues. There was no way in Hell Mr. Harrington wasn't going to make it, that was a determined man.

Rising over the final crest, we saw the famed sign atop Katahdin. The worn trail on a thin layer of topsoil transitions from solid rock, back to dirt to solid rock and stones again. You have risen thousands of feet higher than anything around. Elevated in so many ways. I now understood what I had witnessed just over 2 years ago, in the young man finishing his thru-hike.

This was the peak, the pinnacle, the payday, the northern terminus, the end of the Appalachian Trail. We had the pain, we had the rain, and now we had Maine. My mind was no longer telling my body to walk, but my legs kept moving, inching closer to that sign. That sign meant everything. The last picture I have with Steve was us on either side of it. We had talked at length about completing this journey together and that opportunity had been yanked like a rug from beneath us. Angry at the "why?" of life, 2,175 miles that should have been shared in one way were shared in the complete opposite.

It wasn't all tears atop Maine's highest peak. Ben and I were able to flash an occasional, triumphant smile for the cameras. We hogged the sign for a bit, having to take a few hard-earned photographs. Each of us individually, with the iconic standing on the back of the sign. One of us together, one of us together holding Ben's fraternity flag, one of us holding the BSA Troop 215 flag, one of us holding a running jersey that the Harrington's family friend, Kazem Yayhapour wore in the Boston Marathon, which had printed on it a picture of Steve and read "In Loving Memory of Stephen Harrington." And, of course, one of Ben and me holding the picture I carried the entire way of Steve and me – on the summit holding Payday candy bars, unopened – pointed towards the camera while Ben held his ashes.

Shortly after the photo session at the summit's sign, I documented Mr. Harrington and Ben as they shuffled to the edge of the peak to spread Stephen's ashes. This was the formal goodbye we never got to have. For Mr. Harrington, I can only imagine it to be losing him all over again. The strength it must require for a parent to have to perform such a task is haunting. God Bless the Harringtons. I hope this adventure brought them more good memories than bad. I never intended it to be a constant reminder of their loss; I hope to God that's not how they have ever felt about it. Ben, Garrett, and I hiked this trail to honor him. Ben fetched the bottle of Steve's ashes from his pack, the one we had filled at the Harrington's home 96 days ago. Ninety-five days ago we set foot on this incredible journey.

Always one to crack a joke, as Mr. Harrington unscrewed the top, Steve made his presence known by kicking up a large gust of wind just as the first flick of the his father's wrist flung the ashes towards the edge of the steep mountain below our feet, blowing the first portion all over Tim, Ben, Malinda and me. The second attempt was a much more successful if somber one; as a few shakes emptied the small container, a lone bird streaked just a few feet over heads as the final particles of Steve's remains slipped from the bottle. Seriously, you can't make this shit up. It was beyond a shadow of doubt Steve sending a message. We made it, Buddy, we made it.

With the most difficult task of my life behind me, it was back to worrying about my mom. Tim, Malinda and Ben understood as I began booking it down the mountain to make sure she was descending safely. The climb up Katahdin is certainly a daunting one, but the real potential for injuries occurs on the way down. I raced down the mountain twice as fast as I had sprinted up it, hoping after each turn I would find them safe and well. We had taken a good while at the summit, so I was hoping they were making it down with relative ease. I finally came across them just as the trail became a walking path again instead of a hand-over-hand climbing affair. The behind of Zoezilla's nylon hiking britches were worn slap out. Picked fabric resembling cheese cloth made up the remaining seat of her pants. I can picture her now sliding down each rock. She'd be sore for days.

The quote by Henry David Thoreau that we saw etched in a rock ascending Mt. Greylock in Massachusetts rang clear in my mind once again, "It were as well to be educated in the shadow of a mountain as in more classical shade. Some will remember, no doubt, not only that they went to college, but that they went to the mountain." Life continues past the days of our greatest accomplishments, thus giving us only more experiences to build upon and develop new ambitions, using what we know and what we don't to propel us forward. There is no back and there is no future; if you're not living life in the now, then you aren't living at all. Yes, school awaited me as I returned for the Fall Semester, but I had never considered education outside of that which is institutionalized. It remains clear that setting goals and having big dreams needs to be a more transparent foundation for everyone's life. Again, the trail does not judge who or what we are; it only determines who we will become.

A Trip For Steve
May 21st, 2007-August 23rd, 2007

Spencer McKay

98725618R10130

Made in the USA
Middletown, DE
11 November 2018